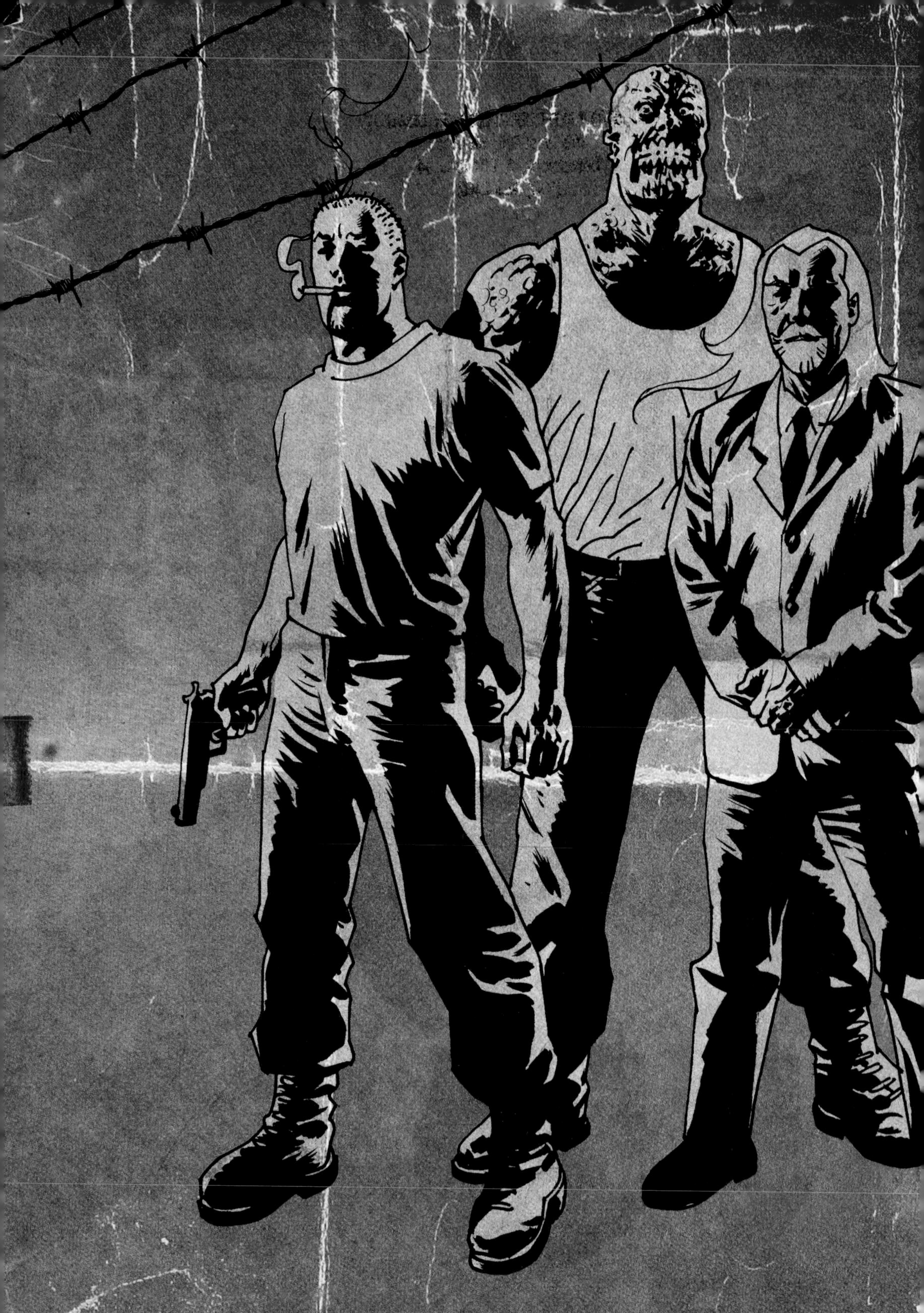

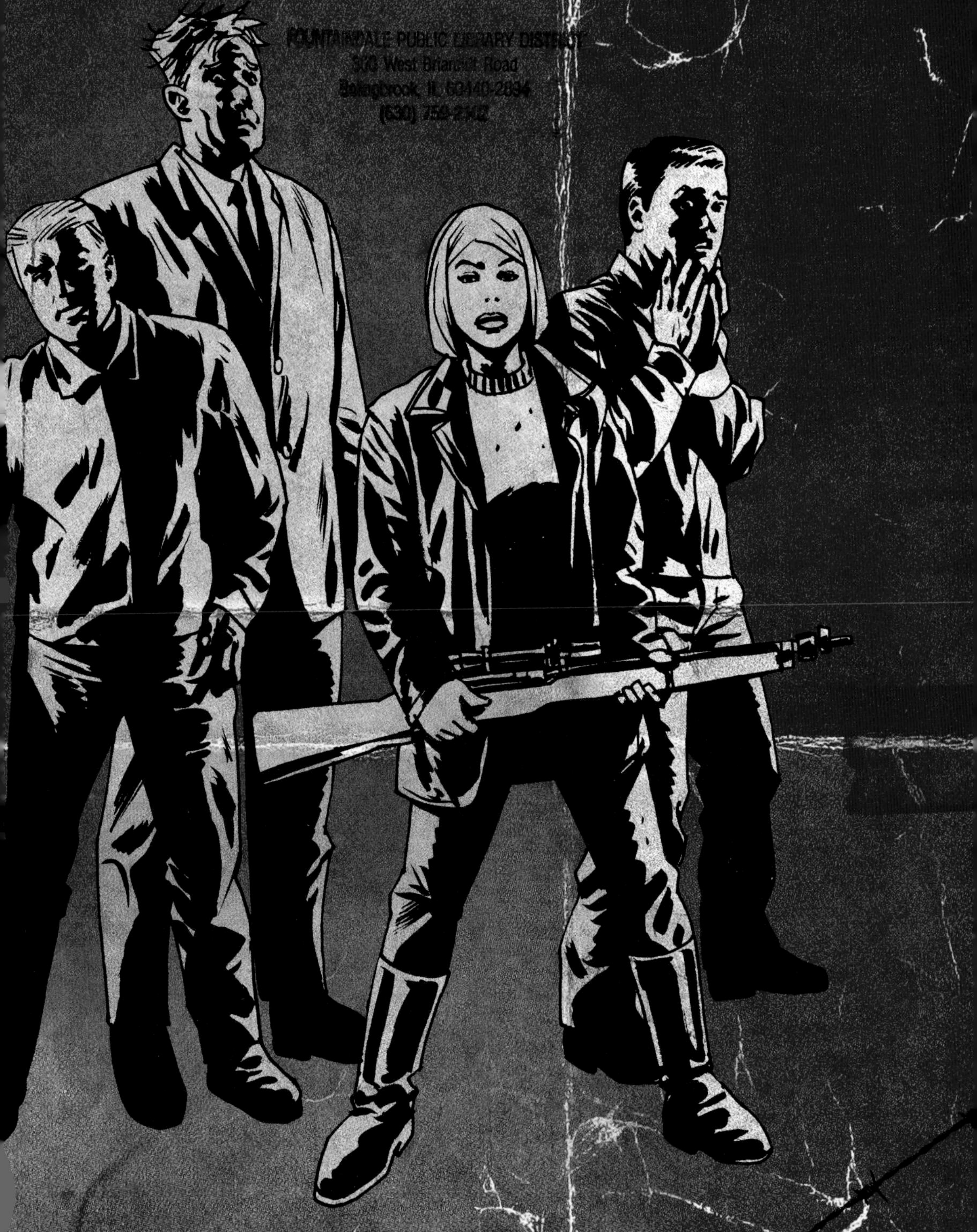

7 PSYCHOPATHS — September 2010 published by BOOM! Studios. 7 Psychopathes, Vehlmann - Phillips © Guy Delcourt Productions – 2007. All rights reserved. BOOM! Studios™ and the BOOM! logo are trademarks of Boom Entertainment, Inc., registered in various countries and categories. All rights reserved. The characters and events depicted herein are fictional. Any similarity to actual persons, demons, anti-Christs, aliens, vampires, face-suckers or political figures, whether living, dead or undead, or to any actual or supernatural events is coincidental and unintentional. So don't come whining to us. Office of publication: 6310 San Vicente Blvd, Ste 404, Los Angeles, CA 90048-5457. For information regarding the CPSIA on this printed material call: 203-595-3636 and provide reference # EAST – 67566

A catalog record for this book is available from OCLC and on our website www.boom-studios.com on the Librarians page.

First Edition: September 2010

10 9 8 7 6 5 4 3 2 1

Printed in U.S.A.

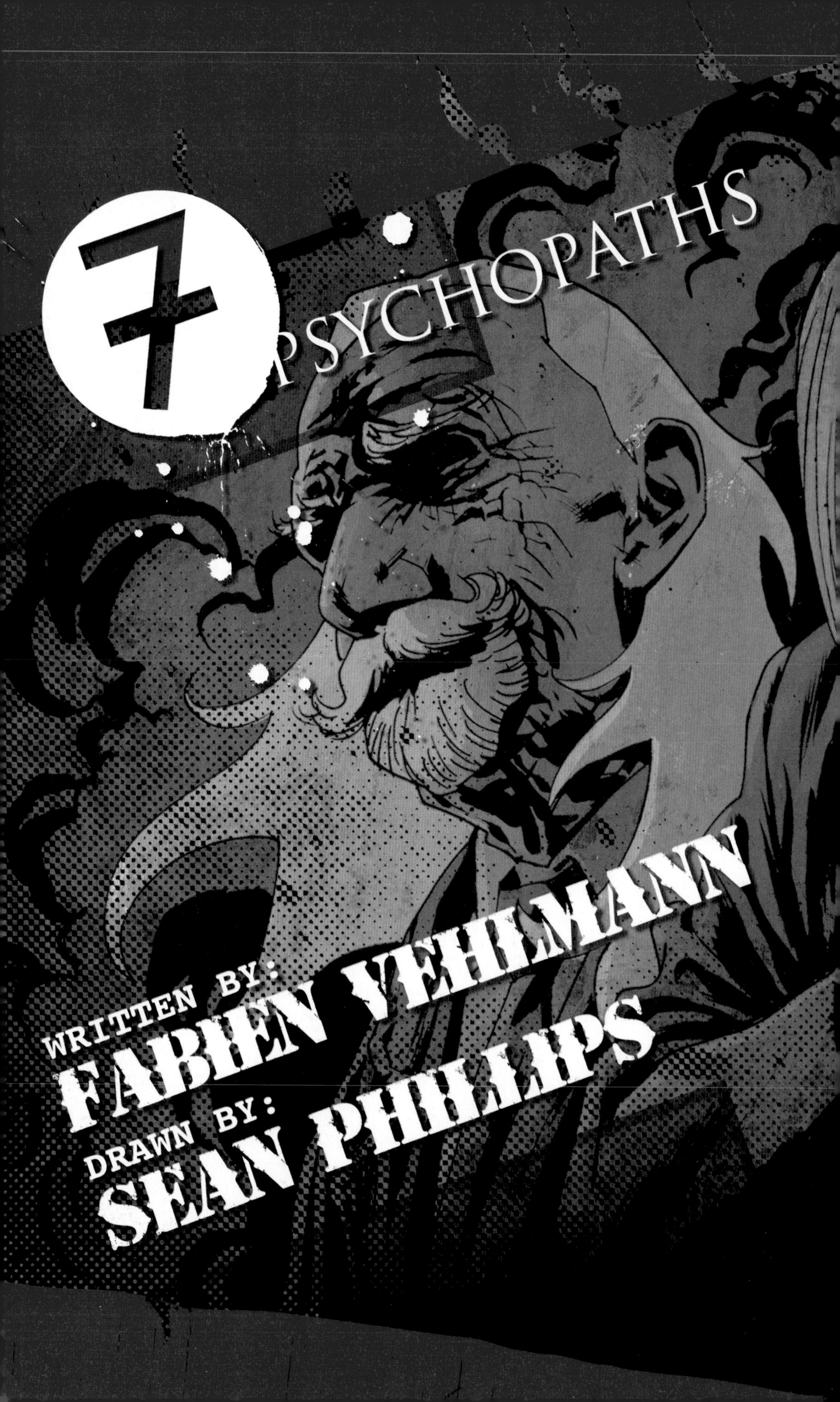

7 PSYCHOPATHS
WRITTEN BY:
FABIEN VEHLMANN
DRAWN BY:
SEAN PHILLIPS

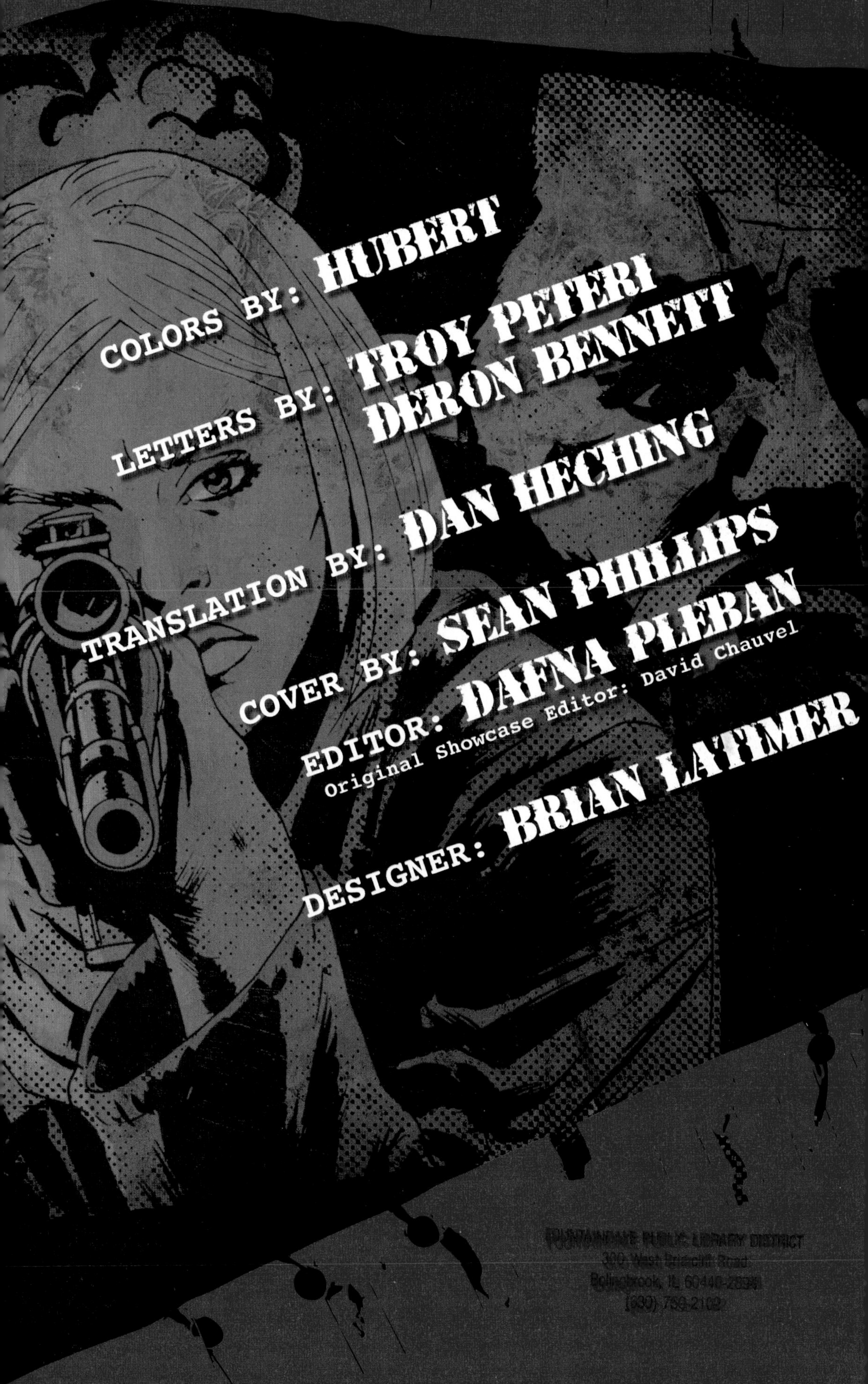
COLORS BY: HUBERT
LETTERS BY: TROY PETERI
DERON BENNETT
TRANSLATION BY: DAN HECHING
COVER BY: SEAN PHILLIPS
EDITOR: DAFNA PLEBAN
Original Showcase Editor: David Chauvel
DESIGNER: BRIAN LATIMER

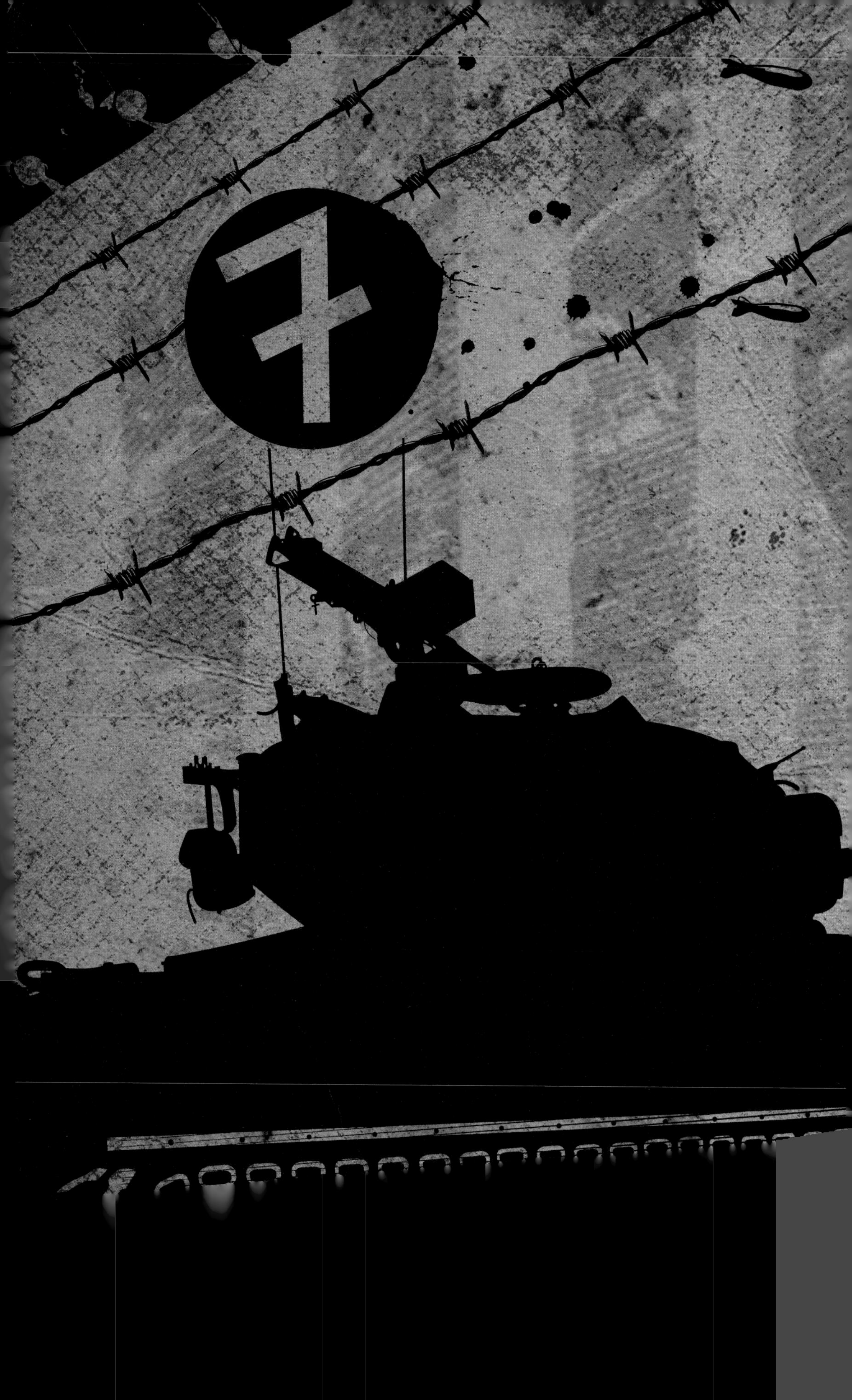

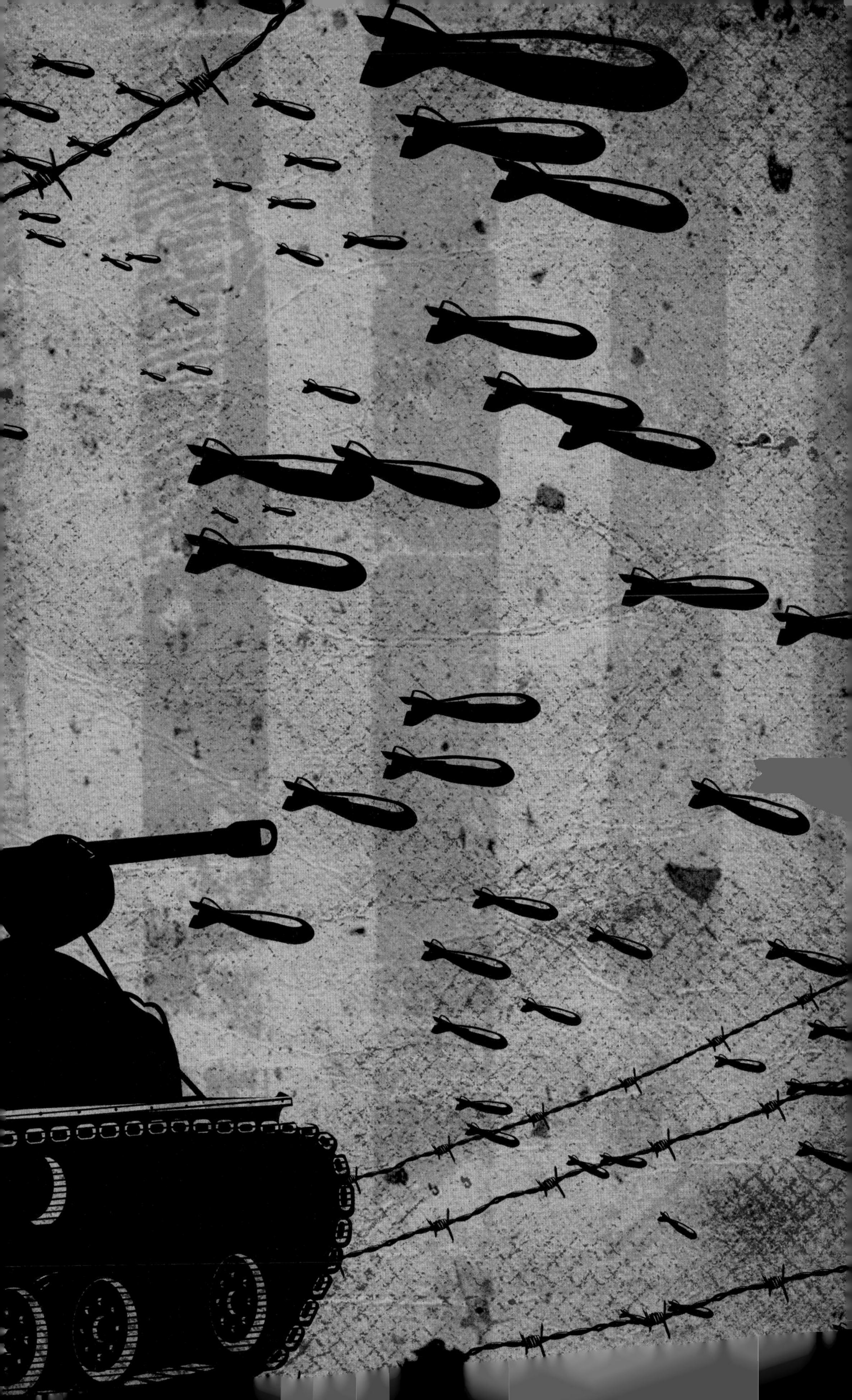

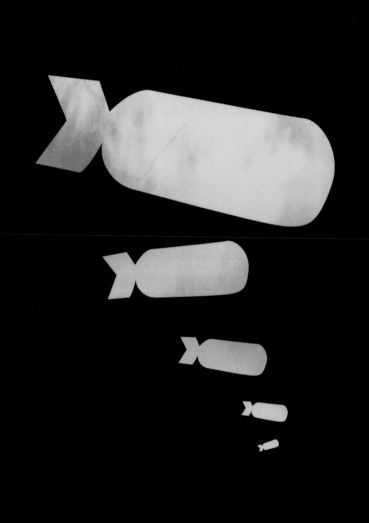

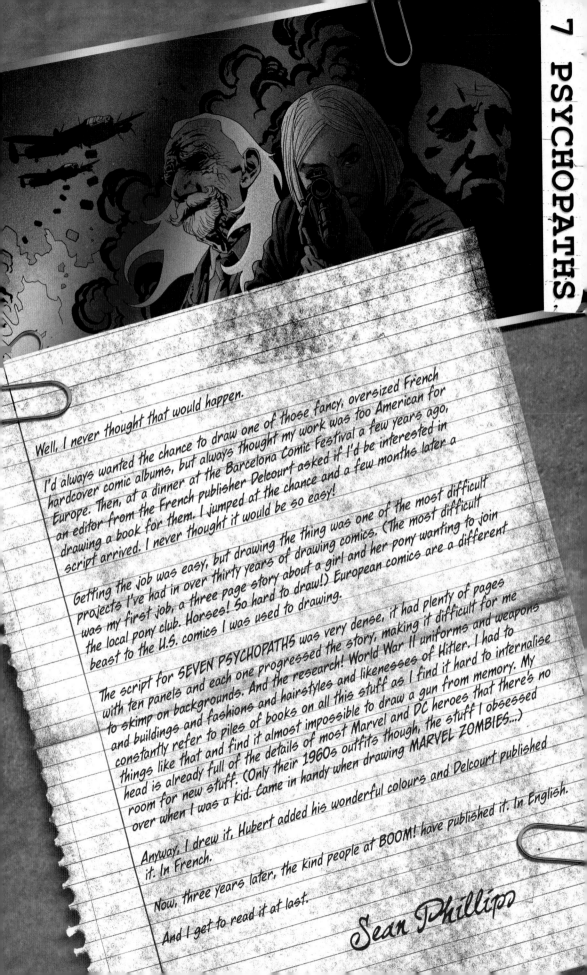

Well, I never thought that would happen.

I'd always wanted the chance to draw one of those fancy, oversized French hardcover comic albums, but always thought my work was too American for Europe. Then, at a dinner at the Barcelona Comic Festival a few years ago, an editor from the French publisher Delcourt asked if I'd be interested in drawing a book for them. I jumped at the chance and a few months later a script arrived. I never thought it would be so easy!

Getting the job was easy, but drawing the thing was one of the most difficult projects I've had in over thirty years of drawing comics. (The most difficult was my first job, a three page story about a girl and her pony wanting to join the local pony club. Horses! So hard to draw!) European comics are a different beast to the U.S. comics I was used to drawing.

The script for SEVEN PSYCHOPATHS was very dense, it had plenty of pages with ten panels and each one progressed the story, making it difficult for me to skimp on backgrounds. And the research! World War II uniforms and weapons and buildings and fashions and hairstyles and likenesses of Hitler. I had to constantly refer to piles of books on all this stuff as I find it hard to internalise things like that and find it almost impossible to draw a gun from memory. My head is already full of the details of most Marvel and DC heroes that there's no room for new stuff. (Only their 1960s outfits though, the stuff I obsessed over when I was a kid. Came in handy when drawing MARVEL ZOMBIES...)

Anyway, I drew it, Hubert added his wonderful colours and Delcourt published it. In French.

Now, three years later, the kind people at BOOM! have published it. In English.

And I get to read it at last.

Sean Phillips

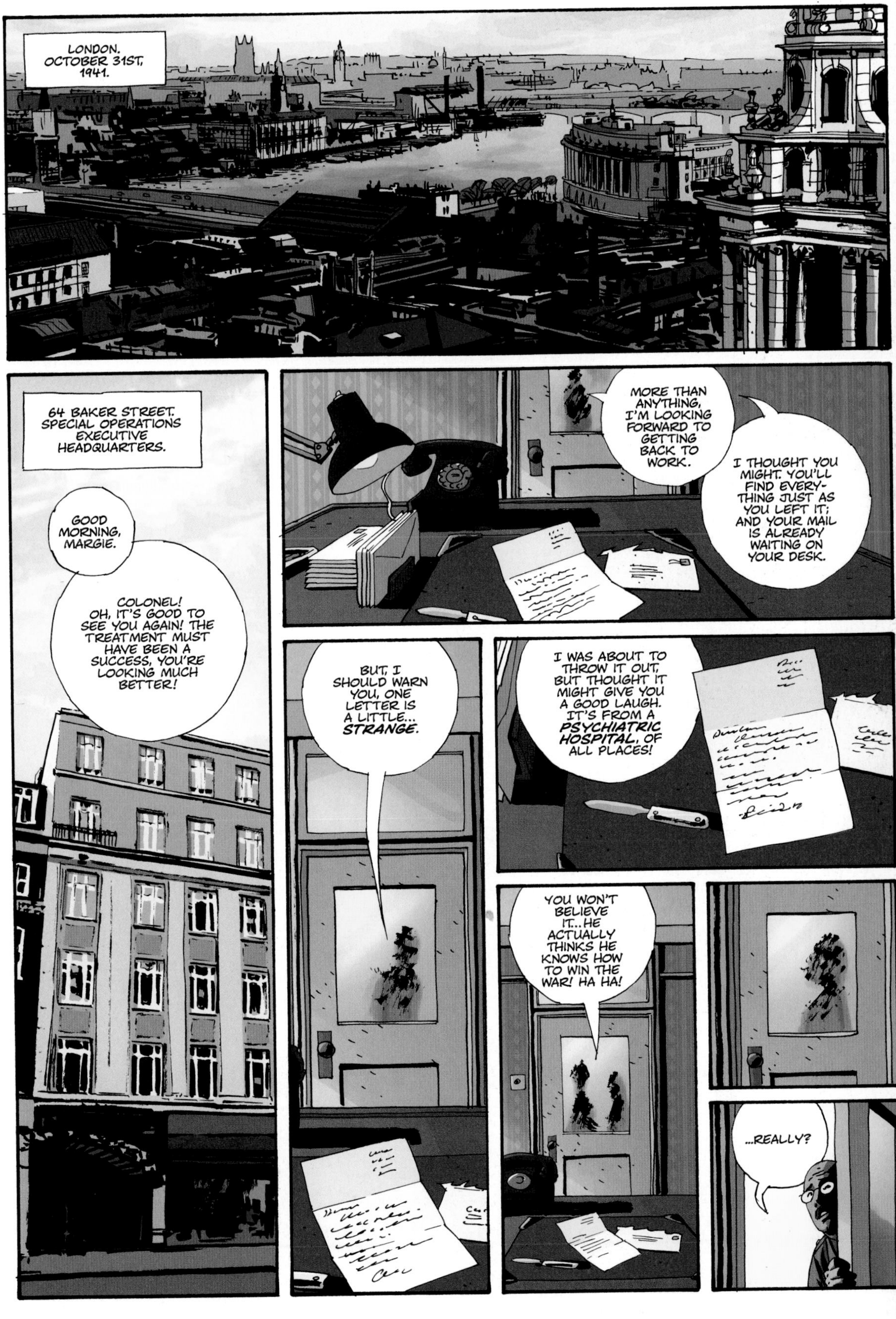
LONDON. OCTOBER 31ST, 1941.
64 BAKER STREET. SPECIAL OPERATIONS EXECUTIVE HEADQUARTERS.
GOOD MORNING, MARGIE.
COLONEL! OH, IT'S GOOD TO SEE YOU AGAIN! THE TREATMENT MUST HAVE BEEN A SUCCESS, YOU'RE LOOKING MUCH BETTER!
MORE THAN ANYTHING, I'M LOOKING FORWARD TO GETTING BACK TO WORK.
I THOUGHT YOU MIGHT. YOU'LL FIND EVERY-THING JUST AS YOU LEFT IT; AND YOUR MAIL IS ALREADY WAITING ON YOUR DESK.
BUT, I SHOULD WARN YOU, ONE LETTER IS A LITTLE... STRANGE.
I WAS ABOUT TO THROW IT OUT, BUT THOUGHT IT MIGHT GIVE YOU A GOOD LAUGH. IT'S FROM A PSYCHIATRIC HOSPITAL, OF ALL PLACES!
YOU WON'T BELIEVE IT...HE ACTUALLY THINKS HE KNOWS HOW TO WIN THE WAR! HA HA!
...REALLY?

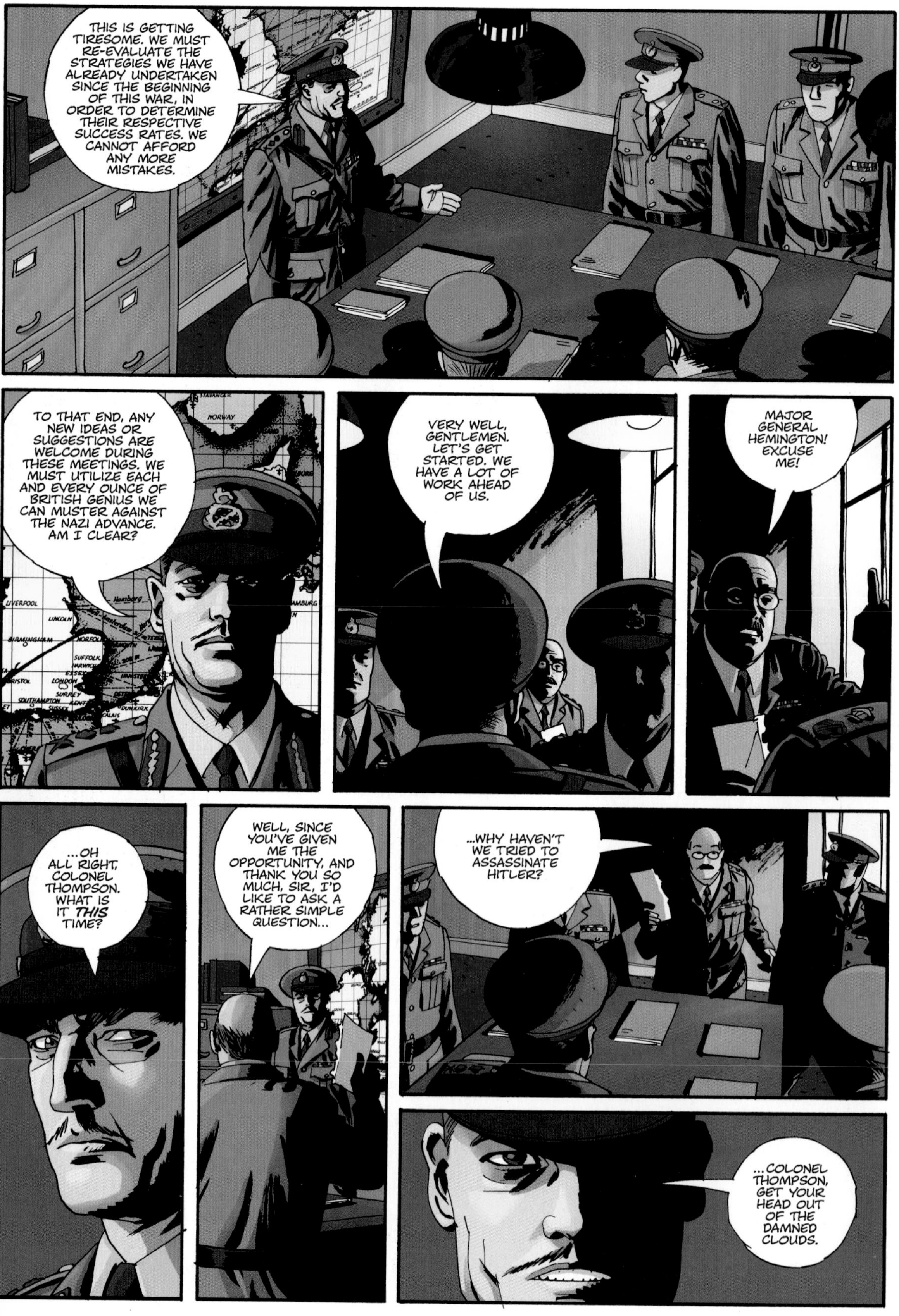
THIS IS GETTING TIRESOME. WE MUST RE-EVALUATE THE STRATEGIES WE HAVE ALREADY UNDERTAKEN SINCE THE BEGINNING OF THIS WAR, IN ORDER TO DETERMINE THEIR RESPECTIVE SUCCESS RATES. WE CANNOT AFFORD ANY MORE MISTAKES.
TO THAT END, ANY NEW IDEAS OR SUGGESTIONS ARE WELCOME DURING THESE MEETINGS. WE MUST UTILIZE EACH AND EVERY OUNCE OF BRITISH GENIUS WE CAN MUSTER AGAINST THE NAZI ADVANCE. AM I CLEAR?
VERY WELL, GENTLEMEN. LET'S GET STARTED. WE HAVE A LOT OF WORK AHEAD OF US.
MAJOR GENERAL HEMINGTON! EXCUSE ME!
...OH ALL RIGHT, COLONEL THOMPSON. WHAT IS IT *THIS* TIME?
WELL, SINCE YOU'VE GIVEN ME THE OPPORTUNITY, AND THANK YOU SO MUCH, SIR, I'D LIKE TO ASK A RATHER SIMPLE QUESTION...
...WHY HAVEN'T WE TRIED TO ASSASSINATE HITLER?
...COLONEL THOMPSON, GET YOUR HEAD OUT OF THE DAMNED CLOUDS.

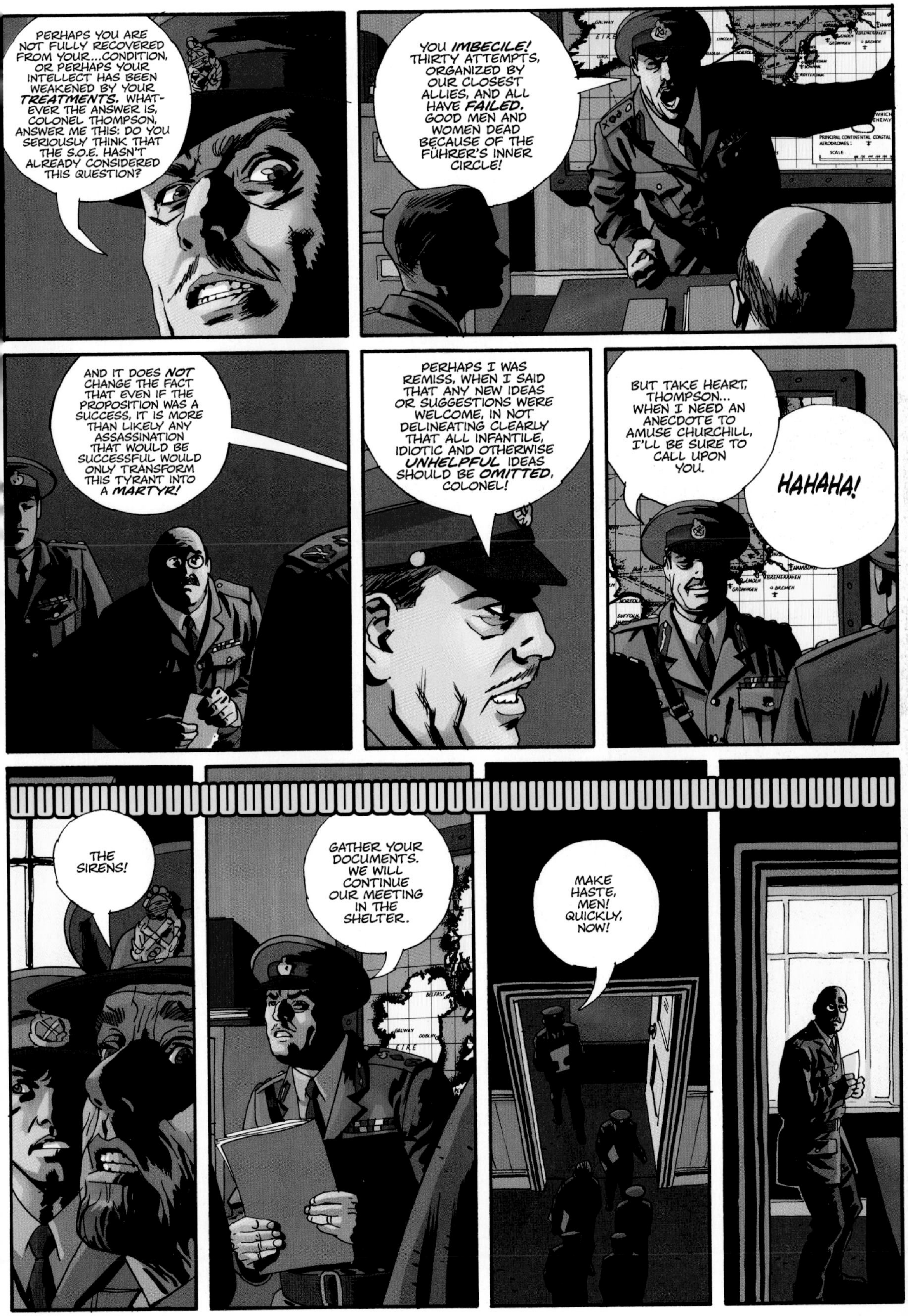
PERHAPS YOU ARE NOT FULLY RECOVERED FROM YOUR...CONDITION, OR PERHAPS YOUR INTELLECT HAS BEEN WEAKENED BY YOUR TREATMENTS. WHATEVER THE ANSWER IS, COLONEL THOMPSON, ANSWER ME THIS: DO YOU SERIOUSLY THINK THAT THE S.O.E. HASN'T ALREADY CONSIDERED THIS QUESTION?
YOU IMBECILE! THIRTY ATTEMPTS, ORGANIZED BY OUR CLOSEST ALLIES, AND ALL HAVE FAILED. GOOD MEN AND WOMEN DEAD BECAUSE OF THE FÜHRER'S INNER CIRCLE!
AND IT DOES NOT CHANGE THE FACT THAT EVEN IF THE PROPOSITION WAS A SUCCESS, IT IS MORE THAN LIKELY ANY ASSASSINATION THAT WOULD BE SUCCESSFUL WOULD ONLY TRANSFORM THIS TYRANT INTO A MARTYR!
PERHAPS I WAS REMISS, WHEN I SAID THAT ANY NEW IDEAS OR SUGGESTIONS WERE WELCOME, IN NOT DELINEATING CLEARLY THAT ALL INFANTILE, IDIOTIC AND OTHERWISE UNHELPFUL IDEAS SHOULD BE OMITTED, COLONEL!
BUT TAKE HEART, THOMPSON... WHEN I NEED AN ANECDOTE TO AMUSE CHURCHILL, I'LL BE SURE TO CALL UPON YOU.
HAHAHA!
WUUUUUUUUUUUUUUWUUUUUUUUUUUUUUUUUUUUWUUUUUUUUUUUUUUUUWUUUUUUUUUUUUUUUU
THE SIRENS!
GATHER YOUR DOCUMENTS. WE WILL CONTINUE OUR MEETING IN THE SHELTER.
MAKE HASTE, MEN! QUICKLY, NOW!

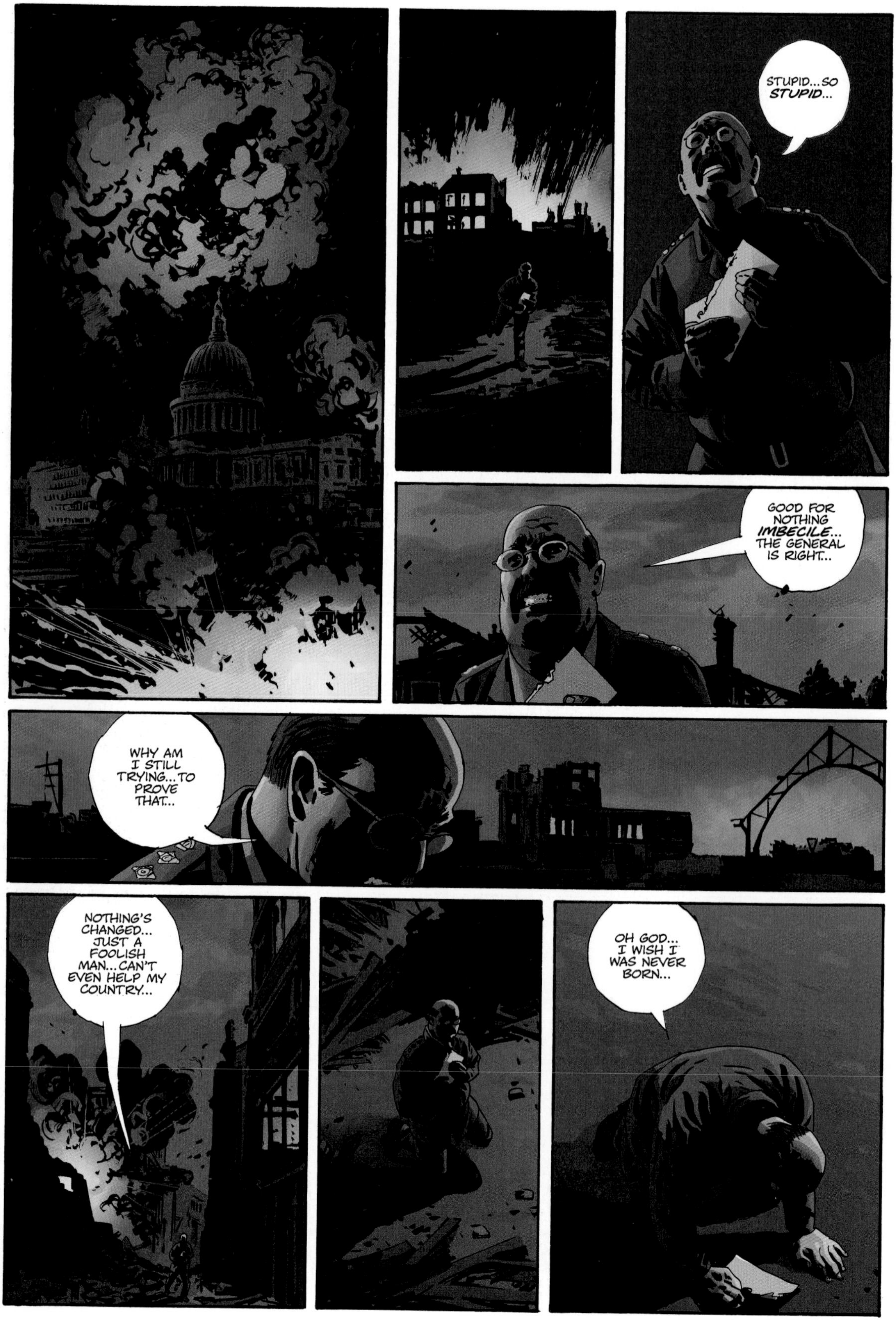
STUPID...SO STUPID...
GOOD FOR NOTHING IMBECILE... THE GENERAL IS RIGHT...
WHY AM I STILL TRYING...TO PROVE THAT...
NOTHING'S CHANGED... JUST A FOOLISH MAN...CAN'T EVEN HELP MY COUNTRY...
OH GOD... I WISH I WAS NEVER BORN...

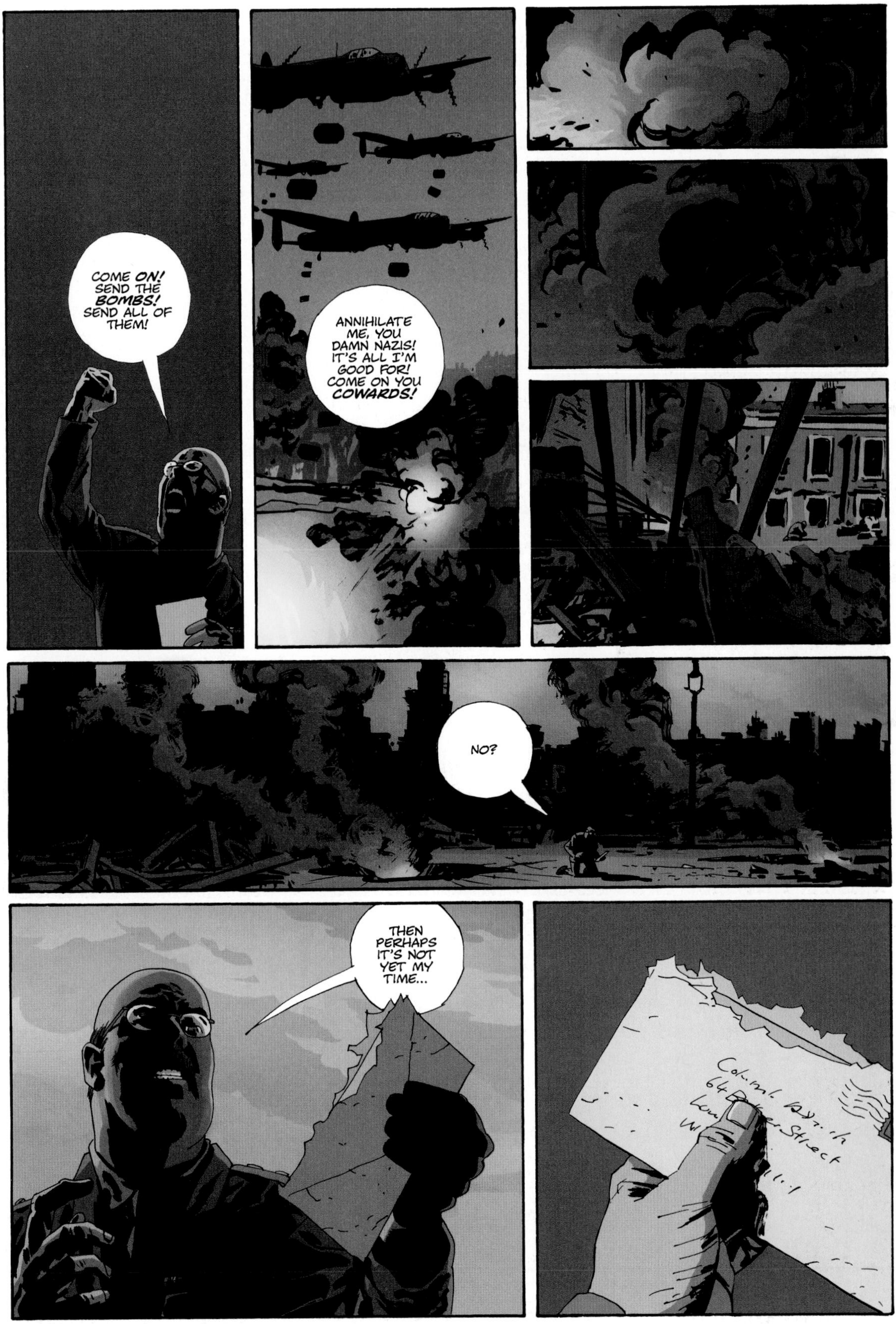
COME ON! SEND THE BOMBS! SEND ALL OF THEM!
ANNIHILATE ME, YOU DAMN NAZIS! IT'S ALL I'M GOOD FOR! COME ON YOU COWARDS!
NO?
THEN PERHAPS IT'S NOT YET MY TIME...

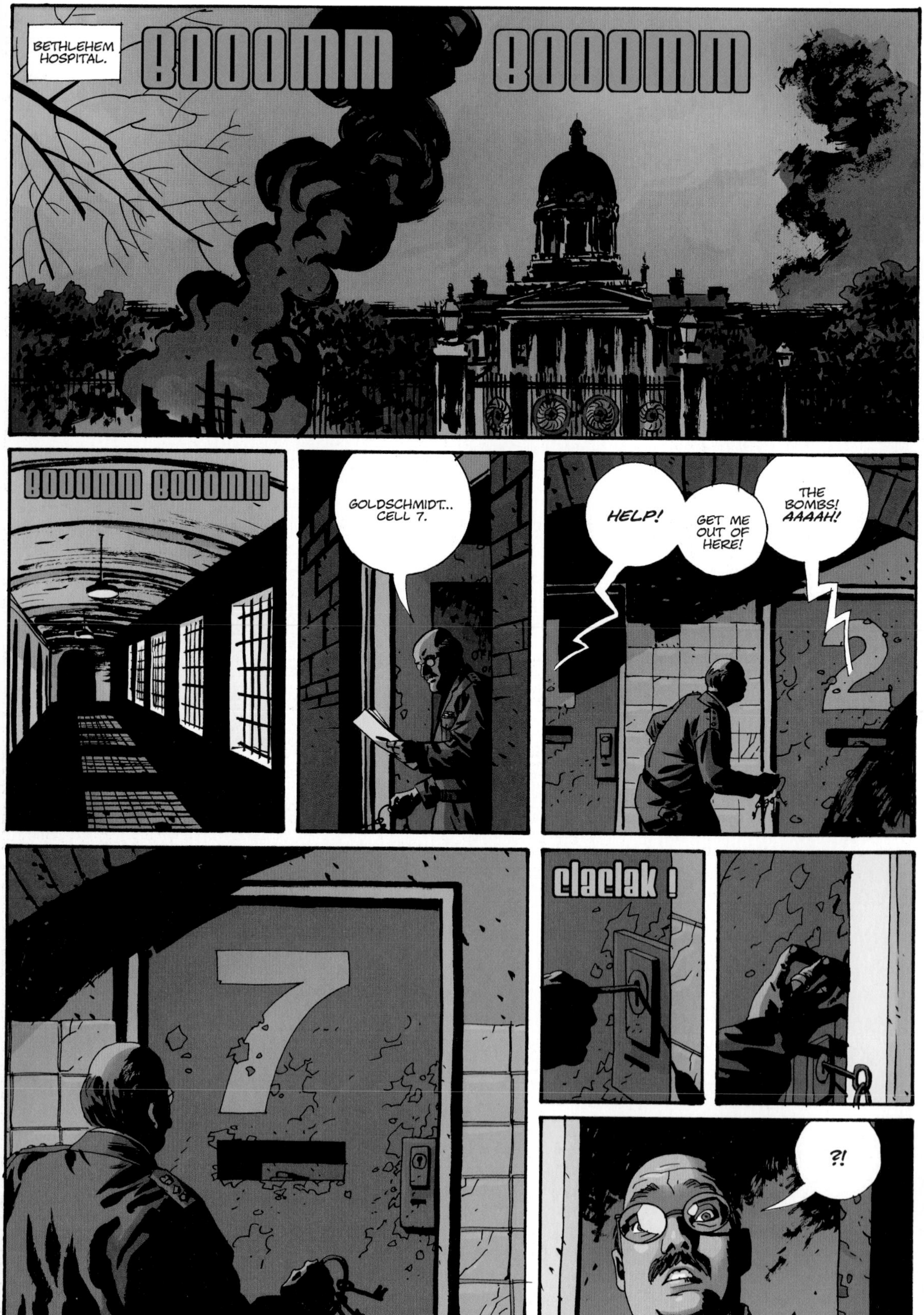
BETHLEHEM HOSPITAL.
BOOOMM
BOOOMM
BOOOMM BOOOMM
GOLDSCHMIDT... CELL 7.
HELP!
GET ME OUT OF HERE!
THE BOMBS! AAAAH!
2
7
CLACLAK !
?!

RIGHT ON TIME, COLONEL THOMPSON. I'VE BEEN WAITING FOR YOU. WELCOME.

WELL...SUCH AS IT IS, ANYWAY. JOSHUA GOLDSCHMIDT, PROFESSOR OF RELIGIOUS HISTORY AT CAMBRIDGE...OR AT LEAST I WAS, BEFORE MY LUDICROUS AND UNJUST INTERNMENT HERE.

WHAT... WHAT WAS THE REASON, IF I MAY BE SO BOLD?

THEY SAY I HAVE A *PERSECUTION COMPLEX*, IF YOU CAN BELIEVE IT.

SHOCKING. HERE I AM, A JEW, WITH HIS PEOPLE BEING EXTERMINATED BY THE NAZIS. THE GENOCIDE OF ONE'S PEOPLE IS MORE THAN REASON ENOUGH FOR ANYONE TO DEVELOP A PERSECUTION COMPLEX, WOULDN'T YOU THINK? BUT LET'S NOT DWELL.

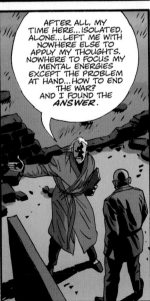

AFTER ALL, MY TIME HERE...ISOLATED, ALONE...LEFT ME WITH NOWHERE ELSE TO APPLY MY THOUGHTS. NOWHERE TO FOCUS MY MENTAL ENERGIES EXCEPT THE PROBLEM AT HAND...HOW TO END THE WAR? AND I FOUND THE *ANSWER*.

WE WILL PARACHUTE SEVEN MEN INTO GERMANY AND THEN *ASSASSINATE HITLER*.

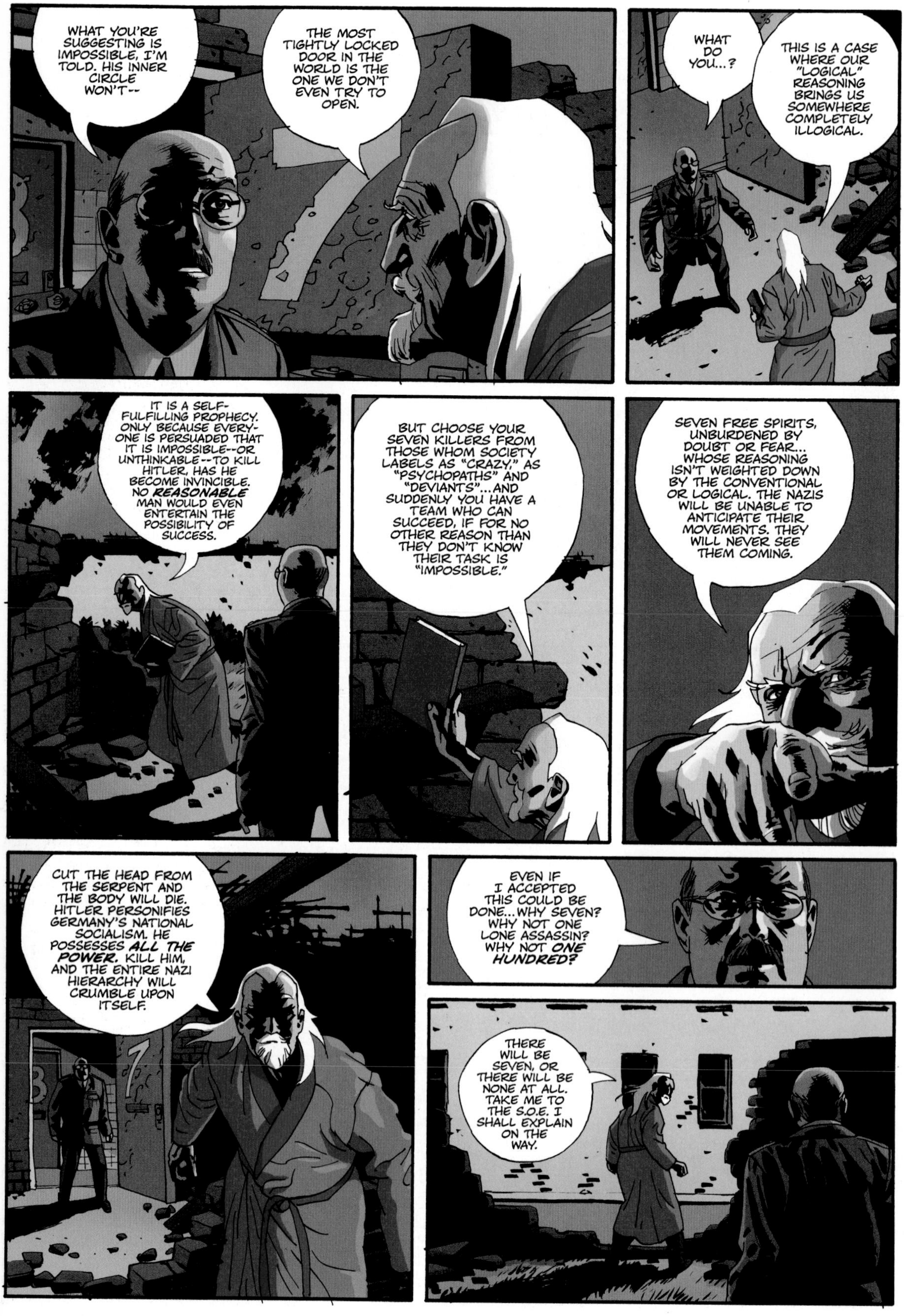
WHAT YOU'RE SUGGESTING IS IMPOSSIBLE, I'M TOLD. HIS INNER CIRCLE WON'T--
THE MOST TIGHTLY LOCKED DOOR IN THE WORLD IS THE ONE WE DON'T EVEN TRY TO OPEN.
WHAT DO YOU...?
THIS IS A CASE WHERE OUR "LOGICAL" REASONING BRINGS US SOMEWHERE COMPLETELY ILLOGICAL.
IT IS A SELF-FULFILLING PROPHECY. ONLY BECAUSE EVERY-ONE IS PERSUADED THAT IT IS IMPOSSIBLE--OR UNTHINKABLE--TO KILL HITLER, HAS HE BECOME INVINCIBLE. NO REASONABLE MAN WOULD EVEN ENTERTAIN THE POSSIBILITY OF SUCCESS.
BUT CHOOSE YOUR SEVEN KILLERS FROM THOSE WHOM SOCIETY LABELS AS "CRAZY," AS "PSYCHOPATHS" AND "DEVIANTS"...AND SUDDENLY YOU HAVE A TEAM WHO CAN SUCCEED, IF FOR NO OTHER REASON THAN THEY DON'T KNOW THEIR TASK IS "IMPOSSIBLE."
SEVEN FREE SPIRITS, UNBURDENED BY DOUBT OR FEAR... WHOSE REASONING ISN'T WEIGHTED DOWN BY THE CONVENTIONAL OR LOGICAL. THE NAZIS WILL BE UNABLE TO ANTICIPATE THEIR MOVEMENTS. THEY WILL NEVER SEE THEM COMING.
CUT THE HEAD FROM THE SERPENT AND THE BODY WILL DIE. HITLER PERSONIFIES GERMANY'S NATIONAL SOCIALISM. HE POSSESSES ALL THE POWER. KILL HIM, AND THE ENTIRE NAZI HIERARCHY WILL CRUMBLE UPON ITSELF.
EVEN IF I ACCEPTED THIS COULD BE DONE...WHY SEVEN? WHY NOT ONE LONE ASSASSIN? WHY NOT ONE HUNDRED?
THERE WILL BE SEVEN, OR THERE WILL BE NONE AT ALL. TAKE ME TO THE S.O.E. I SHALL EXPLAIN ON THE WAY.

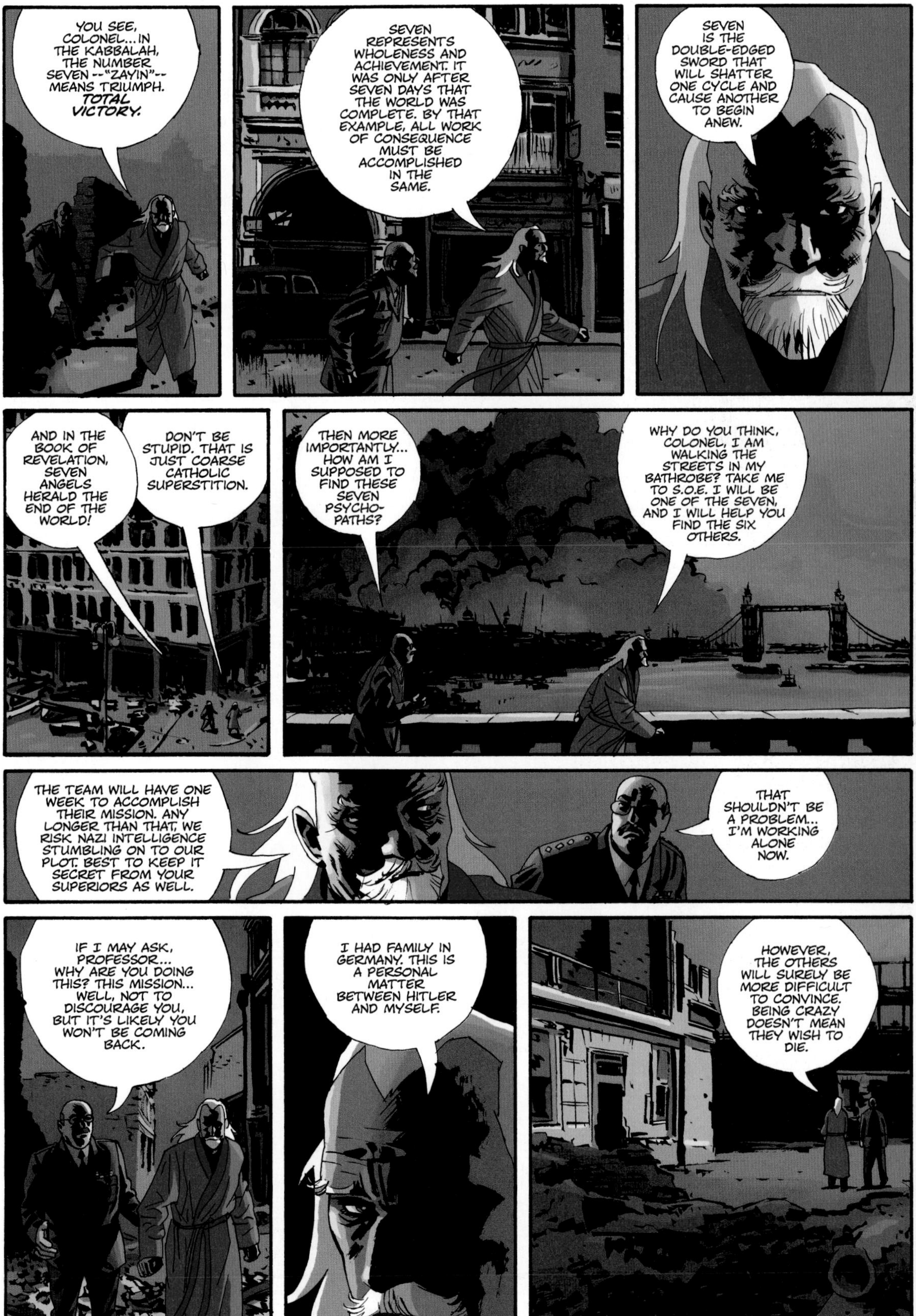
YOU SEE, COLONEL... IN THE KABBALAH, THE NUMBER SEVEN --"ZAYIN"-- MEANS TRIUMPH. TOTAL VICTORY.
SEVEN REPRESENTS WHOLENESS AND ACHIEVEMENT. IT WAS ONLY AFTER SEVEN DAYS THAT THE WORLD WAS COMPLETE. BY THAT EXAMPLE, ALL WORK OF CONSEQUENCE MUST BE ACCOMPLISHED IN THE SAME.
SEVEN IS THE DOUBLE-EDGED SWORD THAT WILL SHATTER ONE CYCLE AND CAUSE ANOTHER TO BEGIN ANEW.
AND IN THE BOOK OF REVELATION, SEVEN ANGELS HERALD THE END OF THE WORLD!
DON'T BE STUPID. THAT IS JUST COARSE CATHOLIC SUPERSTITION.
THEN MORE IMPORTANTLY... HOW AM I SUPPOSED TO FIND THESE SEVEN PSYCHO-PATHS?
WHY DO YOU THINK, COLONEL, I AM WALKING THE STREETS IN MY BATHROBE? TAKE ME TO S.O.E. I WILL BE ONE OF THE SEVEN, AND I WILL HELP YOU FIND THE SIX OTHERS.
THE TEAM WILL HAVE ONE WEEK TO ACCOMPLISH THEIR MISSION. ANY LONGER THAN THAT, WE RISK NAZI INTELLIGENCE STUMBLING ON TO OUR PLOT. BEST TO KEEP IT SECRET FROM YOUR SUPERIORS AS WELL.
THAT SHOULDN'T BE A PROBLEM... I'M WORKING ALONE NOW.
IF I MAY ASK, PROFESSOR... WHY ARE YOU DOING THIS? THIS MISSION... WELL, NOT TO DISCOURAGE YOU, BUT IT'S LIKELY YOU WON'T BE COMING BACK.
I HAD FAMILY IN GERMANY. THIS IS A PERSONAL MATTER BETWEEN HITLER AND MYSELF.
HOWEVER, THE OTHERS WILL SURELY BE MORE DIFFICULT TO CONVINCE. BEING CRAZY DOESN'T MEAN THEY WISH TO DIE.

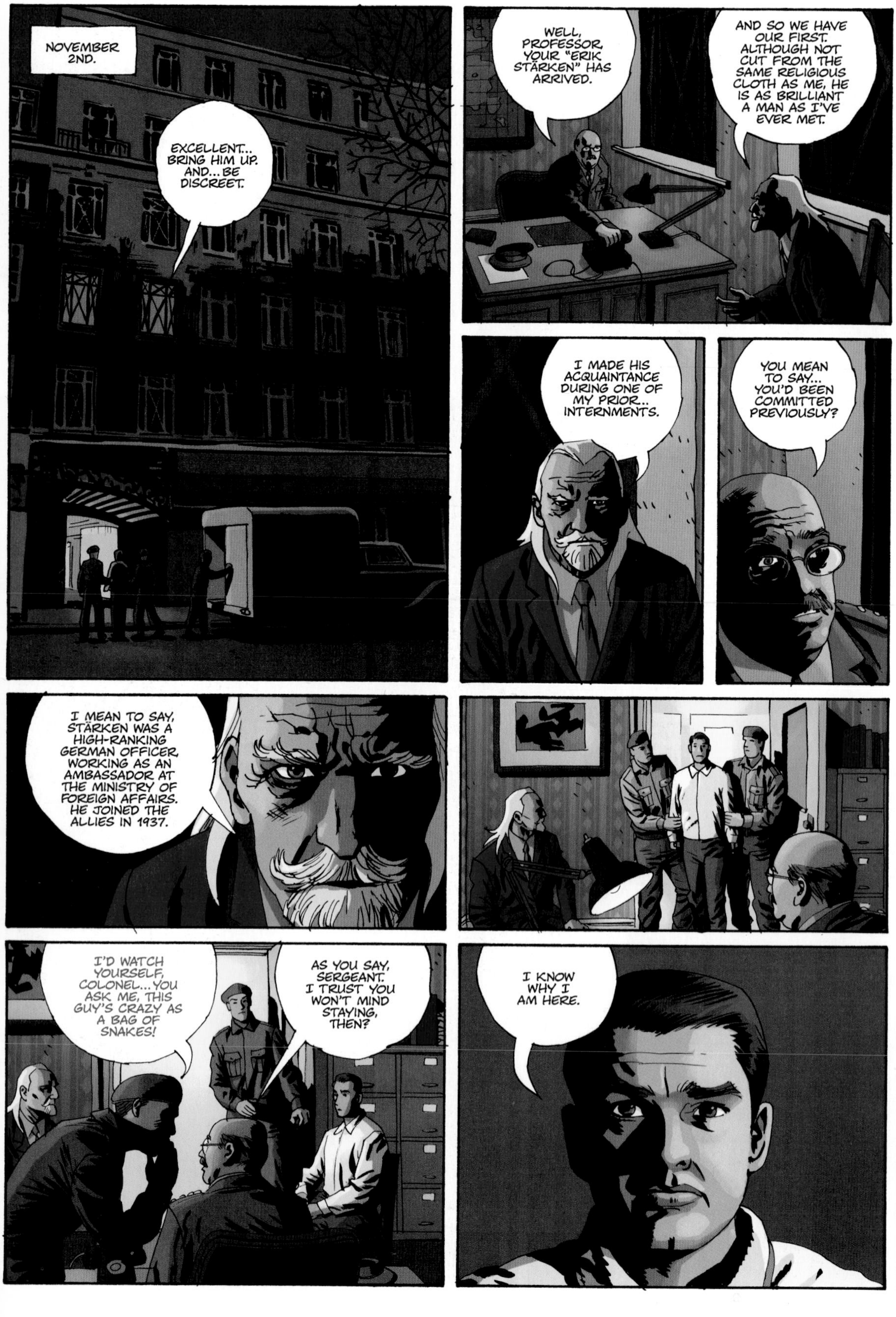
NOVEMBER 2ND.
EXCELLENT... BRING HIM UP. AND... BE DISCREET.
WELL, PROFESSOR, YOUR "ERIK STÄRKEN" HAS ARRIVED.
AND SO WE HAVE OUR FIRST. ALTHOUGH NOT CUT FROM THE SAME RELIGIOUS CLOTH AS ME, HE IS AS BRILLIANT A MAN AS I'VE EVER MET.
I MADE HIS ACQUAINTANCE DURING ONE OF MY PRIOR.. INTERNMENTS.
YOU MEAN TO SAY... YOU'D BEEN COMMITTED PREVIOUSLY?
I MEAN TO SAY, STÄRKEN WAS A HIGH-RANKING GERMAN OFFICER, WORKING AS AN AMBASSADOR AT THE MINISTRY OF FOREIGN AFFAIRS. HE JOINED THE ALLIES IN 1937.
I'D WATCH YOURSELF, COLONEL...YOU ASK ME, THIS GUY'S CRAZY AS A BAG OF SNAKES!
AS YOU SAY, SERGEANT. I TRUST YOU WON'T MIND STAYING, THEN?
I KNOW WHY I AM HERE.

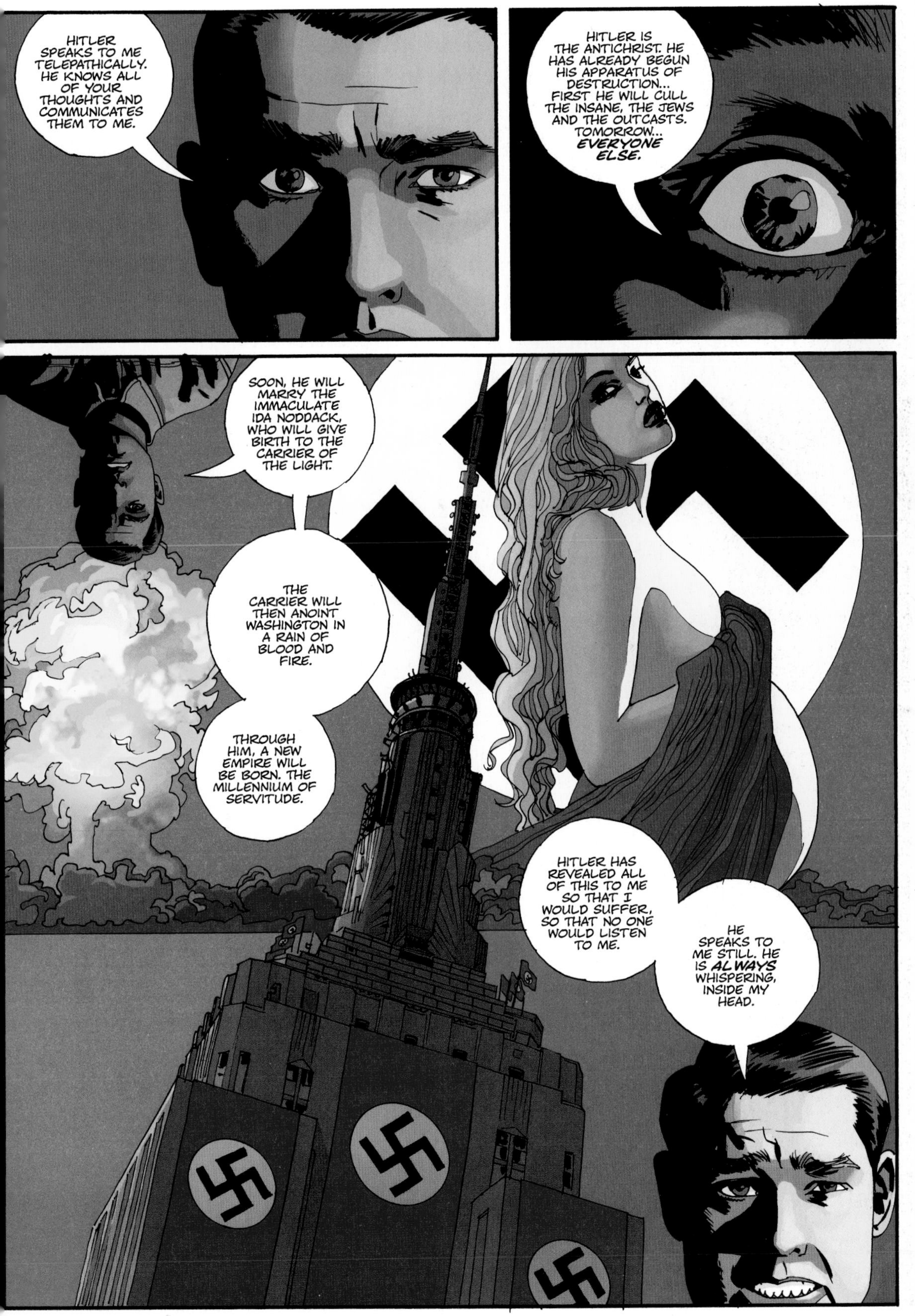
HITLER SPEAKS TO ME TELEPATHICALLY. HE KNOWS ALL OF YOUR THOUGHTS AND COMMUNICATES THEM TO ME.
HITLER IS THE ANTICHRIST. HE HAS ALREADY BEGUN HIS APPARATUS OF DESTRUCTION... FIRST HE WILL CULL THE INSANE, THE JEWS AND THE OUTCASTS. TOMORROW... EVERYONE ELSE.
SOON, HE WILL MARRY THE IMMACULATE IDA NODDACK, WHO WILL GIVE BIRTH TO THE CARRIER OF THE LIGHT.
THE CARRIER WILL THEN ANOINT WASHINGTON IN A RAIN OF BLOOD AND FIRE.
THROUGH HIM, A NEW EMPIRE WILL BE BORN. THE MILLENNIUM OF SERVITUDE.
HITLER HAS REVEALED ALL OF THIS TO ME SO THAT I WOULD SUFFER, SO THAT NO ONE WOULD LISTEN TO ME.
HE SPEAKS TO ME STILL. HE IS ALWAYS WHISPERING, INSIDE MY HEAD.

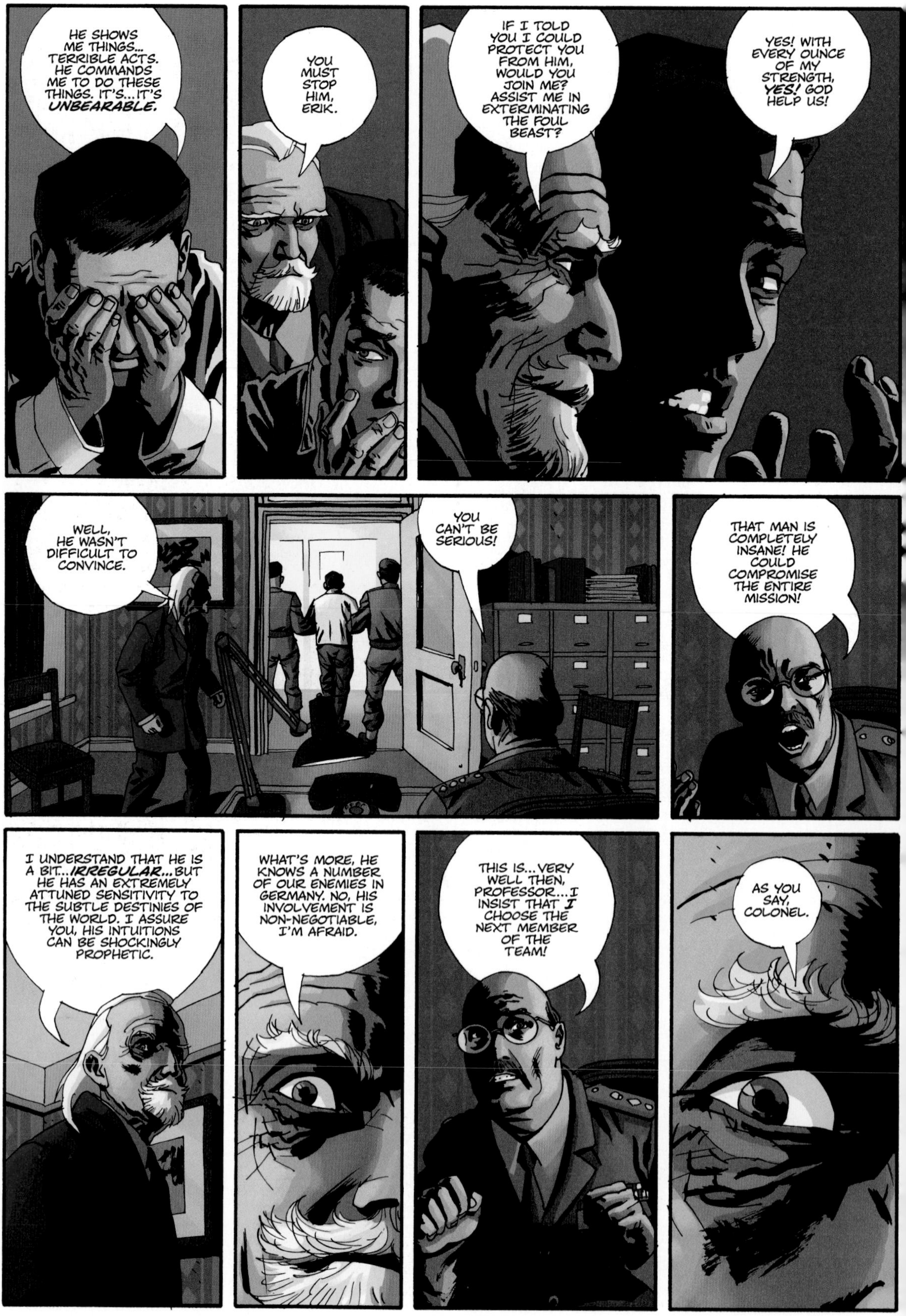
HE SHOWS ME THINGS... TERRIBLE ACTS. HE COMMANDS ME TO DO THESE THINGS. IT'S...IT'S *UNBEARABLE.*
YOU MUST STOP HIM, ERIK.
IF I TOLD YOU I COULD PROTECT YOU FROM HIM, WOULD YOU JOIN ME? ASSIST ME IN EXTERMINATING THE FOUL BEAST?
YES! WITH EVERY OUNCE OF MY STRENGTH, *YES!* GOD HELP US!
WELL, HE WASN'T DIFFICULT TO CONVINCE.
YOU CAN'T BE SERIOUS!
THAT MAN IS COMPLETELY INSANE! HE COULD COMPROMISE THE ENTIRE MISSION!
I UNDERSTAND THAT HE IS A BIT...*IRREGULAR*...BUT HE HAS AN EXTREMELY ATTUNED SENSITIVITY TO THE SUBTLE DESTINIES OF THE WORLD. I ASSURE YOU, HIS INTUITIONS CAN BE SHOCKINGLY PROPHETIC.
WHAT'S MORE, HE KNOWS A NUMBER OF OUR ENEMIES IN GERMANY. NO, HIS INVOLVEMENT IS NON-NEGOTIABLE, I'M AFRAID.
THIS IS...VERY WELL THEN, PROFESSOR...I INSIST THAT *I* CHOOSE THE NEXT MEMBER OF THE TEAM!
AS YOU SAY, COLONEL.

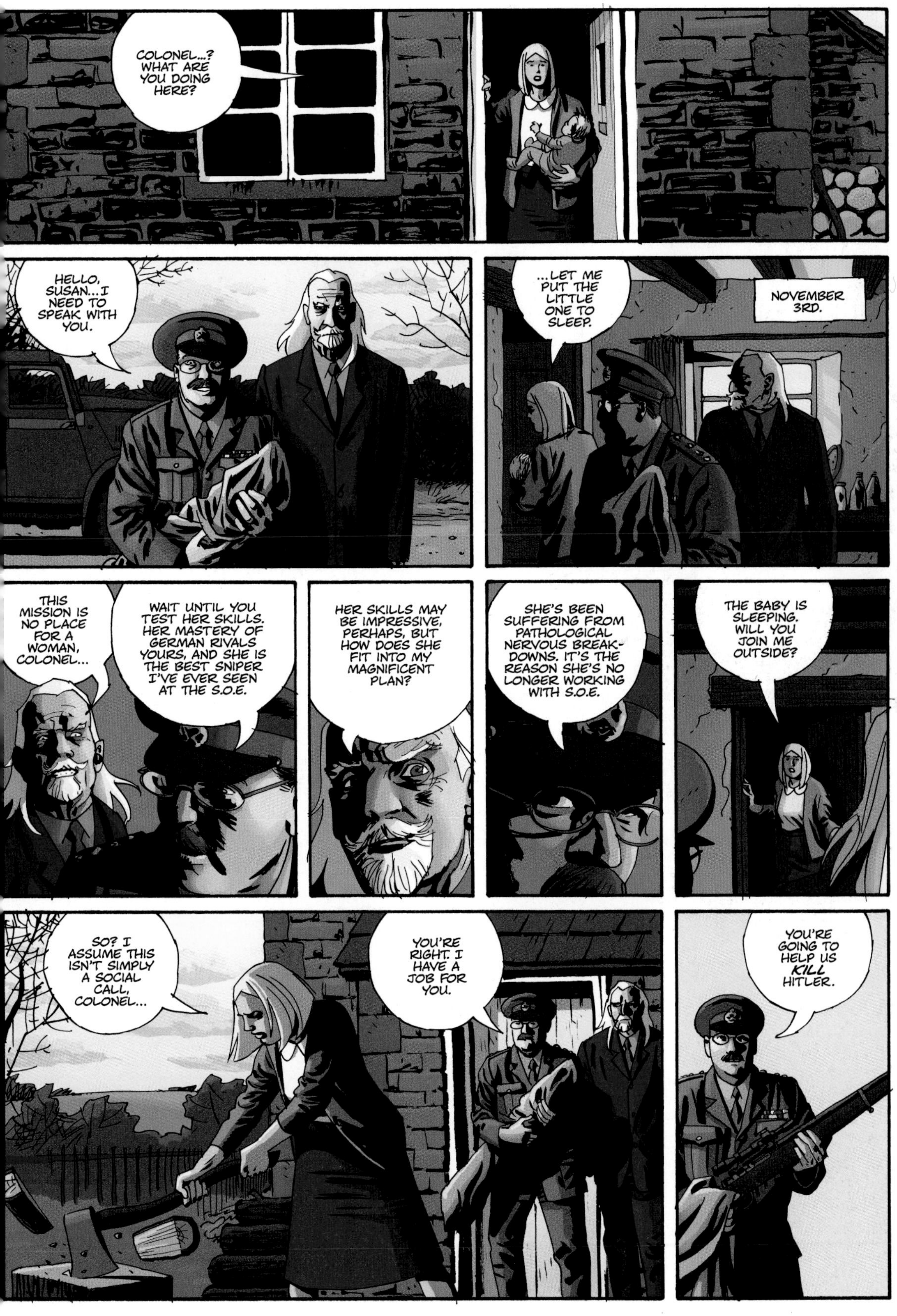
COLONEL...? WHAT ARE YOU DOING HERE?
HELLO, SUSAN... I NEED TO SPEAK WITH YOU.
...LET ME PUT THE LITTLE ONE TO SLEEP.
NOVEMBER 3RD.
THIS MISSION IS NO PLACE FOR A WOMAN, COLONEL...
WAIT UNTIL YOU TEST HER SKILLS. HER MASTERY OF GERMAN RIVALS YOURS, AND SHE IS THE BEST SNIPER I'VE EVER SEEN AT THE S.O.E.
HER SKILLS MAY BE IMPRESSIVE, PERHAPS, BUT HOW DOES SHE FIT INTO MY MAGNIFICENT PLAN?
SHE'S BEEN SUFFERING FROM PATHOLOGICAL NERVOUS BREAK-DOWNS. IT'S THE REASON SHE'S NO LONGER WORKING WITH S.O.E.
THE BABY IS SLEEPING. WILL YOU JOIN ME OUTSIDE?
SO? I ASSUME THIS ISN'T SIMPLY A SOCIAL CALL, COLONEL...
YOU'RE RIGHT. I HAVE A JOB FOR YOU.
YOU'RE GOING TO HELP US *KILL* HITLER.

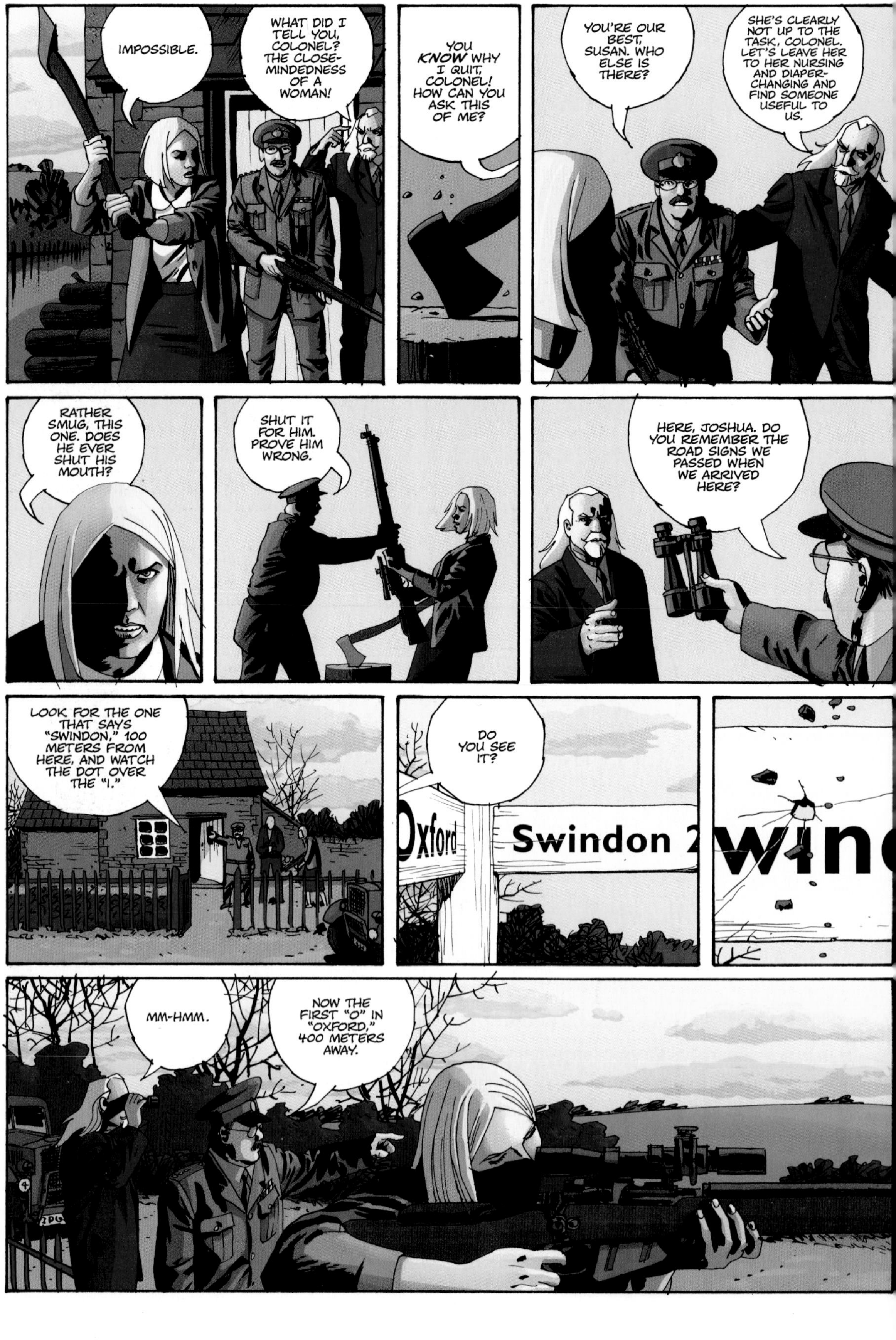
IMPOSSIBLE.
WHAT DID I TELL YOU, COLONEL? THE CLOSE-MINDEDNESS OF A WOMAN!
YOU *KNOW* WHY I QUIT, COLONEL! HOW CAN YOU ASK THIS OF ME?
YOU'RE OUR BEST, SUSAN. WHO ELSE IS THERE?
SHE'S CLEARLY NOT UP TO THE TASK, COLONEL. LET'S LEAVE HER TO HER NURSING AND DIAPER-CHANGING AND FIND SOMEONE USEFUL TO US.
RATHER SMUG, THIS ONE. DOES HE EVER SHUT HIS MOUTH?
SHUT IT FOR HIM. PROVE HIM WRONG.
HERE, JOSHUA. DO YOU REMEMBER THE ROAD SIGNS WE PASSED WHEN WE ARRIVED HERE?
LOOK FOR THE ONE THAT SAYS "SWINDON," 100 METERS FROM HERE, AND WATCH THE DOT OVER THE "I."
DO YOU SEE IT?
Oxford
Swindon 2
wind
MM-HMM.
NOW THE FIRST "O" IN "OXFORD," 400 METERS AWAY.

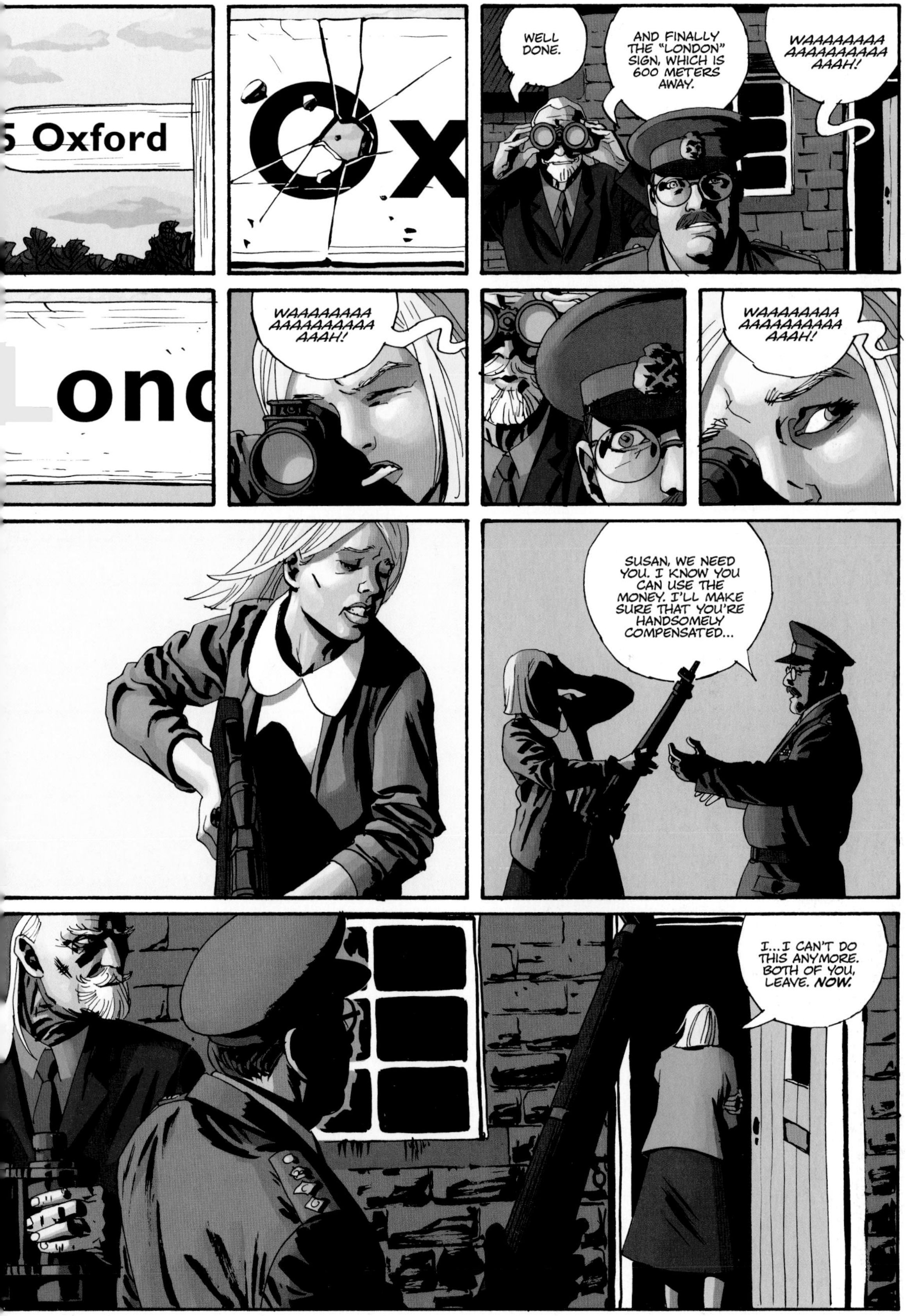
5 Oxford
Ox
WELL DONE.
AND FINALLY THE "LONDON" SIGN, WHICH IS 600 METERS AWAY.
WAAAAAAAA AAAAAAAAAA AAAH!
Lond
WAAAAAAAA AAAAAAAAAA AAAH!
WAAAAAAAA AAAAAAAAAA AAAH!
SUSAN, WE NEED YOU. I KNOW YOU CAN USE THE MONEY. I'LL MAKE SURE THAT YOU'RE HANDSOMELY COMPENSATED...
I...I CAN'T DO THIS ANYMORE. BOTH OF YOU, LEAVE. *NOW.*

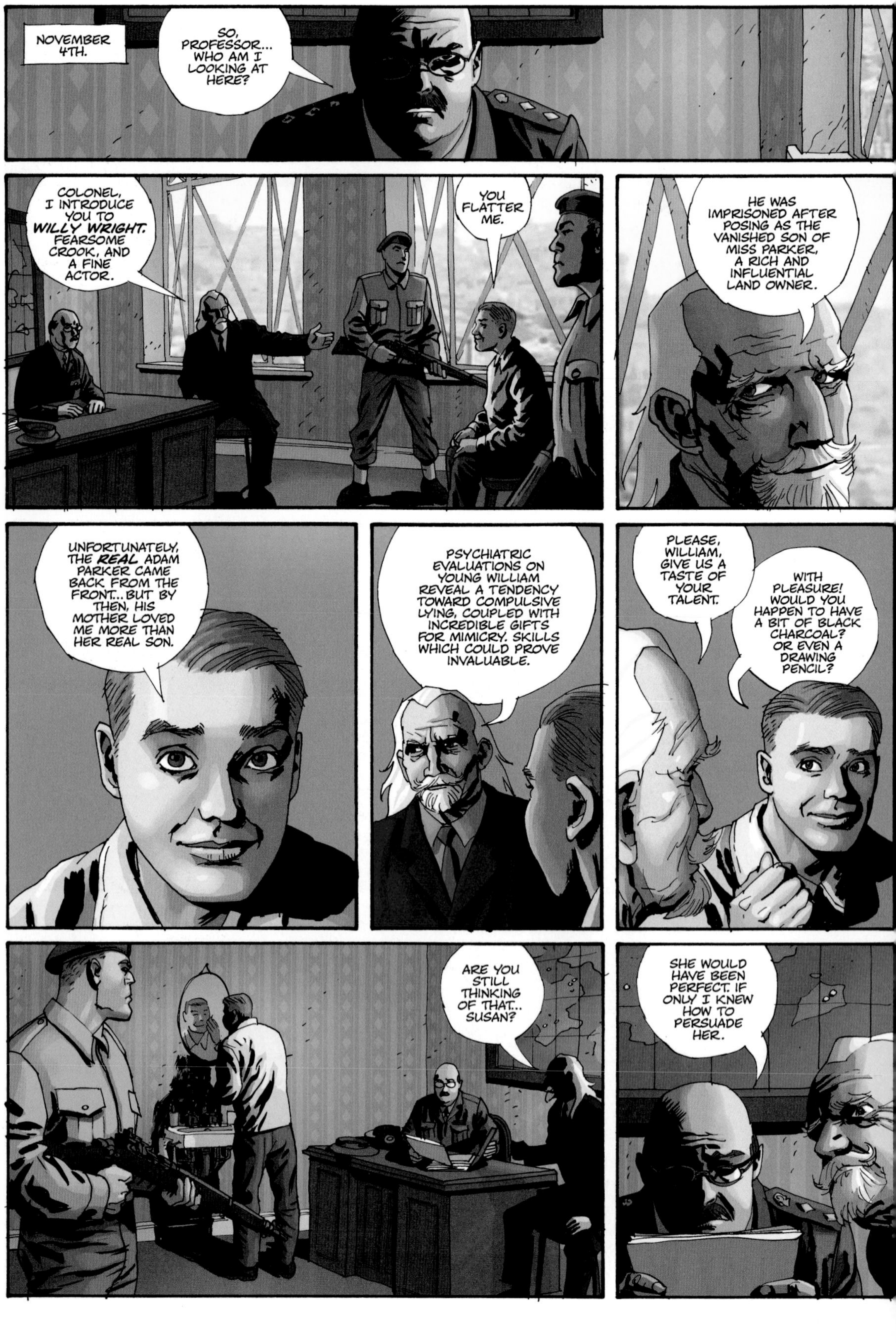
NOVEMBER 4TH.
SO, PROFESSOR... WHO AM I LOOKING AT HERE?
COLONEL, I INTRODUCE YOU TO WILLY WRIGHT. FEARSOME CROOK, AND A FINE ACTOR.
YOU FLATTER ME.
HE WAS IMPRISONED AFTER POSING AS THE VANISHED SON OF MISS PARKER, A RICH AND INFLUENTIAL LAND OWNER.
UNFORTUNATELY, THE REAL ADAM PARKER CAME BACK FROM THE FRONT... BUT BY THEN, HIS MOTHER LOVED ME MORE THAN HER REAL SON.
PSYCHIATRIC EVALUATIONS ON YOUNG WILLIAM REVEAL A TENDENCY TOWARD COMPULSIVE LYING, COUPLED WITH INCREDIBLE GIFTS FOR MIMICRY. SKILLS WHICH COULD PROVE INVALUABLE.
PLEASE, WILLIAM, GIVE US A TASTE OF YOUR TALENT.
WITH PLEASURE! WOULD YOU HAPPEN TO HAVE A BIT OF BLACK CHARCOAL? OR EVEN A DRAWING PENCIL?
ARE YOU STILL THINKING OF THAT... SUSAN?
SHE WOULD HAVE BEEN PERFECT. IF ONLY I KNEW HOW TO PERSUADE HER.

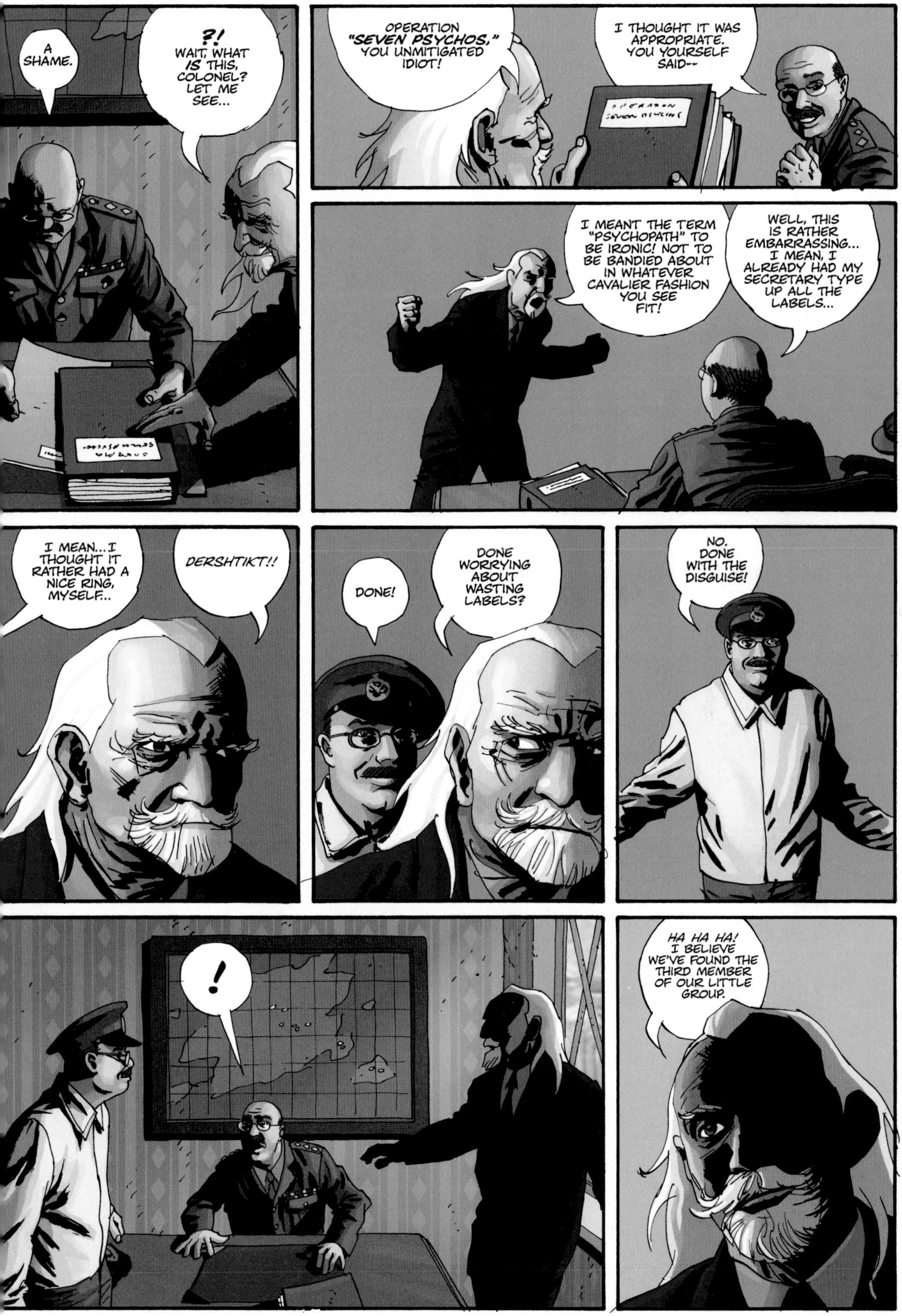
A SHAME.
?! WAIT, WHAT IS THIS, COLONEL? LET ME SEE...
OPERATION "SEVEN PSYCHOS," YOU UNMITIGATED IDIOT!
I THOUGHT IT WAS APPROPRIATE. YOU YOURSELF SAID--
I MEANT THE TERM "PSYCHOPATH" TO BE IRONIC! NOT TO BE BANDIED ABOUT IN WHATEVER CAVALIER FASHION YOU SEE FIT!
WELL, THIS IS RATHER EMBARRASSING... I MEAN, I ALREADY HAD MY SECRETARY TYPE UP ALL THE LABELS...
I MEAN...I THOUGHT IT RATHER HAD A NICE RING, MYSELF...
DERSHTIKT!!
DONE!
DONE WORRYING ABOUT WASTING LABELS?
NO. DONE WITH THE DISGUISE!
!
HA HA HA! I BELIEVE WE'VE FOUND THE THIRD MEMBER OF OUR LITTLE GROUP.

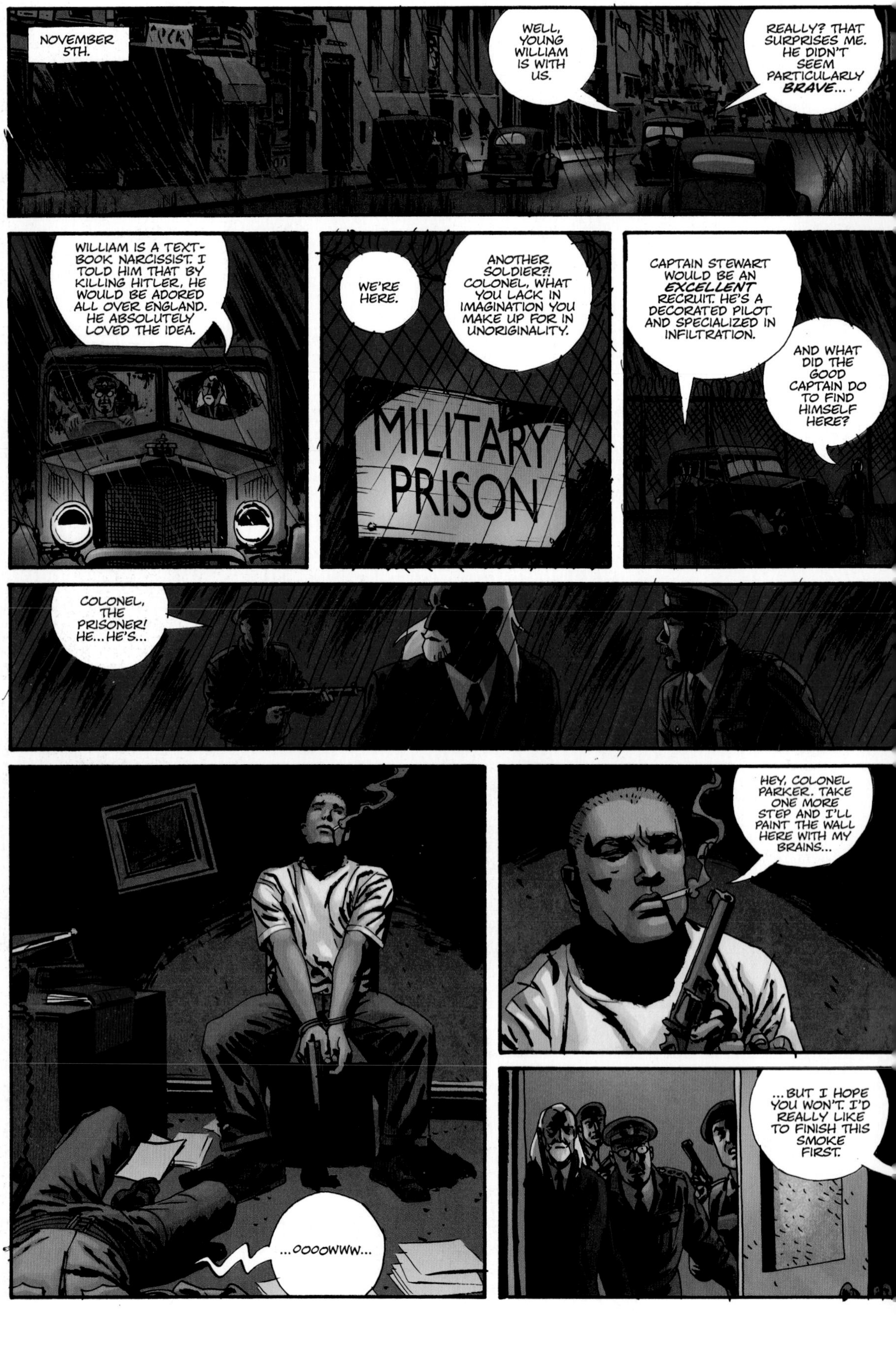
NOVEMBER 5TH.
WELL, YOUNG WILLIAM IS WITH US.
REALLY? THAT SURPRISES ME. HE DIDN'T SEEM PARTICULARLY BRAVE...
WILLIAM IS A TEXT-BOOK NARCISSIST. I TOLD HIM THAT BY KILLING HITLER, HE WOULD BE ADORED ALL OVER ENGLAND. HE ABSOLUTELY LOVED THE IDEA.
WE'RE HERE.
ANOTHER SOLDIER?! COLONEL, WHAT YOU LACK IN IMAGINATION YOU MAKE UP FOR IN UNORIGINALITY.
MILITARY PRISON
CAPTAIN STEWART WOULD BE AN EXCELLENT RECRUIT. HE'S A DECORATED PILOT AND SPECIALIZED IN INFILTRATION.
AND WHAT DID THE GOOD CAPTAIN DO TO FIND HIMSELF HERE?
COLONEL, THE PRISONER! HE... HE'S...
...OOOOWWW...
HEY, COLONEL PARKER. TAKE ONE MORE STEP AND I'LL PAINT THE WALL HERE WITH MY BRAINS...
...BUT I HOPE YOU WON'T. I'D REALLY LIKE TO FINISH THIS SMOKE FIRST.

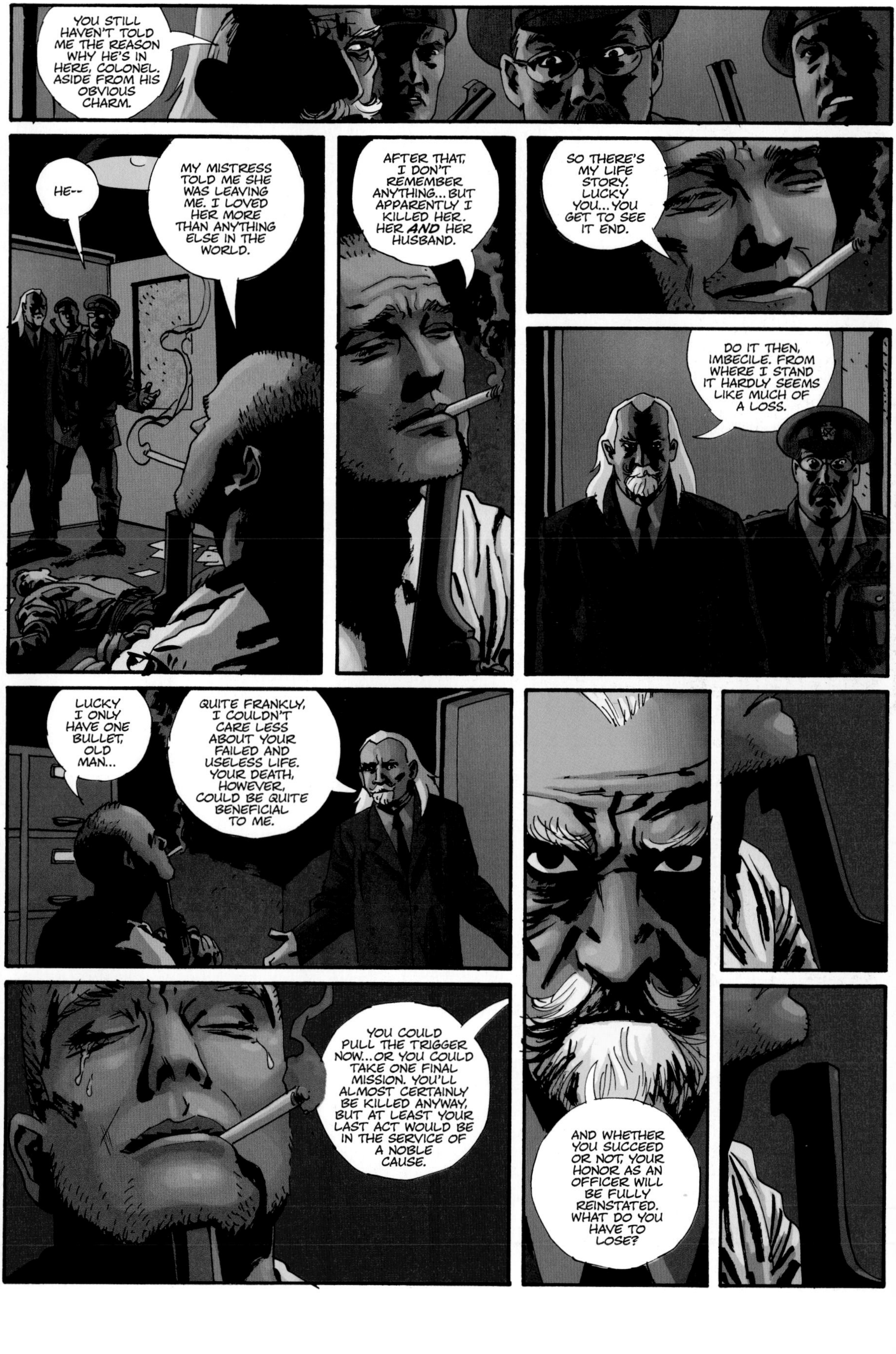
YOU STILL HAVEN'T TOLD ME THE REASON WHY HE'S IN HERE, COLONEL. ASIDE FROM HIS OBVIOUS CHARM.
HE--
MY MISTRESS TOLD ME SHE WAS LEAVING ME. I LOVED HER MORE THAN ANYTHING ELSE IN THE WORLD.
AFTER THAT, I DON'T REMEMBER ANYTHING... BUT APPARENTLY I KILLED HER. HER AND HER HUSBAND.
SO THERE'S MY LIFE STORY. LUCKY YOU... YOU GET TO SEE IT END.
DO IT THEN, IMBECILE. FROM WHERE I STAND IT HARDLY SEEMS LIKE MUCH OF A LOSS.
LUCKY I ONLY HAVE ONE BULLET, OLD MAN...
QUITE FRANKLY, I COULDN'T CARE LESS ABOUT YOUR FAILED AND USELESS LIFE. YOUR DEATH, HOWEVER, COULD BE QUITE BENEFICIAL TO ME.
YOU COULD PULL THE TRIGGER NOW... OR YOU COULD TAKE ONE FINAL MISSION. YOU'LL ALMOST CERTAINLY BE KILLED ANYWAY, BUT AT LEAST YOUR LAST ACT WOULD BE IN THE SERVICE OF A NOBLE CAUSE.
AND WHETHER YOU SUCCEED OR NOT, YOUR HONOR AS AN OFFICER WILL BE FULLY REINSTATED. WHAT DO YOU HAVE TO LOSE?

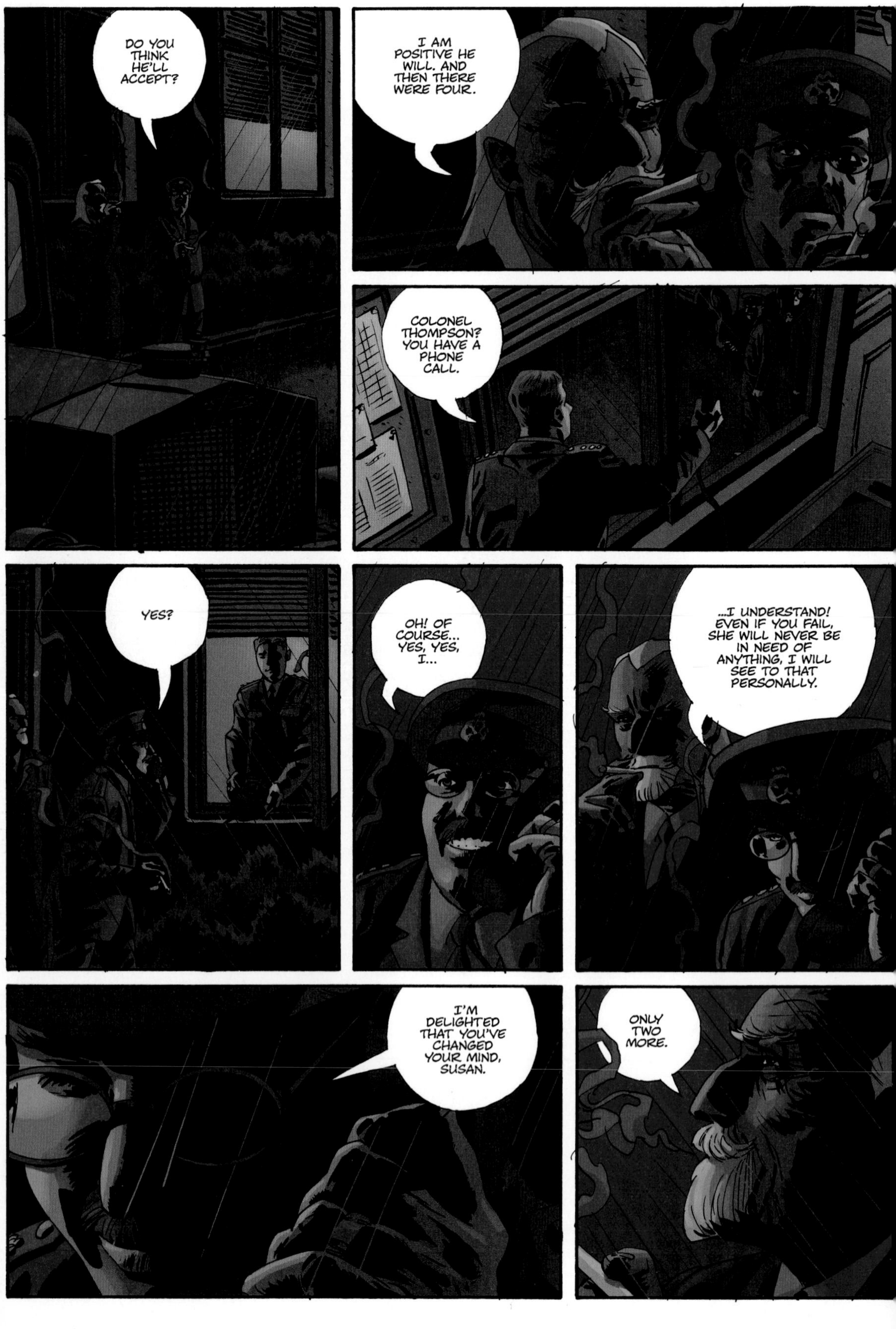
DO YOU THINK HE'LL ACCEPT?
I AM POSITIVE HE WILL. AND THEN THERE WERE FOUR.
COLONEL THOMPSON? YOU HAVE A PHONE CALL.
YES?
OH! OF COURSE... YES, YES, I...
...I UNDERSTAND! EVEN IF YOU FAIL, SHE WILL NEVER BE IN NEED OF ANYTHING, I WILL SEE TO THAT PERSONALLY.
I'M DELIGHTED THAT YOU'VE CHANGED YOUR MIND, SUSAN.
ONLY TWO MORE.

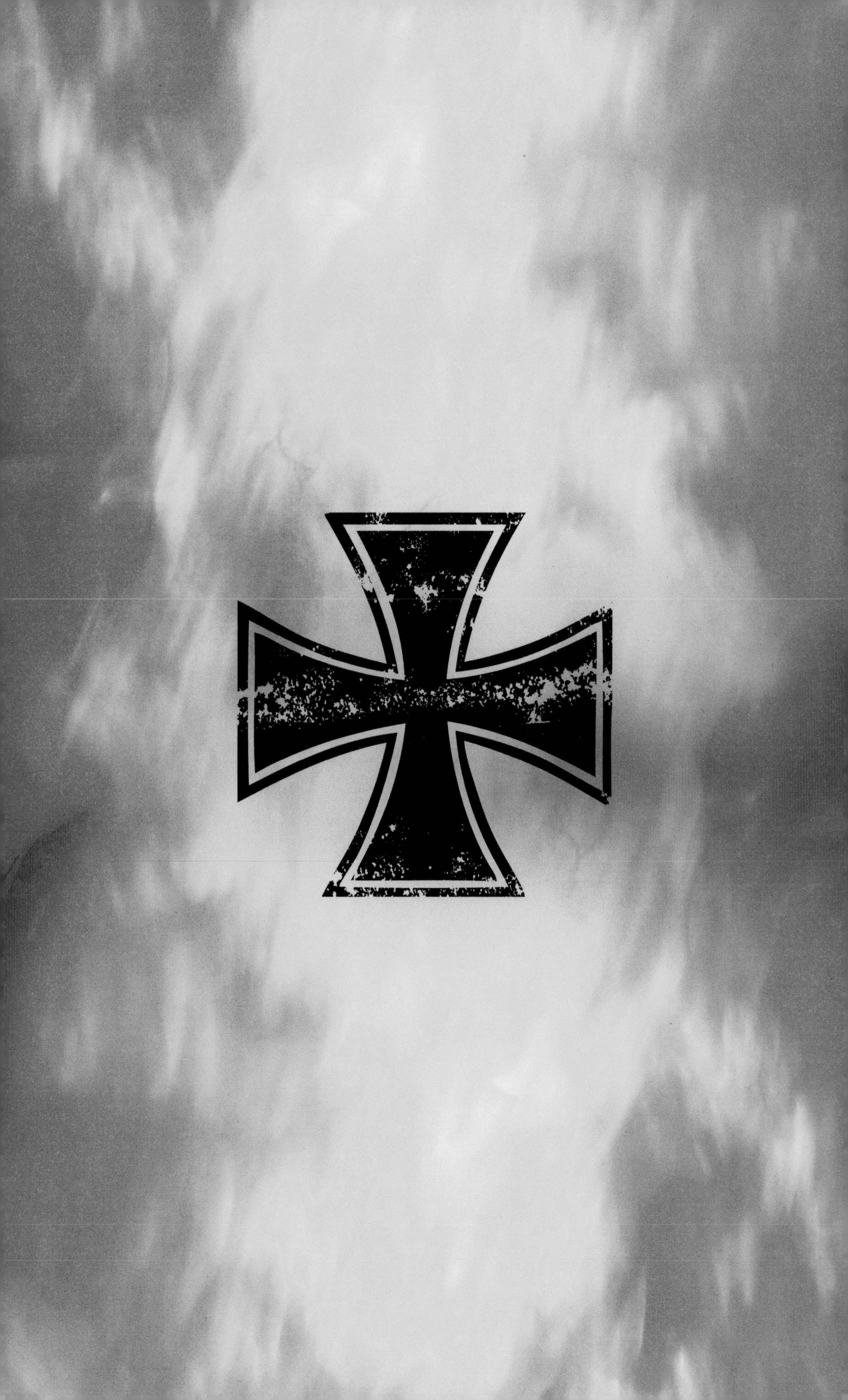

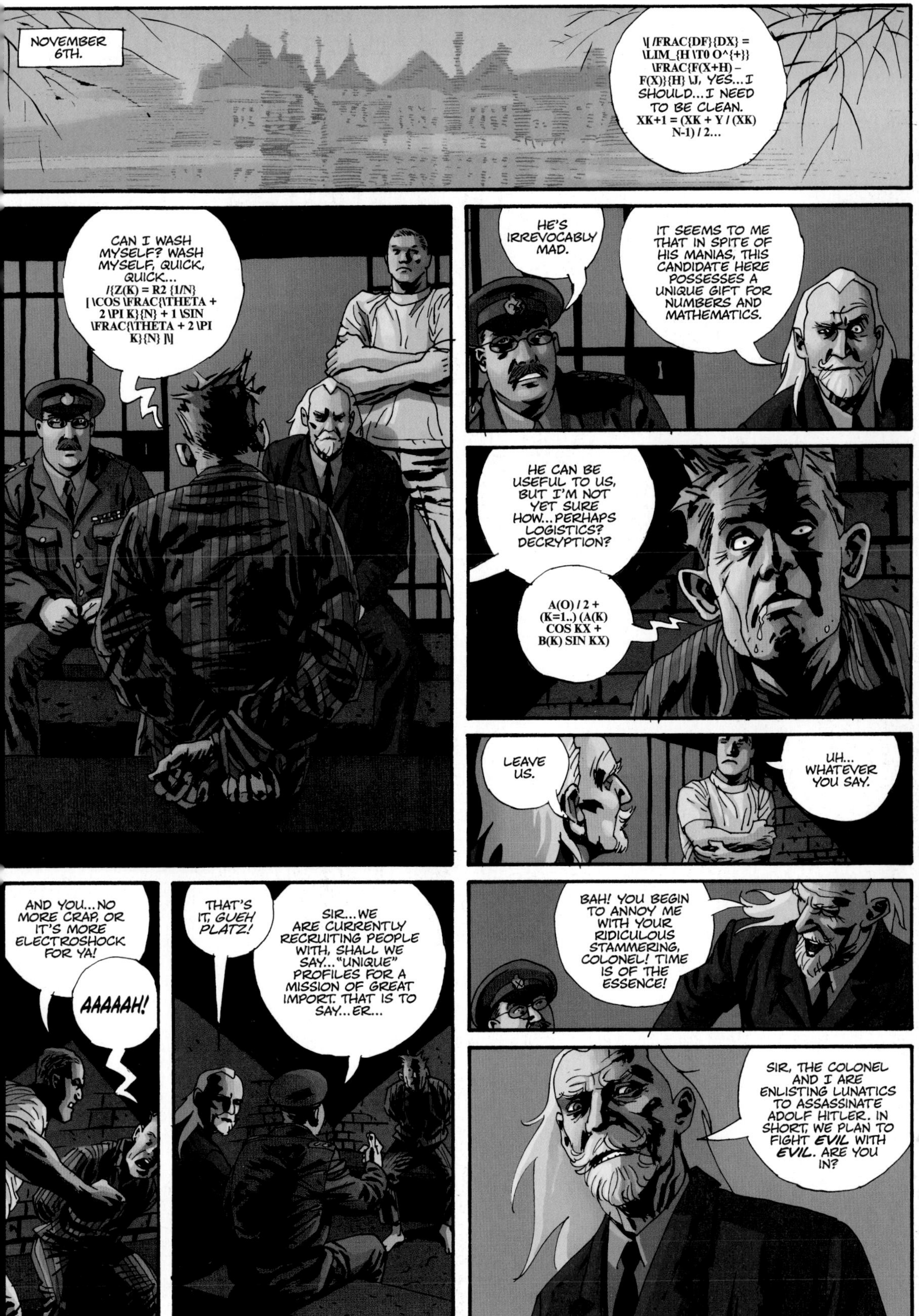

NOVEMBER 6TH.
\[/FRAC{DF}{DX} = \LIM_{H \T0 O^{+}} \FRAC{F(X+H) – F(X)}{H} \J, YES...I SHOULD...I NEED TO BE CLEAN. XK+1 = (XK + Y / (XK) N-1) / 2...
CAN I WASH MYSELF? WASH MYSELF, QUICK, QUICK... /{Z(K) = R2 {1/N} [\COS \FRAC{\THETA + 2 \PI K}{N} + 1 \SIN \FRAC{\THETA + 2 \PI K}{N}]\]
HE'S IRREVOCABLY MAD.
IT SEEMS TO ME THAT IN SPITE OF HIS MANIAS, THIS CANDIDATE HERE POSSESSES A UNIQUE GIFT FOR NUMBERS AND MATHEMATICS.
HE CAN BE USEFUL TO US, BUT I'M NOT YET SURE HOW...PERHAPS LOGISTICS? DECRYPTION?
A(O) / 2 + (K=1..) (A(K) COS KX + B(K) SIN KX)
LEAVE US.
UH... WHATEVER YOU SAY.
AND YOU...NO MORE CRAP, OR IT'S MORE ELECTROSHOCK FOR YA!
AAAAAH!
THAT'S IT, GUEH PLATZ!
SIR...WE ARE CURRENTLY RECRUITING PEOPLE WITH, SHALL WE SAY..."UNIQUE" PROFILES FOR A MISSION OF GREAT IMPORT. THAT IS TO SAY...ER...
BAH! YOU BEGIN TO ANNOY ME WITH YOUR RIDICULOUS STAMMERING, COLONEL! TIME IS OF THE ESSENCE!
SIR, THE COLONEL AND I ARE ENLISTING LUNATICS TO ASSASSINATE ADOLF HITLER. IN SHORT, WE PLAN TO FIGHT EVIL WITH EVIL. ARE YOU IN?

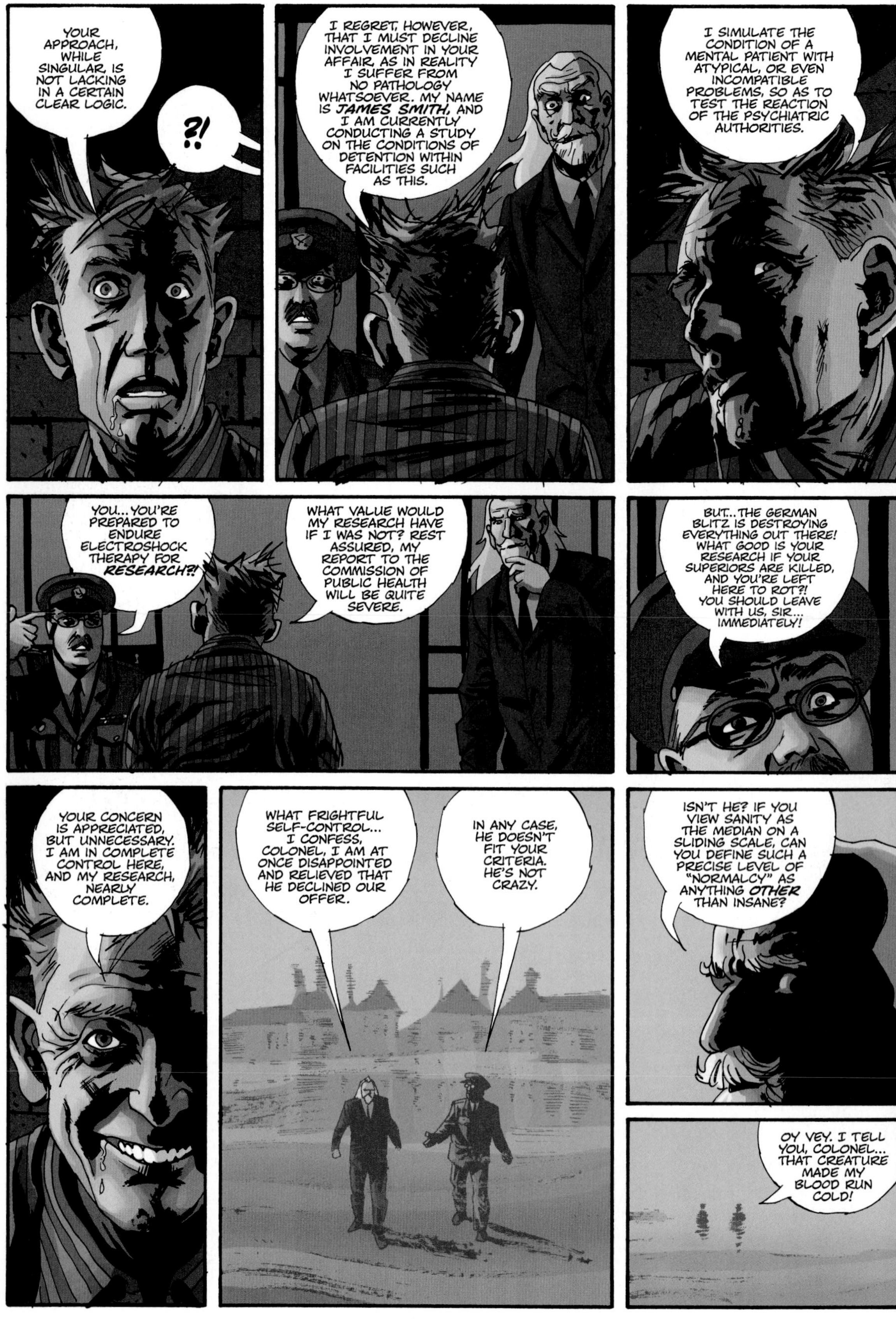
YOUR APPROACH, WHILE SINGULAR, IS NOT LACKING IN A CERTAIN CLEAR LOGIC.
?!
I REGRET, HOWEVER, THAT I MUST DECLINE INVOLVEMENT IN YOUR AFFAIR, AS IN REALITY I SUFFER FROM NO PATHOLOGY WHATSOEVER. MY NAME IS JAMES SMITH, AND I AM CURRENTLY CONDUCTING A STUDY ON THE CONDITIONS OF DETENTION WITHIN FACILITIES SUCH AS THIS.
I SIMULATE THE CONDITION OF A MENTAL PATIENT WITH ATYPICAL, OR EVEN INCOMPATIBLE PROBLEMS, SO AS TO TEST THE REACTION OF THE PSYCHIATRIC AUTHORITIES.
YOU... YOU'RE PREPARED TO ENDURE ELECTROSHOCK THERAPY FOR RESEARCH?!
WHAT VALUE WOULD MY RESEARCH HAVE IF I WAS NOT? REST ASSURED, MY REPORT TO THE COMMISSION OF PUBLIC HEALTH WILL BE QUITE SEVERE.
BUT... THE GERMAN BLITZ IS DESTROYING EVERYTHING OUT THERE! WHAT GOOD IS YOUR RESEARCH IF YOUR SUPERIORS ARE KILLED, AND YOU'RE LEFT HERE TO ROT?! YOU SHOULD LEAVE WITH US, SIR... IMMEDIATELY!
YOUR CONCERN IS APPRECIATED, BUT UNNECESSARY. I AM IN COMPLETE CONTROL HERE, AND MY RESEARCH, NEARLY COMPLETE.
WHAT FRIGHTFUL SELF-CONTROL... I CONFESS, COLONEL, I AM AT ONCE DISAPPOINTED AND RELIEVED THAT HE DECLINED OUR OFFER.
IN ANY CASE, HE DOESN'T FIT YOUR CRITERIA. HE'S NOT CRAZY.
ISN'T HE? IF YOU VIEW SANITY AS THE MEDIAN ON A SLIDING SCALE, CAN YOU DEFINE SUCH A PRECISE LEVEL OF "NORMALCY" AS ANYTHING OTHER THAN INSANE?
OY VEY. I TELL YOU, COLONEL... THAT CREATURE MADE MY BLOOD RUN COLD!

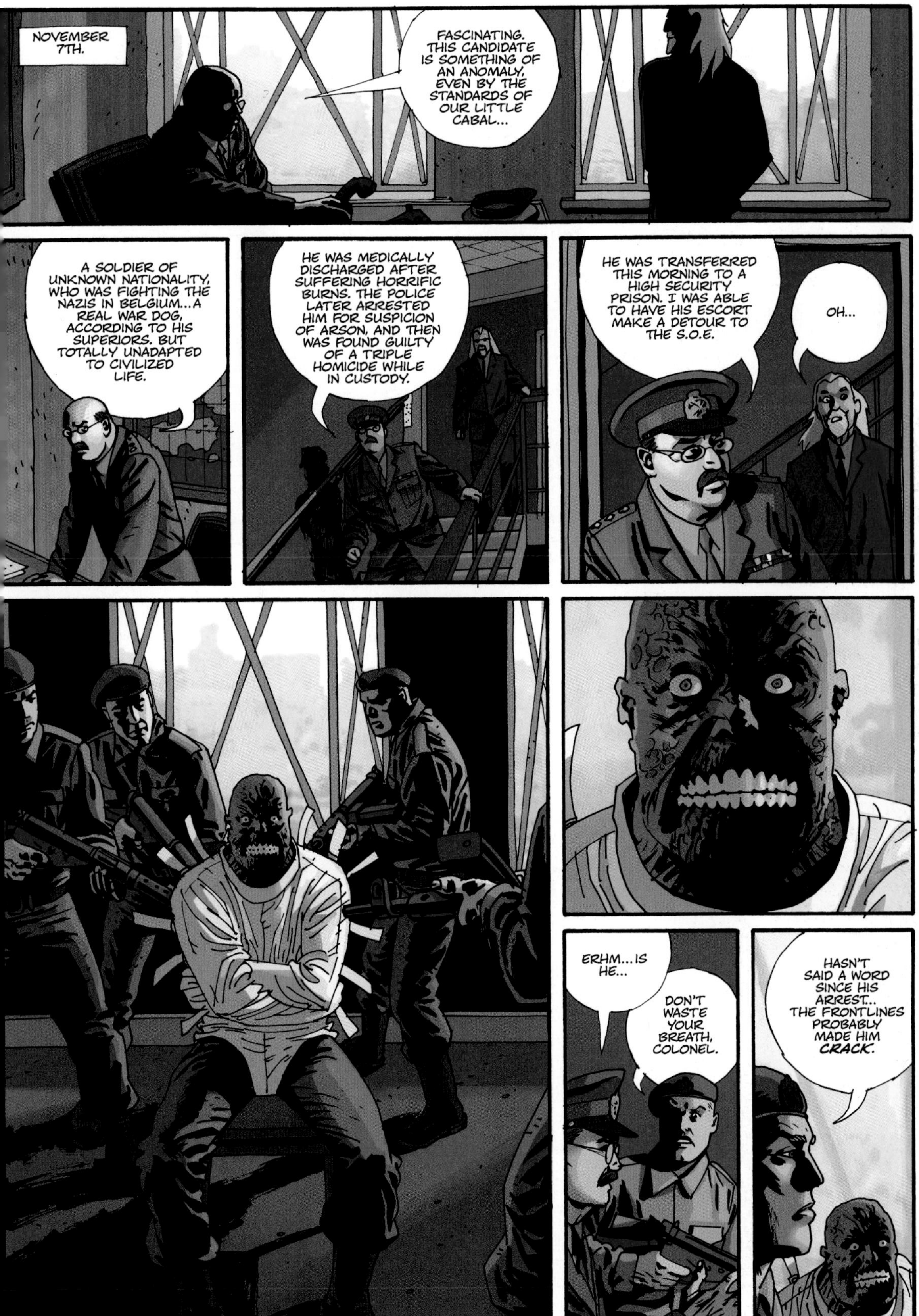
NOVEMBER 7TH.
FASCINATING. THIS CANDIDATE IS SOMETHING OF AN ANOMALY, EVEN BY THE STANDARDS OF OUR LITTLE CABAL...
A SOLDIER OF UNKNOWN NATIONALITY, WHO WAS FIGHTING THE NAZIS IN BELGIUM...A REAL WAR DOG, ACCORDING TO HIS SUPERIORS. BUT TOTALLY UNADAPTED TO CIVILIZED LIFE.
HE WAS MEDICALLY DISCHARGED AFTER SUFFERING HORRIFIC BURNS. THE POLICE LATER ARRESTED HIM FOR SUSPICION OF ARSON, AND THEN WAS FOUND GUILTY OF A TRIPLE HOMICIDE WHILE IN CUSTODY.
HE WAS TRANSFERRED THIS MORNING TO A HIGH SECURITY PRISON. I WAS ABLE TO HAVE HIS ESCORT MAKE A DETOUR TO THE S.O.E.
OH...
ERHM...IS HE...
DON'T WASTE YOUR BREATH, COLONEL.
HASN'T SAID A WORD SINCE HIS ARREST... THE FRONTLINES PROBABLY MADE HIM CRACK.

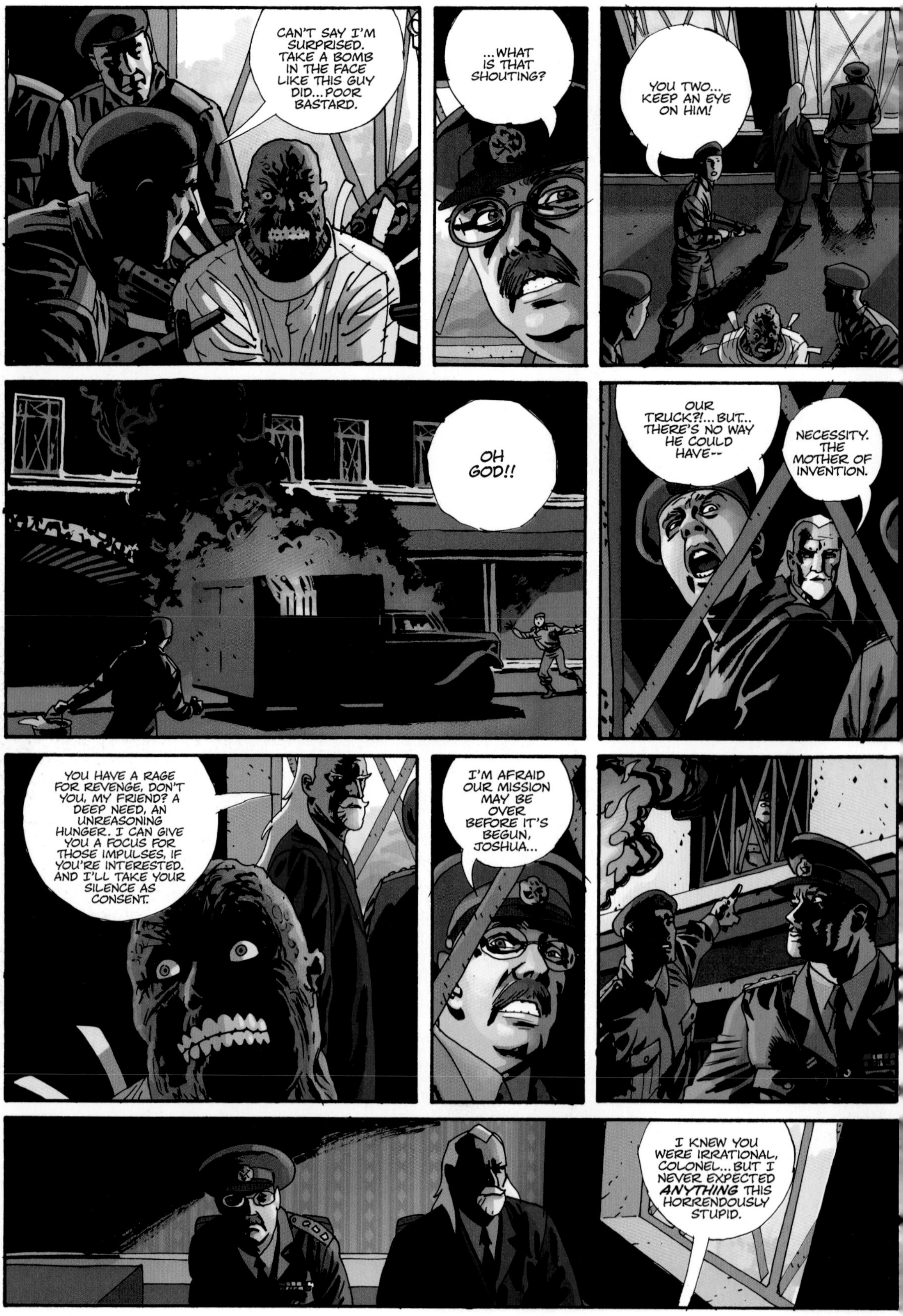
CAN'T SAY I'M SURPRISED. TAKE A BOMB IN THE FACE LIKE THIS GUY DID...POOR BASTARD.
...WHAT IS THAT SHOUTING?
YOU TWO... KEEP AN EYE ON HIM!
OH GOD!!
OUR TRUCK?!...BUT... THERE'S NO WAY HE COULD HAVE--
NECESSITY. THE MOTHER OF INVENTION.
YOU HAVE A RAGE FOR REVENGE, DON'T YOU, MY FRIEND? A DEEP NEED, AN UNREASONING HUNGER. I CAN GIVE YOU A FOCUS FOR THOSE IMPULSES, IF YOU'RE INTERESTED. AND I'LL TAKE YOUR SILENCE AS CONSENT.
I'M AFRAID OUR MISSION MAY BE OVER BEFORE IT'S BEGUN, JOSHUA...
I KNEW YOU WERE IRRATIONAL, COLONEL...BUT I NEVER EXPECTED *ANYTHING* THIS HORRENDOUSLY STUPID.

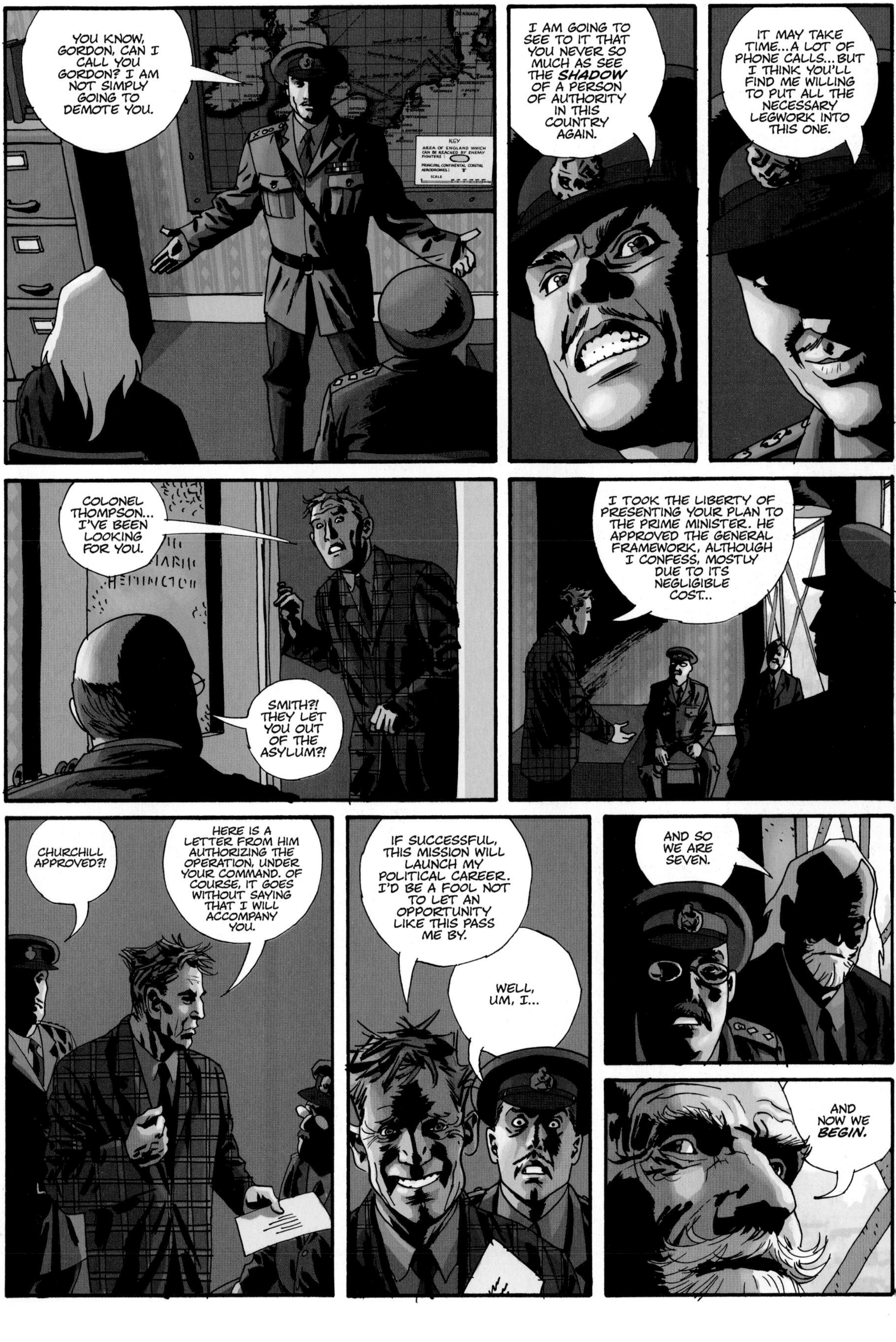
YOU KNOW, GORDON, CAN I CALL YOU GORDON? I AM NOT SIMPLY GOING TO DEMOTE YOU.
I AM GOING TO SEE TO IT THAT YOU NEVER SO MUCH AS SEE THE SHADOW OF A PERSON OF AUTHORITY IN THIS COUNTRY AGAIN.
IT MAY TAKE TIME...A LOT OF PHONE CALLS...BUT I THINK YOU'LL FIND ME WILLING TO PUT ALL THE NECESSARY LEGWORK INTO THIS ONE.
COLONEL THOMPSON... I'VE BEEN LOOKING FOR YOU.
SMITH?! THEY LET YOU OUT OF THE ASYLUM?!
I TOOK THE LIBERTY OF PRESENTING YOUR PLAN TO THE PRIME MINISTER. HE APPROVED THE GENERAL FRAMEWORK, ALTHOUGH I CONFESS, MOSTLY DUE TO ITS NEGLIGIBLE COST...
CHURCHILL APPROVED?!
HERE IS A LETTER FROM HIM AUTHORIZING THE OPERATION, UNDER YOUR COMMAND. OF COURSE, IT GOES WITHOUT SAYING THAT I WILL ACCOMPANY YOU.
IF SUCCESSFUL, THIS MISSION WILL LAUNCH MY POLITICAL CAREER. I'D BE A FOOL NOT TO LET AN OPPORTUNITY LIKE THIS PASS ME BY.
WELL, UM, I...
AND SO WE ARE SEVEN.
AND NOW WE BEGIN.

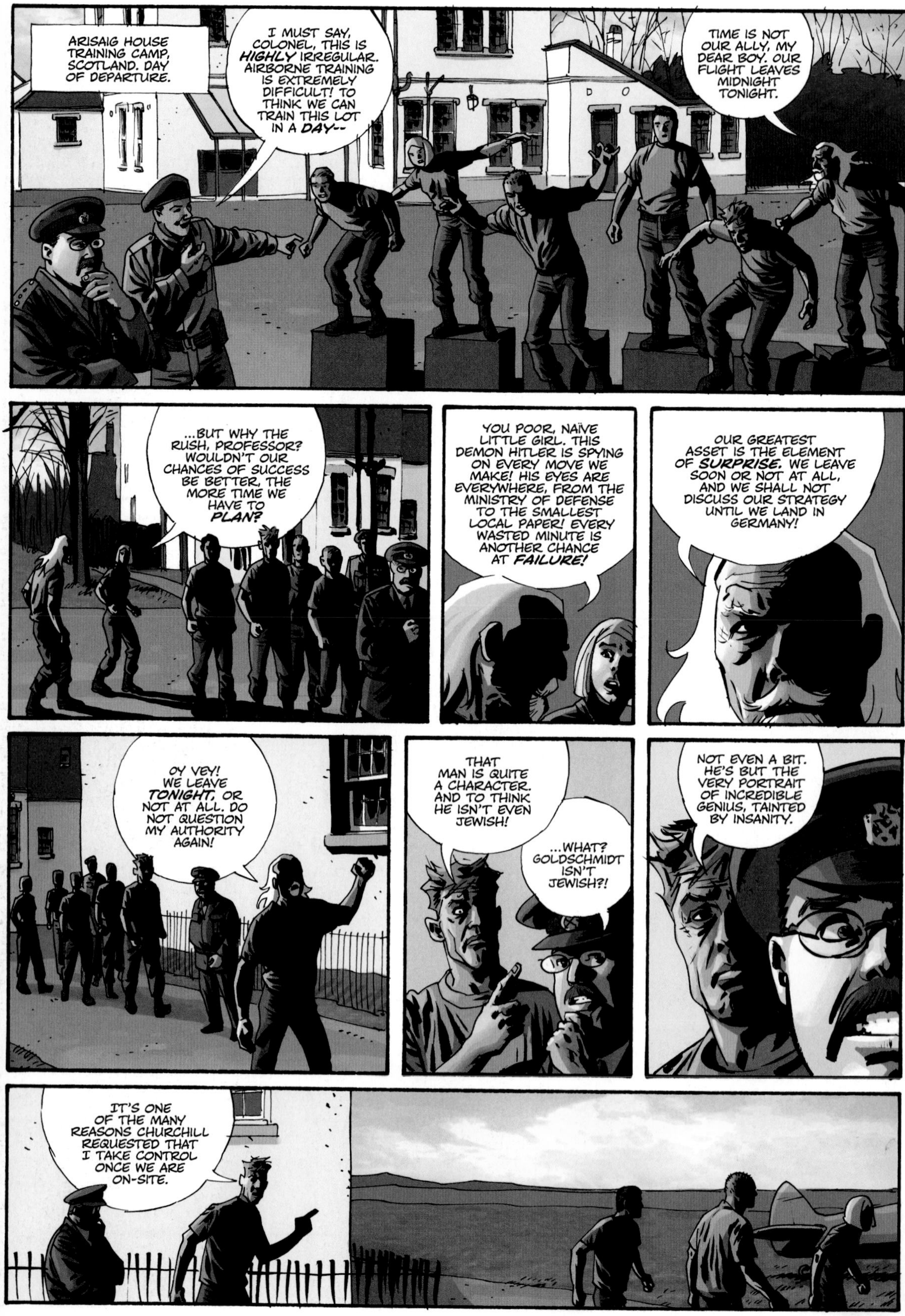
ARISAIG HOUSE TRAINING CAMP, SCOTLAND. DAY OF DEPARTURE.
I MUST SAY, COLONEL, THIS IS *HIGHLY* IRREGULAR. AIRBORNE TRAINING IS EXTREMELY DIFFICULT! TO THINK WE CAN TRAIN THIS LOT IN A *DAY*--
TIME IS NOT OUR ALLY, MY DEAR BOY. OUR FLIGHT LEAVES MIDNIGHT TONIGHT.
...BUT WHY THE RUSH, PROFESSOR? WOULDN'T OUR CHANCES OF SUCCESS BE BETTER, THE MORE TIME WE HAVE TO *PLAN?*
YOU POOR, NAÏVE LITTLE GIRL. THIS DEMON HITLER IS SPYING ON EVERY MOVE WE MAKE! HIS EYES ARE EVERYWHERE, FROM THE MINISTRY OF DEFENSE TO THE SMALLEST LOCAL PAPER! EVERY WASTED MINUTE IS ANOTHER CHANCE AT *FAILURE!*
OUR GREATEST ASSET IS THE ELEMENT OF *SURPRISE.* WE LEAVE SOON OR NOT AT ALL, AND WE SHALL NOT DISCUSS OUR STRATEGY UNTIL WE LAND IN GERMANY!
OY VEY! WE LEAVE *TONIGHT,* OR NOT AT ALL. DO NOT QUESTION MY AUTHORITY AGAIN!
THAT MAN IS QUITE A CHARACTER. AND TO THINK HE ISN'T EVEN JEWISH!
...WHAT? GOLDSCHMIDT ISN'T JEWISH?!
NOT EVEN A BIT. HE'S BUT THE VERY PORTRAIT OF INCREDIBLE GENIUS, TAINTED BY INSANITY.
IT'S ONE OF THE MANY REASONS CHURCHILL REQUESTED THAT I TAKE CONTROL ONCE WE ARE ON-SITE.

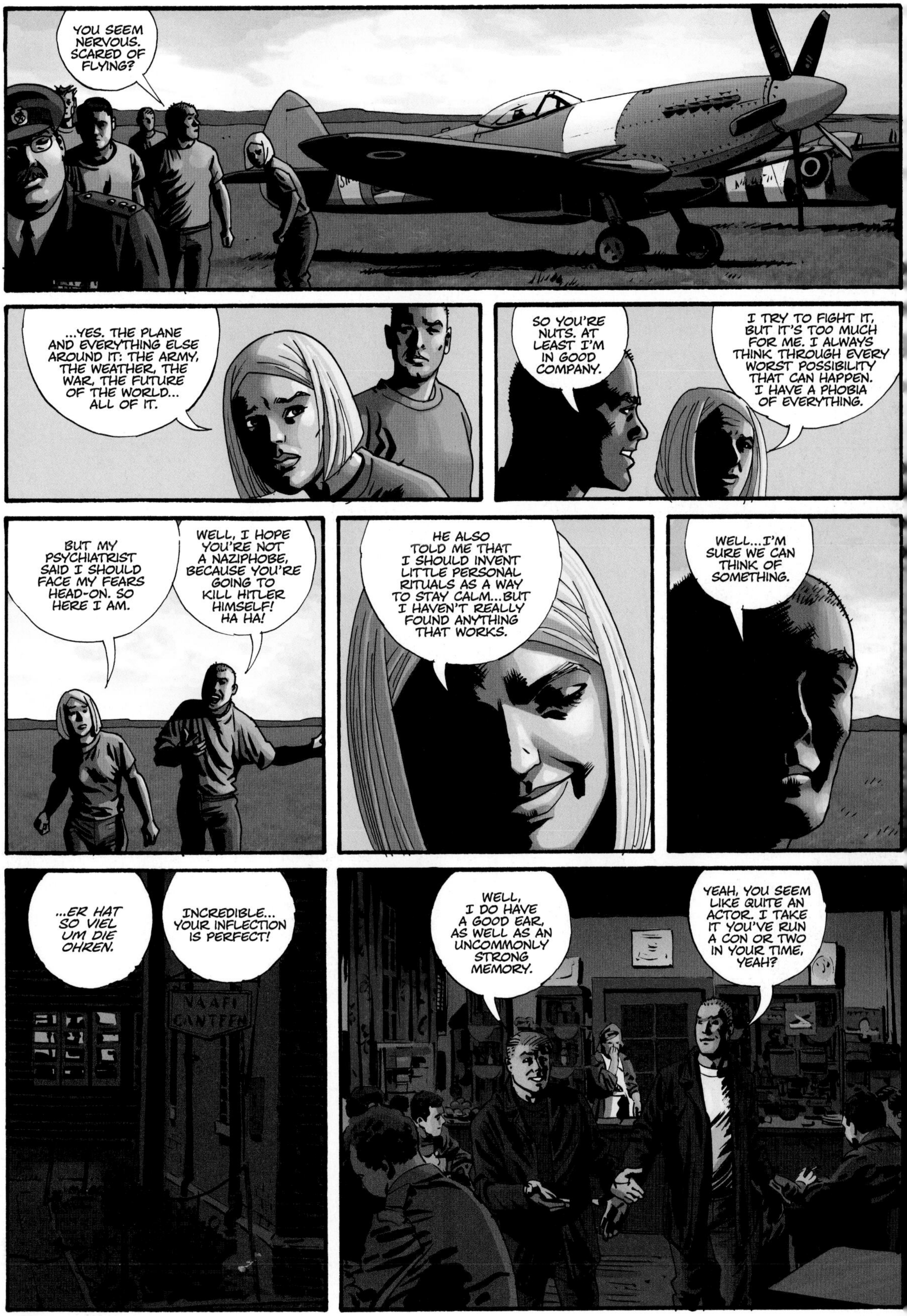
YOU SEEM NERVOUS. SCARED OF FLYING?
...YES. THE PLANE AND EVERYTHING ELSE AROUND IT: THE ARMY, THE WEATHER, THE WAR, THE FUTURE OF THE WORLD... ALL OF IT.
SO YOU'RE NUTS. AT LEAST I'M IN GOOD COMPANY.
I TRY TO FIGHT IT, BUT IT'S TOO MUCH FOR ME. I ALWAYS THINK THROUGH EVERY WORST POSSIBILITY THAT CAN HAPPEN. I HAVE A PHOBIA OF EVERYTHING.
BUT MY PSYCHIATRIST SAID I SHOULD FACE MY FEARS HEAD-ON. SO HERE I AM.
WELL, I HOPE YOU'RE NOT A NAZIPHOBE, BECAUSE YOU'RE GOING TO KILL HITLER HIMSELF! HA HA!
HE ALSO TOLD ME THAT I SHOULD INVENT LITTLE PERSONAL RITUALS AS A WAY TO STAY CALM...BUT I HAVEN'T REALLY FOUND ANYTHING THAT WORKS.
WELL...I'M SURE WE CAN THINK OF SOMETHING.
...ER HAT SO VIEL UM DIE OHREN.
INCREDIBLE... YOUR INFLECTION IS PERFECT!
NAAFI CANTEEN
WELL, I DO HAVE A GOOD EAR, AS WELL AS AN UNCOMMONLY STRONG MEMORY.
YEAH, YOU SEEM LIKE QUITE AN ACTOR. I TAKE IT YOU'VE RUN A CON OR TWO IN YOUR TIME, YEAH?

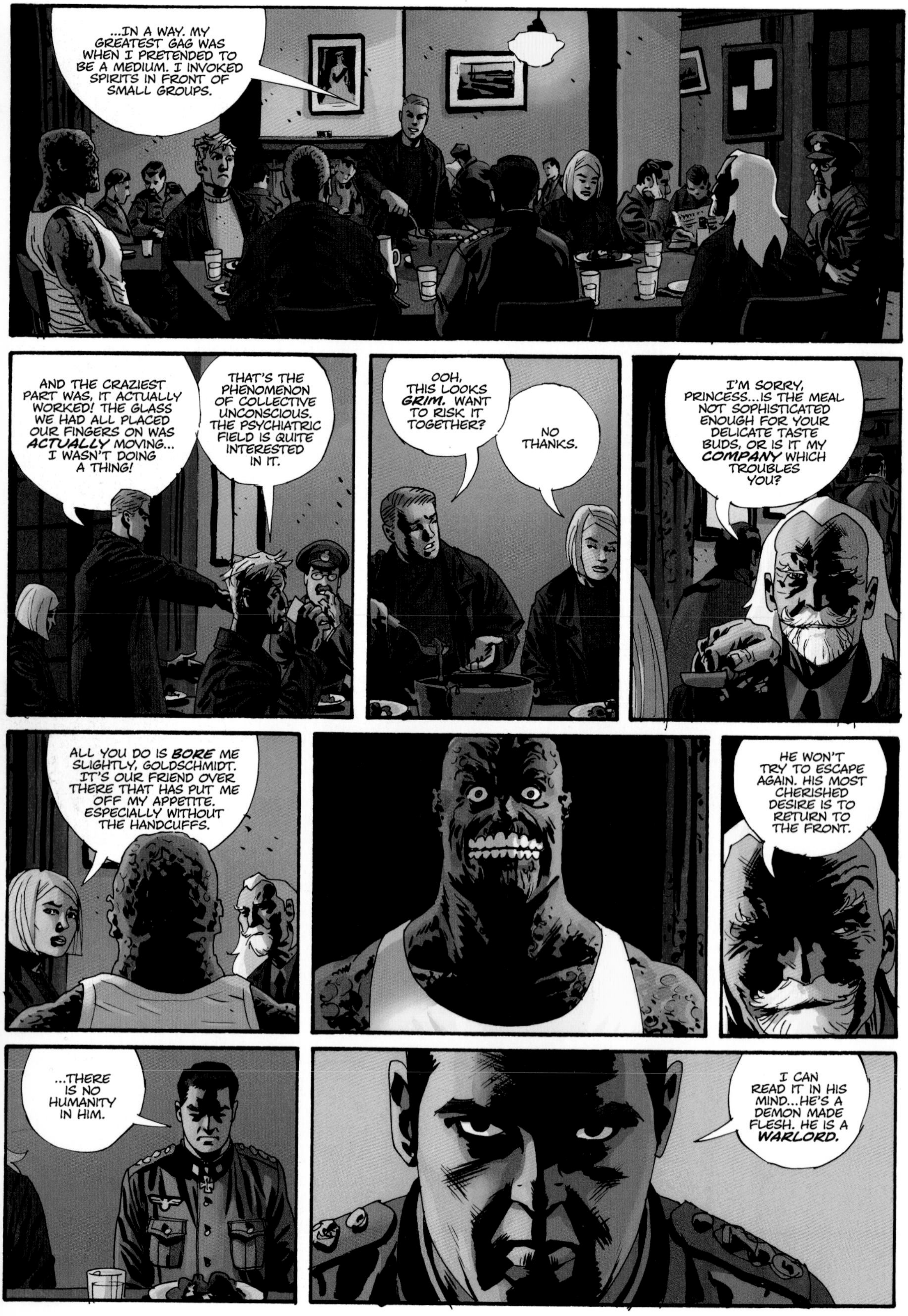
...IN A WAY. MY GREATEST GAG WAS WHEN I PRETENDED TO BE A MEDIUM. I INVOKED SPIRITS IN FRONT OF SMALL GROUPS.
AND THE CRAZIEST PART WAS, IT ACTUALLY WORKED! THE GLASS WE HAD ALL PLACED OUR FINGERS ON WAS ACTUALLY MOVING... I WASN'T DOING A THING!
THAT'S THE PHENOMENON OF COLLECTIVE UNCONSCIOUS. THE PSYCHIATRIC FIELD IS QUITE INTERESTED IN IT.
OOH, THIS LOOKS GRIM. WANT TO RISK IT TOGETHER?
NO THANKS.
I'M SORRY, PRINCESS...IS THE MEAL NOT SOPHISTICATED ENOUGH FOR YOUR DELICATE TASTE BUDS, OR IS IT MY COMPANY WHICH TROUBLES YOU?
ALL YOU DO IS BORE ME SLIGHTLY, GOLDSCHMIDT. IT'S OUR FRIEND OVER THERE THAT HAS PUT ME OFF MY APPETITE. ESPECIALLY WITHOUT THE HANDCUFFS.
HE WON'T TRY TO ESCAPE AGAIN. HIS MOST CHERISHED DESIRE IS TO RETURN TO THE FRONT.
...THERE IS NO HUMANITY IN HIM.
I CAN READ IT IN HIS MIND...HE'S A DEMON MADE FLESH. HE IS A WARLORD.

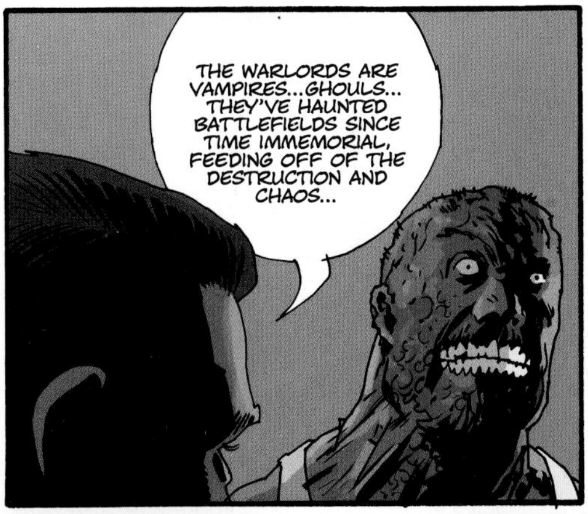
THE WARLORDS ARE VAMPIRES...GHOULS... THEY'VE HAUNTED BATTLEFIELDS SINCE TIME IMMEMORIAL, FEEDING OFF OF THE DESTRUCTION AND CHAOS...

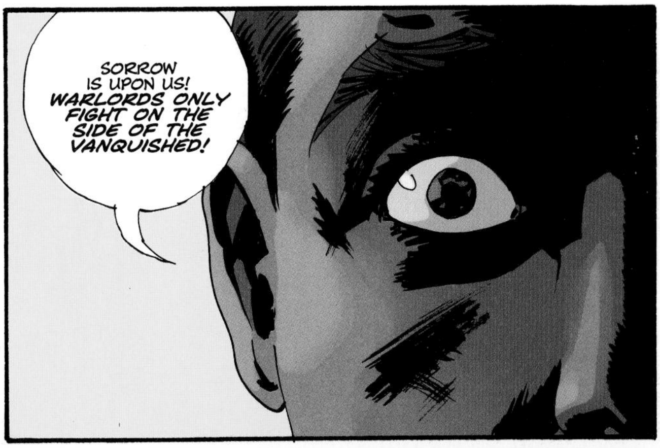
SORROW IS UPON US! *WARLORDS ONLY FIGHT ON THE SIDE OF THE VANQUISHED!*

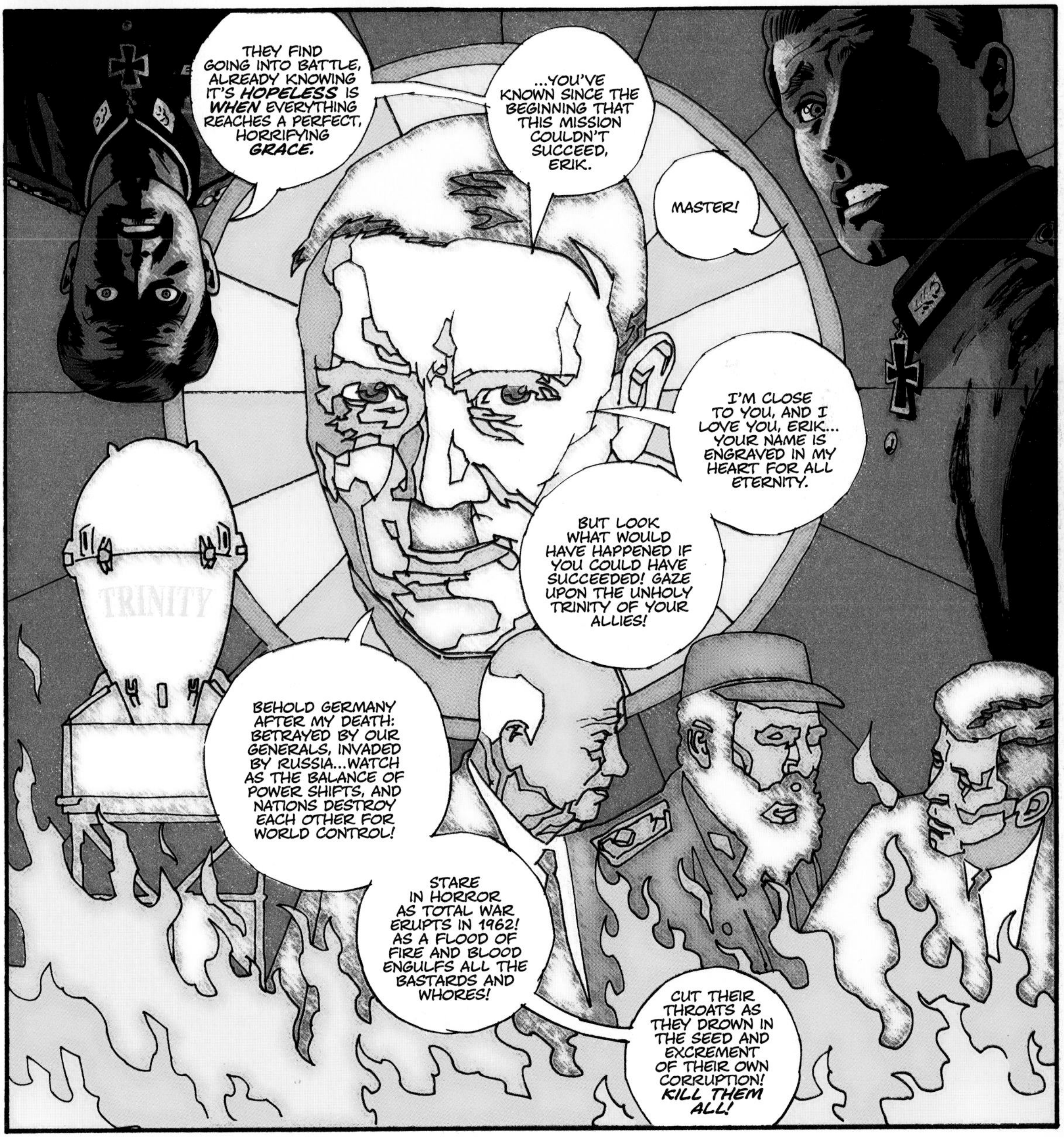
THEY FIND GOING INTO BATTLE, ALREADY KNOWING IT'S *HOPELESS* IS *WHEN* EVERYTHING REACHES A PERFECT, HORRIFYING *GRACE.*
...YOU'VE KNOWN SINCE THE BEGINNING THAT THIS MISSION COULDN'T SUCCEED, ERIK.
MASTER!
I'M CLOSE TO YOU, AND I LOVE YOU, ERIK... YOUR NAME IS ENGRAVED IN MY HEART FOR ALL ETERNITY.
BUT LOOK WHAT WOULD HAVE HAPPENED IF YOU COULD HAVE SUCCEEDED! GAZE UPON THE UNHOLY TRINITY OF YOUR ALLIES!
TRINITY
BEHOLD GERMANY AFTER MY DEATH: BETRAYED BY OUR GENERALS, INVADED BY RUSSIA...WATCH AS THE BALANCE OF POWER SHIFTS, AND NATIONS DESTROY EACH OTHER FOR WORLD CONTROL!
STARE IN HORROR AS TOTAL WAR ERUPTS IN 1962! AS A FLOOD OF FIRE AND BLOOD ENGULFS ALL THE BASTARDS AND WHORES!
CUT THEIR THROATS AS THEY DROWN IN THE SEED AND EXCREMENT OF THEIR OWN CORRUPTION! *KILL THEM ALL!*

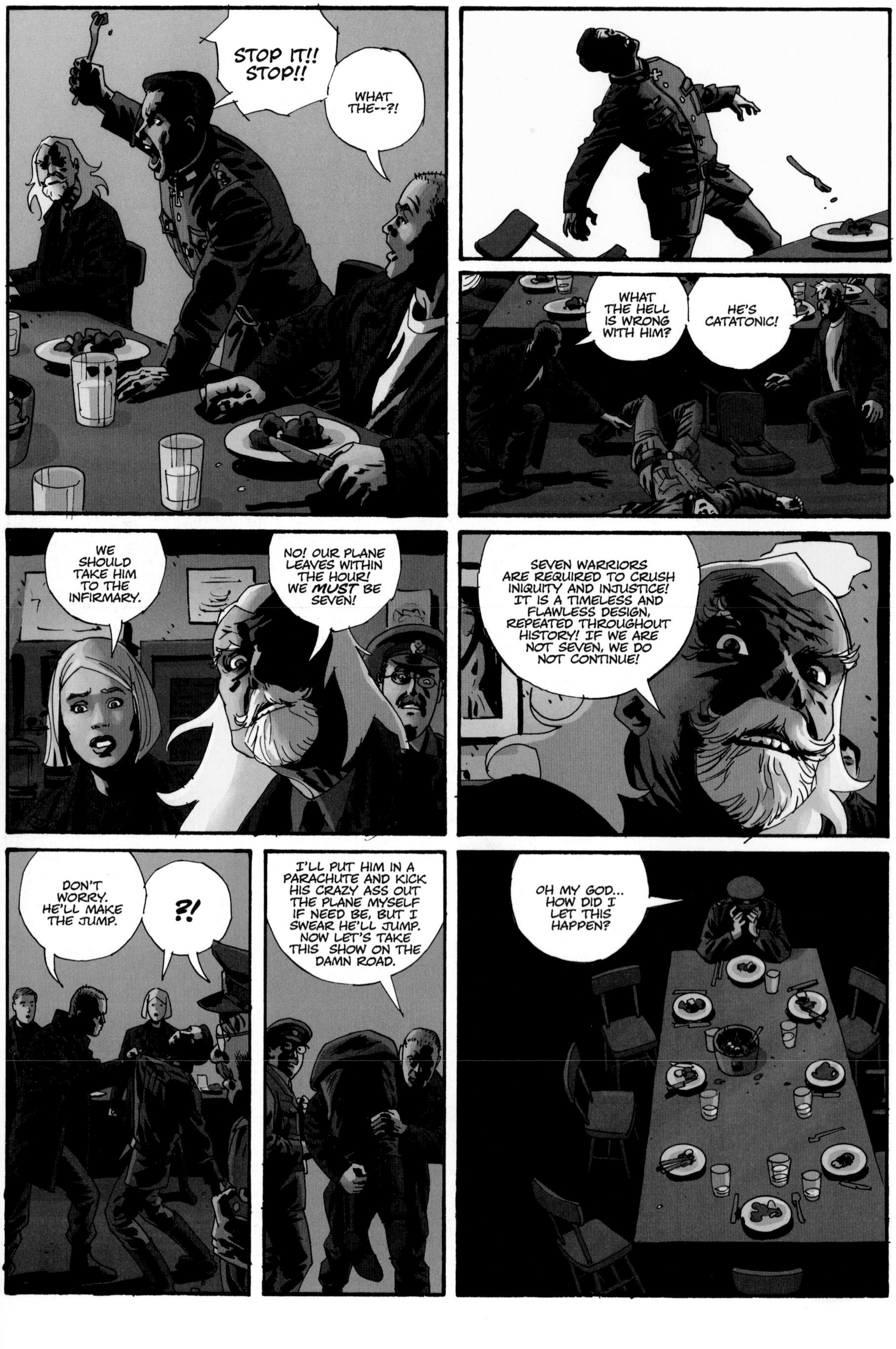
STOP IT!! STOP!!
WHAT THE--?!
WHAT THE HELL IS WRONG WITH HIM?
HE'S CATATONIC!
WE SHOULD TAKE HIM TO THE INFIRMARY.
NO! OUR PLANE LEAVES WITHIN THE HOUR! WE *MUST* BE SEVEN!
SEVEN WARRIORS ARE REQUIRED TO CRUSH INIQUITY AND INJUSTICE! IT IS A TIMELESS AND FLAWLESS DESIGN, REPEATED THROUGHOUT HISTORY! IF WE ARE NOT SEVEN, WE DO NOT CONTINUE!
DON'T WORRY. HE'LL MAKE THE JUMP.
?!
I'LL PUT HIM IN A PARACHUTE AND KICK HIS CRAZY ASS OUT THE PLANE MYSELF IF NEED BE, BUT I SWEAR HE'LL JUMP. NOW LET'S TAKE THIS SHOW ON THE DAMN ROAD.
OH MY GOD... HOW DID I LET THIS HAPPEN?

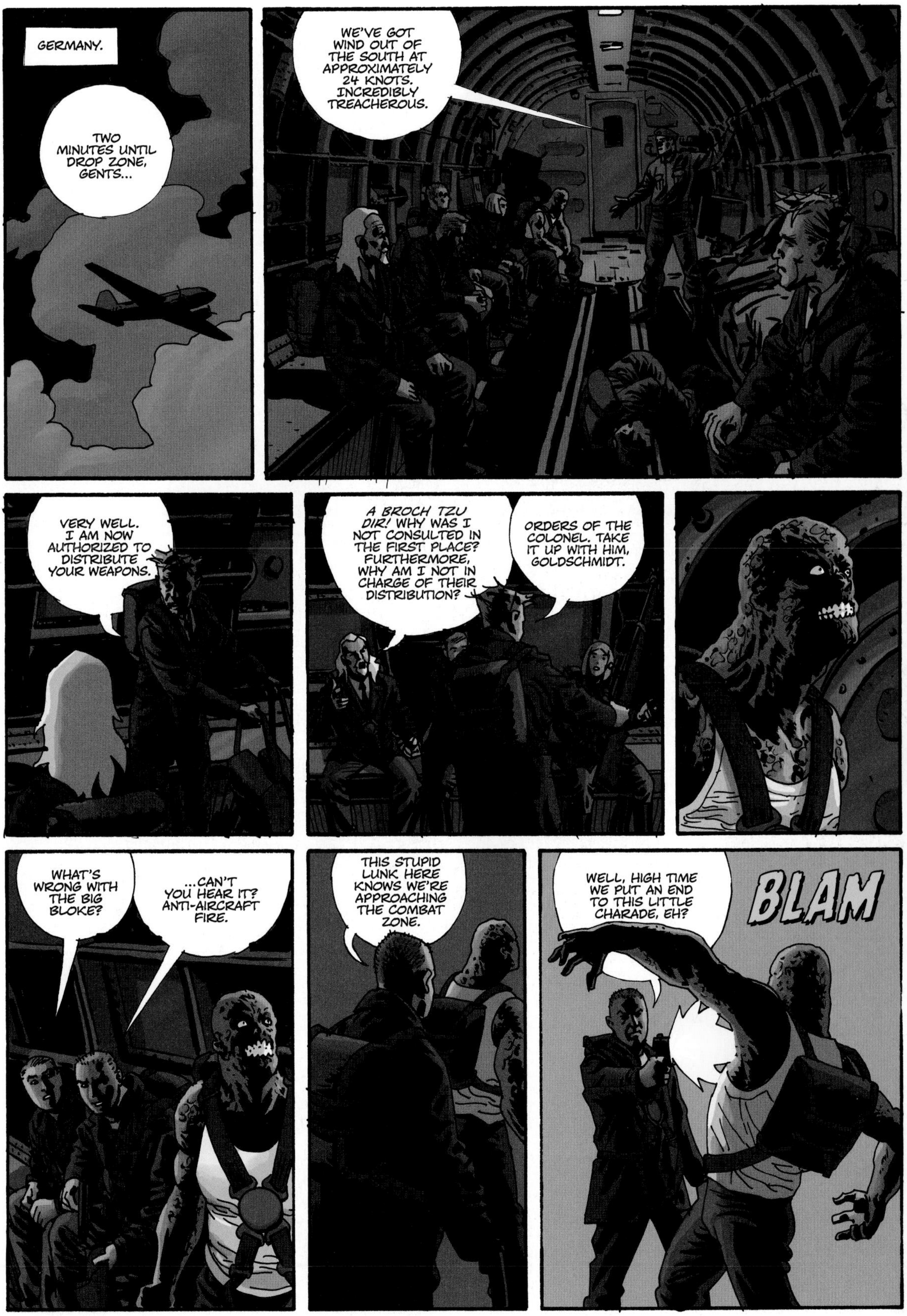
GERMANY.
TWO MINUTES UNTIL DROP ZONE, GENTS...
WE'VE GOT WIND OUT OF THE SOUTH AT APPROXIMATELY 24 KNOTS. INCREDIBLY TREACHEROUS.
VERY WELL. I AM NOW AUTHORIZED TO DISTRIBUTE YOUR WEAPONS.
A BROCH TZU DIR! WHY WAS I NOT CONSULTED IN THE FIRST PLACE? FURTHERMORE, WHY AM I NOT IN CHARGE OF THEIR DISTRIBUTION?
ORDERS OF THE COLONEL. TAKE IT UP WITH HIM, GOLDSCHMIDT.
WHAT'S WRONG WITH THE BIG BLOKE?
...CAN'T YOU HEAR IT? ANTI-AIRCRAFT FIRE.
THIS STUPID LUNK HERE KNOWS WE'RE APPROACHING THE COMBAT ZONE.
WELL, HIGH TIME WE PUT AN END TO THIS LITTLE CHARADE, EH?
BLAM

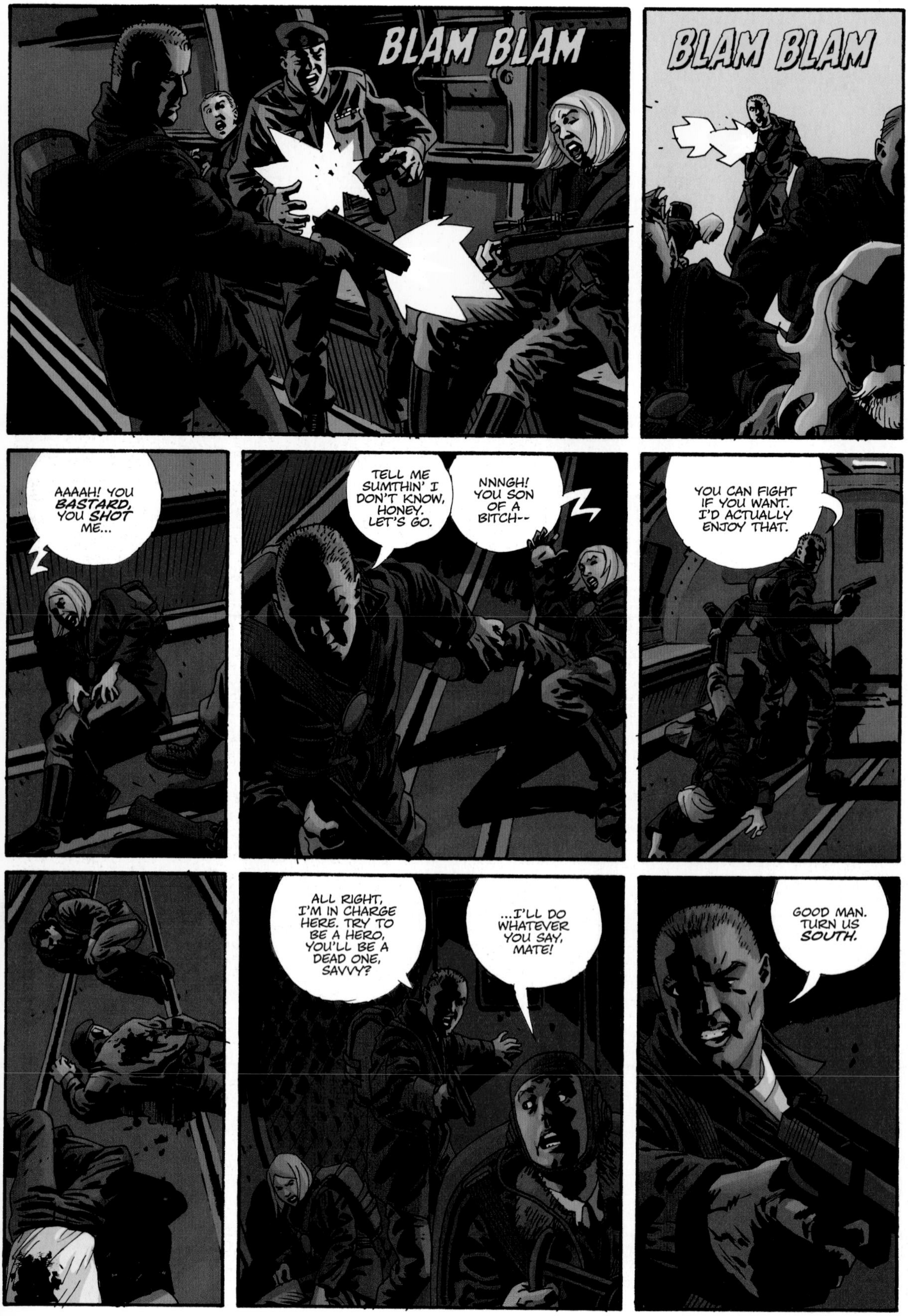
BLAM BLAM
BLAM BLAM
AAAAH! YOU BASTARD, YOU SHOT ME...
TELL ME SUMTHIN' I DON'T KNOW, HONEY. LET'S GO.
NNNGH! YOU SON OF A BITCH--
YOU CAN FIGHT IF YOU WANT. I'D ACTUALLY ENJOY THAT.
ALL RIGHT, I'M IN CHARGE HERE. TRY TO BE A HERO, YOU'LL BE A DEAD ONE, SAVVY?
...I'LL DO WHATEVER YOU SAY, MATE!
GOOD MAN. TURN US SOUTH.

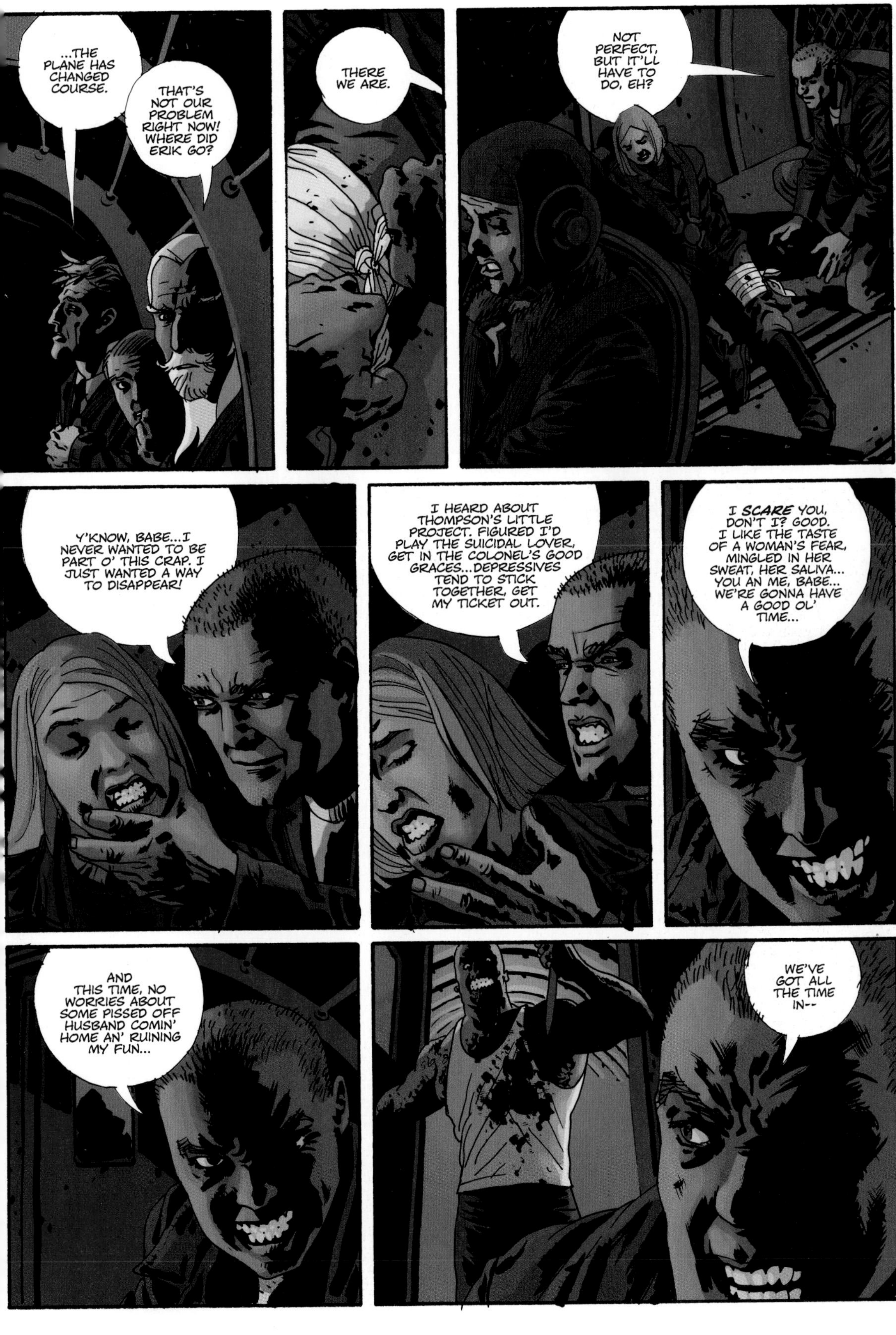
...THE PLANE HAS CHANGED COURSE.
THAT'S NOT OUR PROBLEM RIGHT NOW! WHERE DID ERIK GO?
THERE WE ARE.
NOT PERFECT, BUT IT'LL HAVE TO DO, EH?
Y'KNOW, BABE...I NEVER WANTED TO BE PART O' THIS CRAP. I JUST WANTED A WAY TO DISAPPEAR!
I HEARD ABOUT THOMPSON'S LITTLE PROJECT. FIGURED I'D PLAY THE SUICIDAL LOVER, GET IN THE COLONEL'S GOOD GRACES...DEPRESSIVES TEND TO STICK TOGETHER, GET MY TICKET OUT.
I SCARE YOU, DON'T I? GOOD. I LIKE THE TASTE OF A WOMAN'S FEAR, MINGLED IN HER SWEAT, HER SALIVA... YOU AN ME, BABE... WE'RE GONNA HAVE A GOOD OL' TIME...
AND THIS TIME, NO WORRIES ABOUT SOME PISSED OFF HUSBAND COMIN' HOME AN' RUINING MY FUN...
WE'VE GOT ALL THE TIME IN--

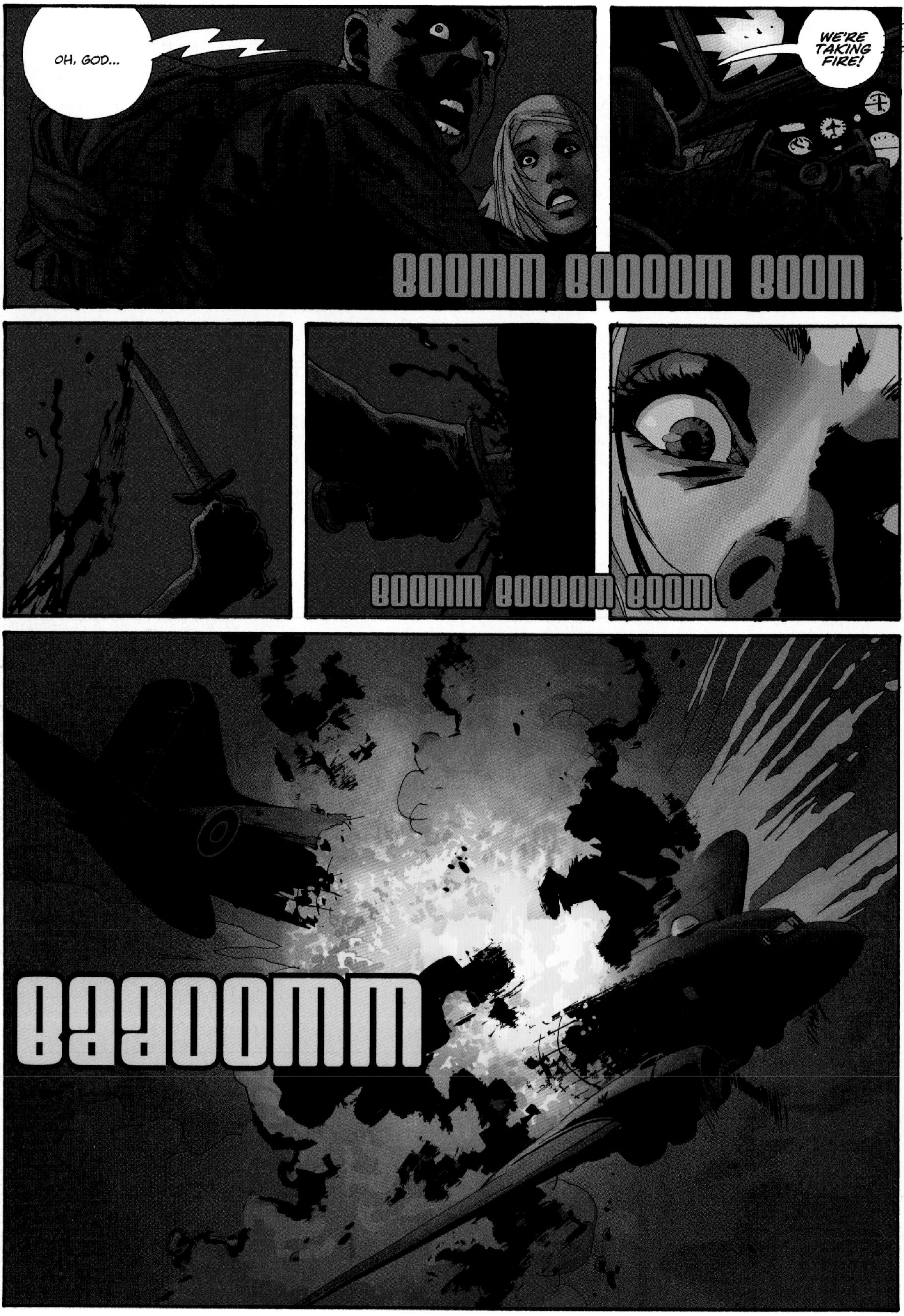
OH, GOD...
WE'RE TAKING FIRE!
BOOMM BOOOOM BOOM
BOOMM BOOOOM BOOM
BAAOOMM

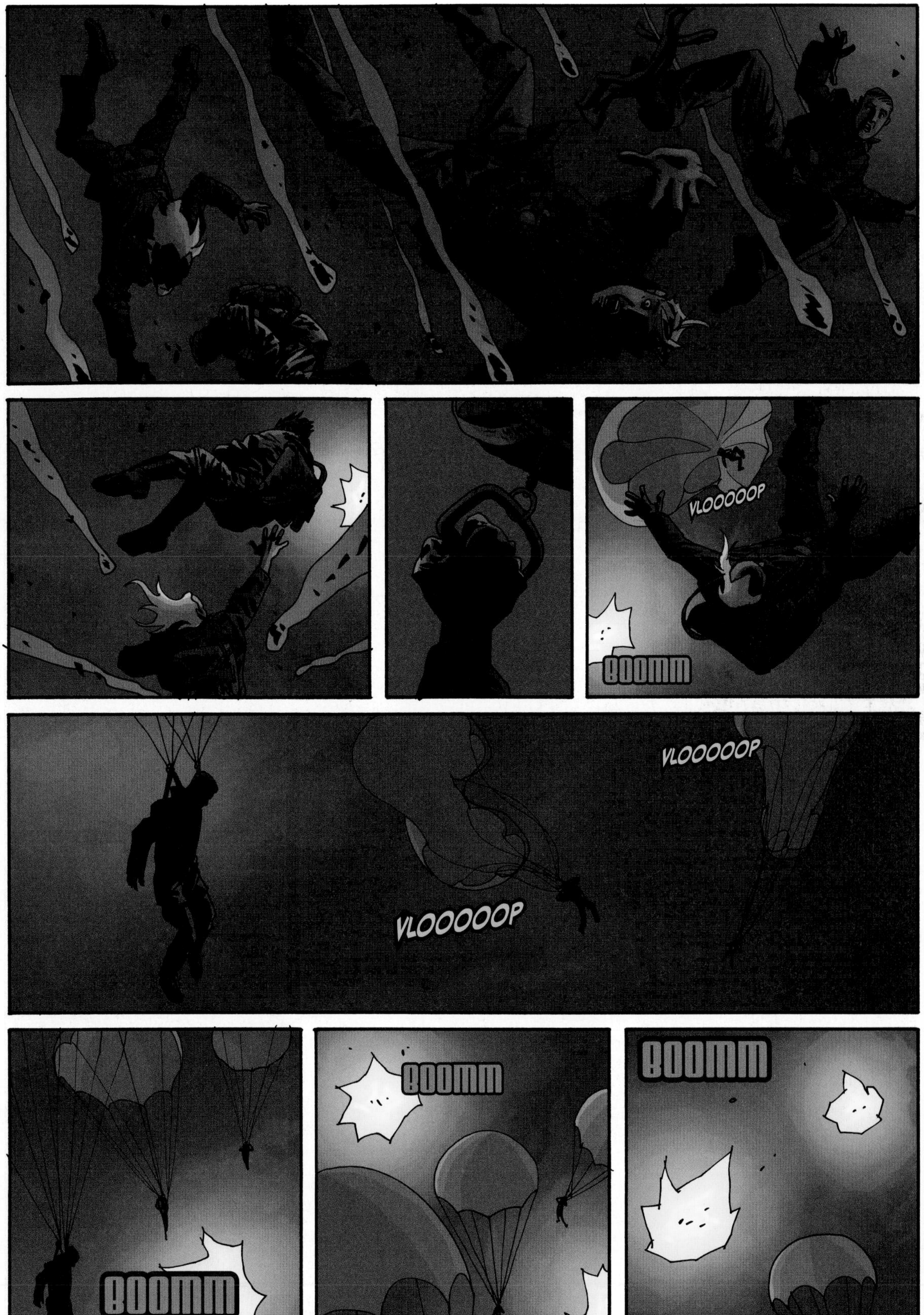
VLOOOOOP
BOOMM
VLOOOOOP
VLOOOOOP
BOOMM
BOOMM
BOOMM

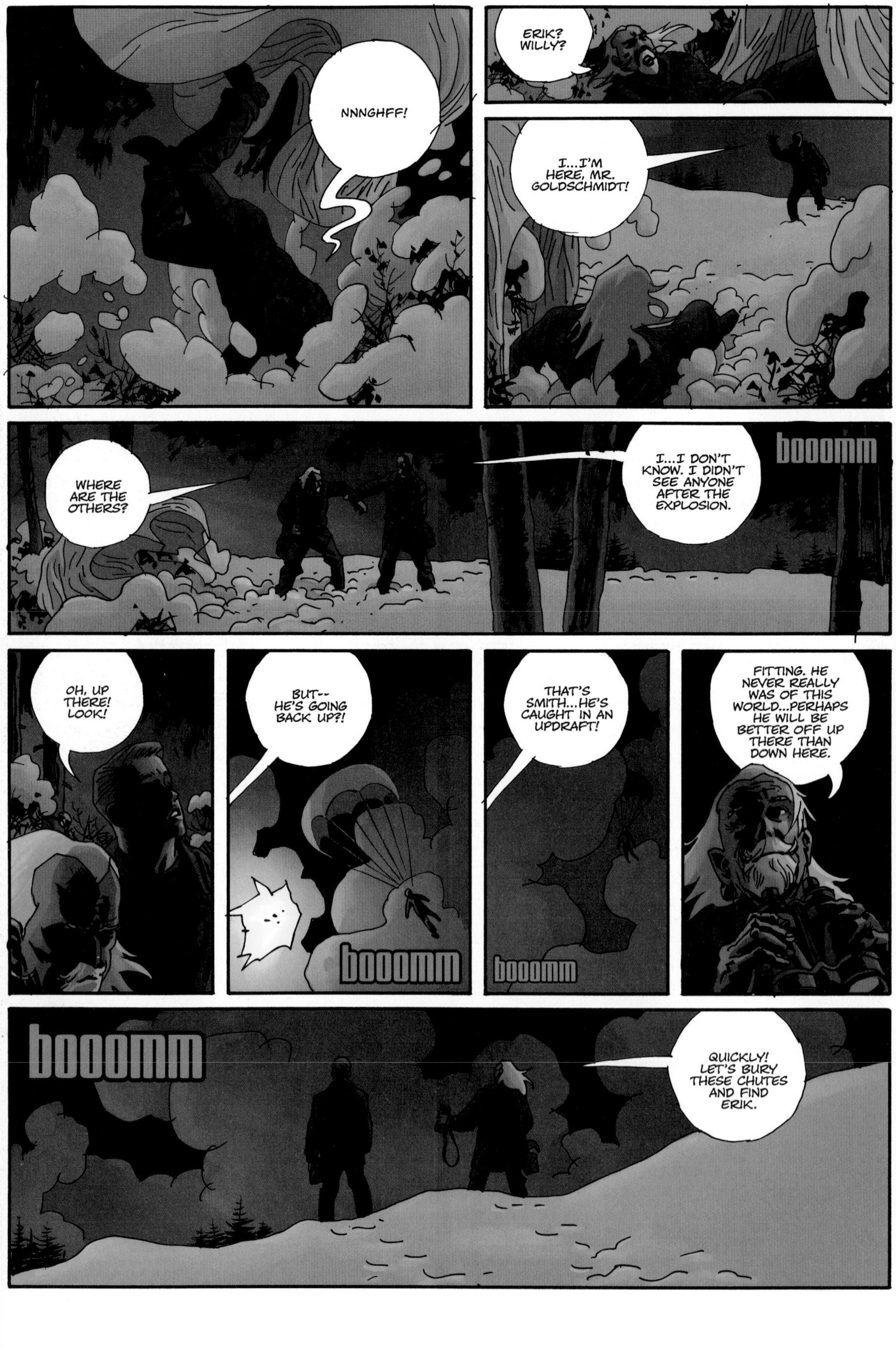
NNNGHFF!
ERIK? WILLY?
I...I'M HERE, MR. GOLDSCHMIDT!
WHERE ARE THE OTHERS?
I...I DON'T KNOW. I DIDN'T SEE ANYONE AFTER THE EXPLOSION.
booomm
OH, UP THERE! LOOK!
BUT-- HE'S GOING BACK UP?!
booomm
THAT'S SMITH...HE'S CAUGHT IN AN UPDRAFT!
booomm
FITTING. HE NEVER REALLY WAS OF THIS WORLD...PERHAPS HE WILL BE BETTER OFF UP THERE THAN DOWN HERE.
booomm
QUICKLY! LET'S BURY THESE CHUTES AND FIND ERIK.

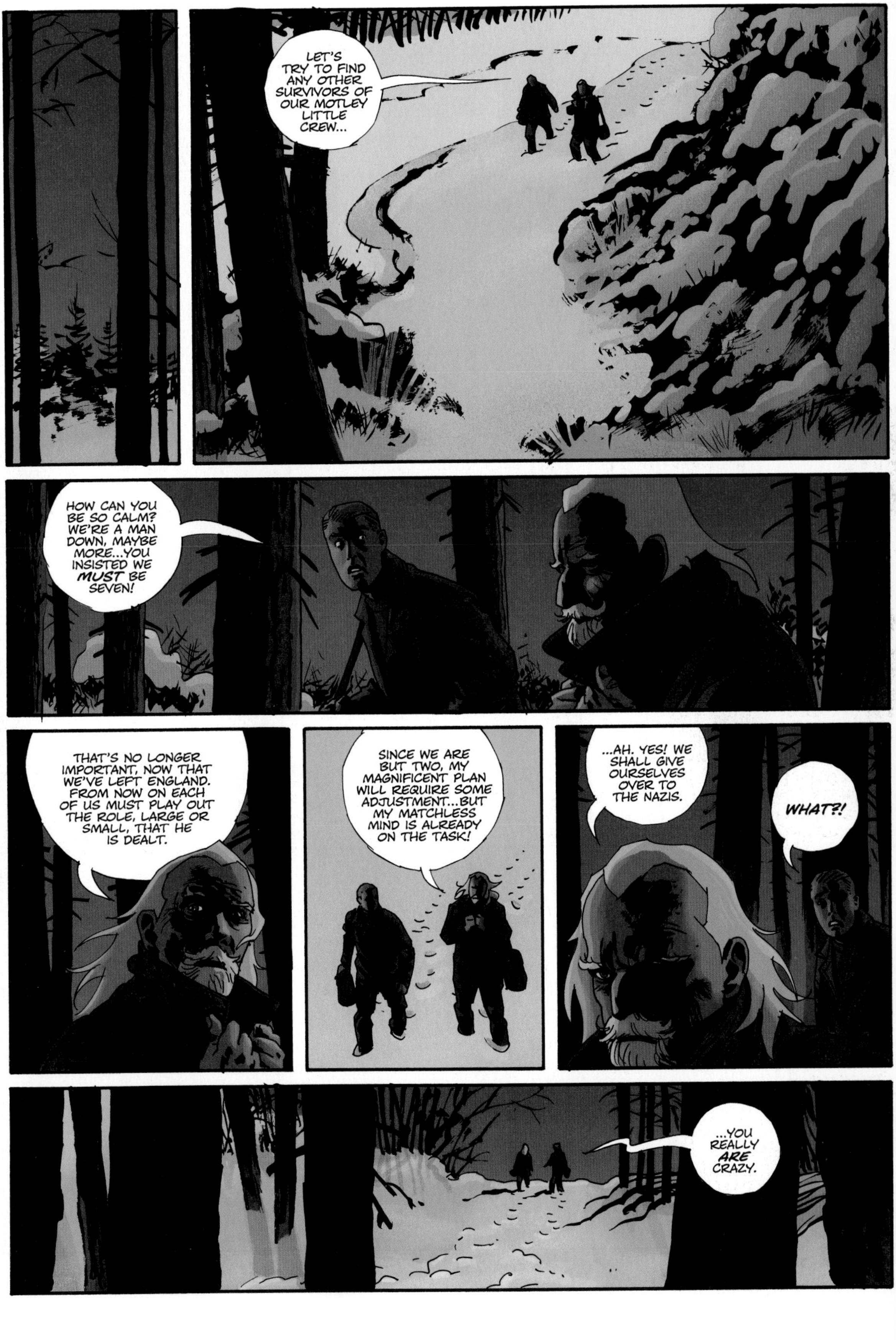
LET'S TRY TO FIND ANY OTHER SURVIVORS OF OUR MOTLEY LITTLE CREW...
HOW CAN YOU BE SO CALM? WE'RE A MAN DOWN, MAYBE MORE...YOU INSISTED WE *MUST* BE SEVEN!
THAT'S NO LONGER IMPORTANT, NOW THAT WE'VE LEFT ENGLAND. FROM NOW ON EACH OF US MUST PLAY OUT THE ROLE, LARGE OR SMALL, THAT HE IS DEALT.
SINCE WE ARE BUT TWO, MY MAGNIFICENT PLAN WILL REQUIRE SOME ADJUSTMENT...BUT MY MATCHLESS MIND IS ALREADY ON THE TASK!
...AH. YES! WE SHALL GIVE OURSELVES OVER TO THE NAZIS.
WHAT?!
...YOU REALLY *ARE* CRAZY.

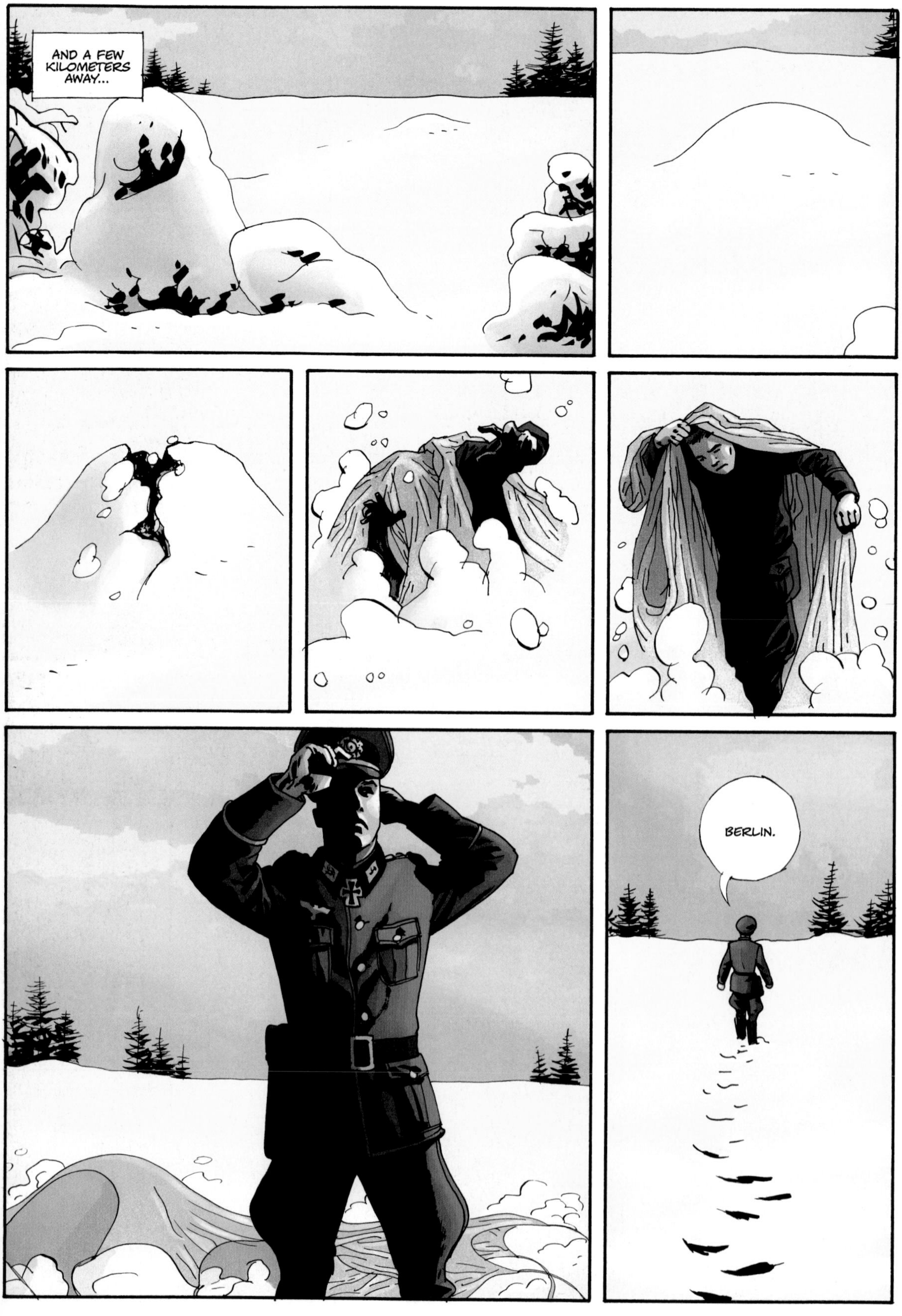
AND A FEW KILOMETERS AWAY...
BERLIN.

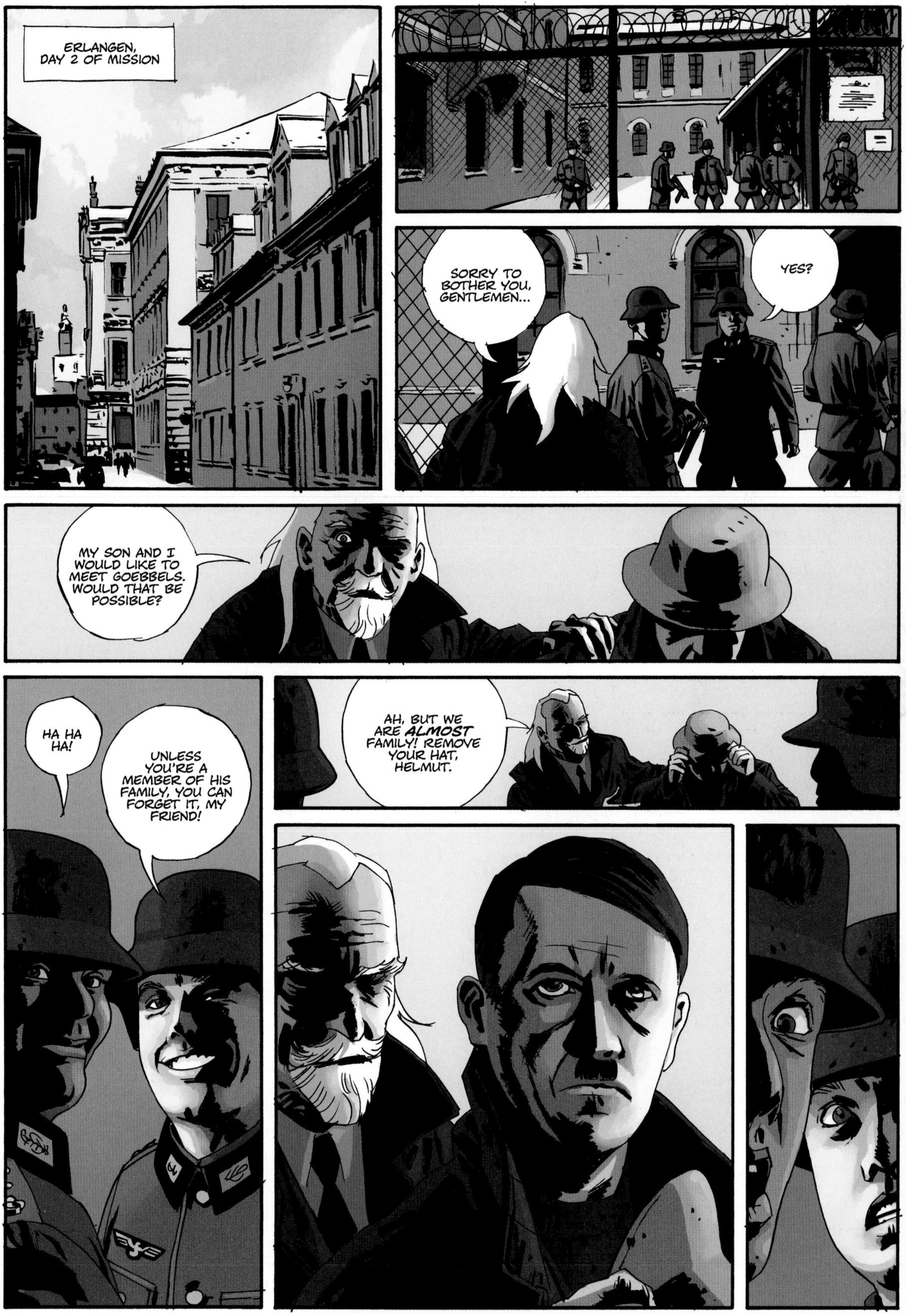

ERLANGEN, DAY 2 OF MISSION
SORRY TO BOTHER YOU, GENTLEMEN...
YES?
MY SON AND I WOULD LIKE TO MEET GOEBBELS. WOULD THAT BE POSSIBLE?
HA HA HA!
UNLESS YOU'RE A MEMBER OF HIS FAMILY, YOU CAN FORGET IT, MY FRIEND!
AH, BUT WE ARE ALMOST FAMILY! REMOVE YOUR HAT, HELMUT.

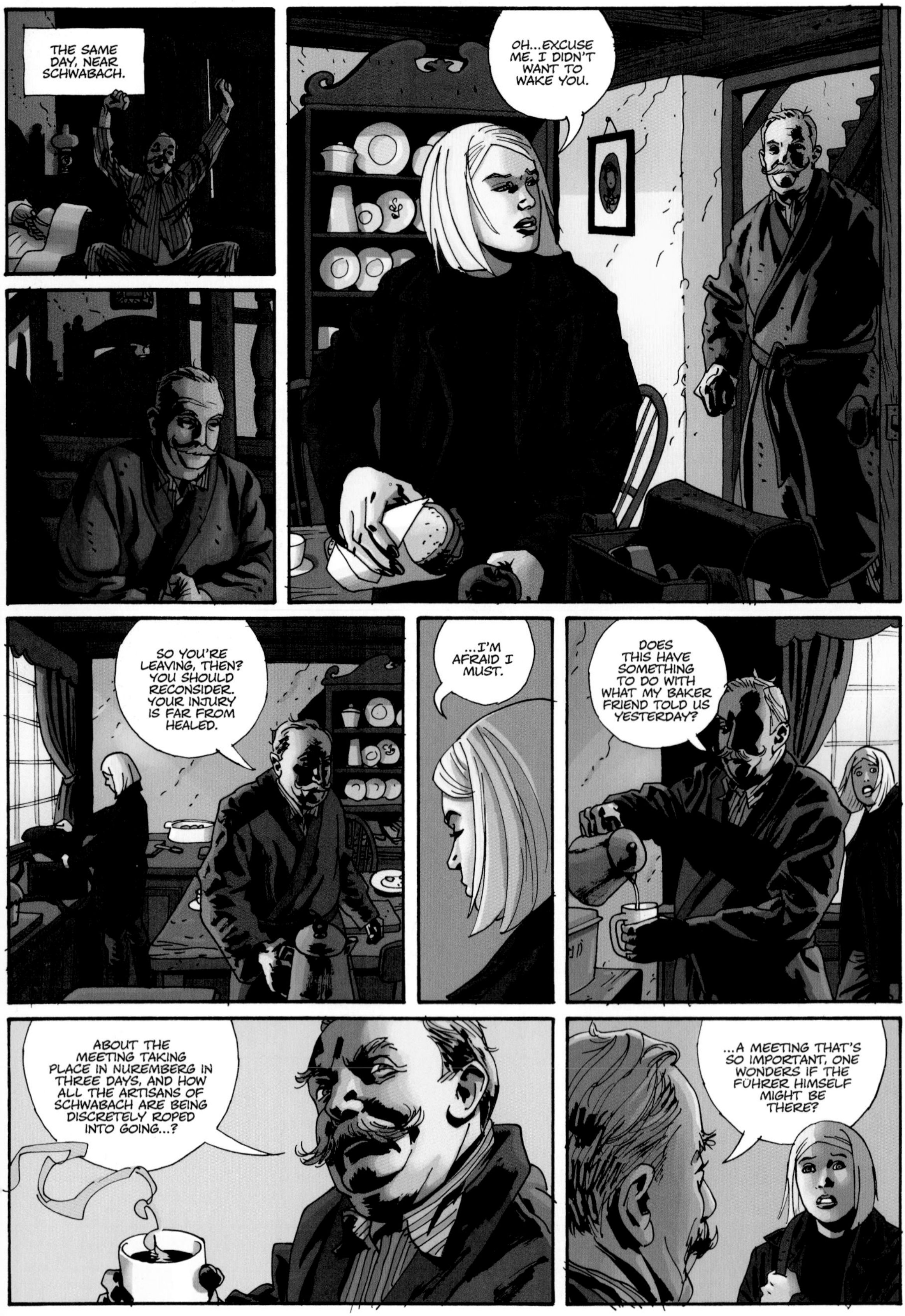
THE SAME DAY, NEAR SCHWABACH.
OH...EXCUSE ME. I DIDN'T WANT TO WAKE YOU.
SO YOU'RE LEAVING, THEN? YOU SHOULD RECONSIDER. YOUR INJURY IS FAR FROM HEALED.
...I'M AFRAID I MUST.
DOES THIS HAVE SOMETHING TO DO WITH WHAT MY BAKER FRIEND TOLD US YESTERDAY?
ABOUT THE MEETING TAKING PLACE IN NUREMBERG IN THREE DAYS, AND HOW ALL THE ARTISANS OF SCHWABACH ARE BEING DISCRETELY ROPED INTO GOING...?
...A MEETING THAT'S SO IMPORTANT, ONE WONDERS IF THE FÜHRER HIMSELF MIGHT BE THERE?

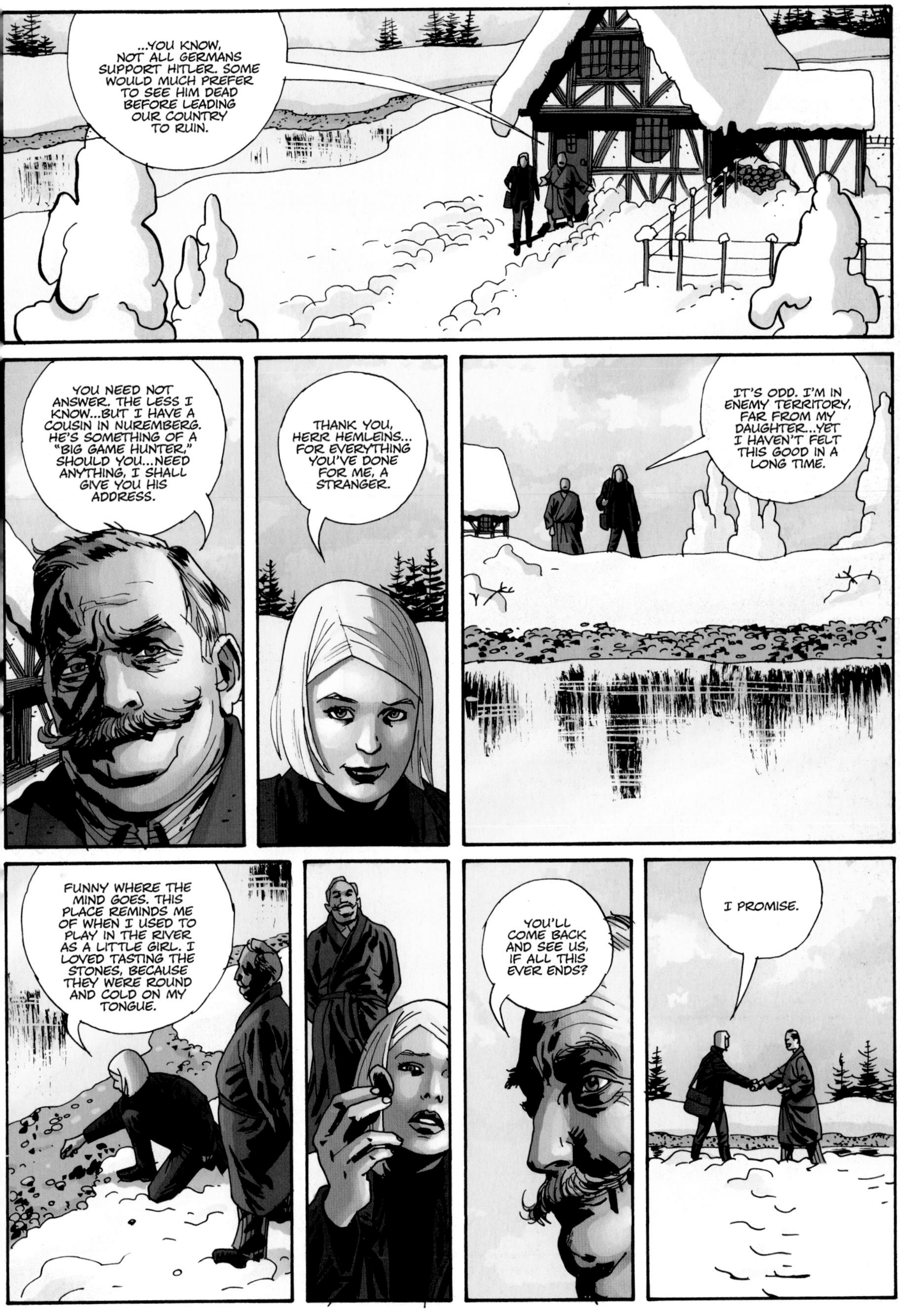
...YOU KNOW, NOT ALL GERMANS SUPPORT HITLER. SOME WOULD MUCH PREFER TO SEE HIM DEAD BEFORE LEADING OUR COUNTRY TO RUIN.
YOU NEED NOT ANSWER. THE LESS I KNOW...BUT I HAVE A COUSIN IN NUREMBERG. HE'S SOMETHING OF A "BIG GAME HUNTER," SHOULD YOU...NEED ANYTHING, I SHALL GIVE YOU HIS ADDRESS.
THANK YOU, HERR HEMLEINS... FOR EVERYTHING YOU'VE DONE FOR ME, A STRANGER.
IT'S ODD. I'M IN ENEMY TERRITORY, FAR FROM MY DAUGHTER...YET I HAVEN'T FELT THIS GOOD IN A LONG TIME.
FUNNY WHERE THE MIND GOES. THIS PLACE REMINDS ME OF WHEN I USED TO PLAY IN THE RIVER AS A LITTLE GIRL. I LOVED TASTING THE STONES, BECAUSE THEY WERE ROUND AND COLD ON MY TONGUE.
YOU'LL COME BACK AND SEE US, IF ALL THIS EVER ENDS?
I PROMISE.

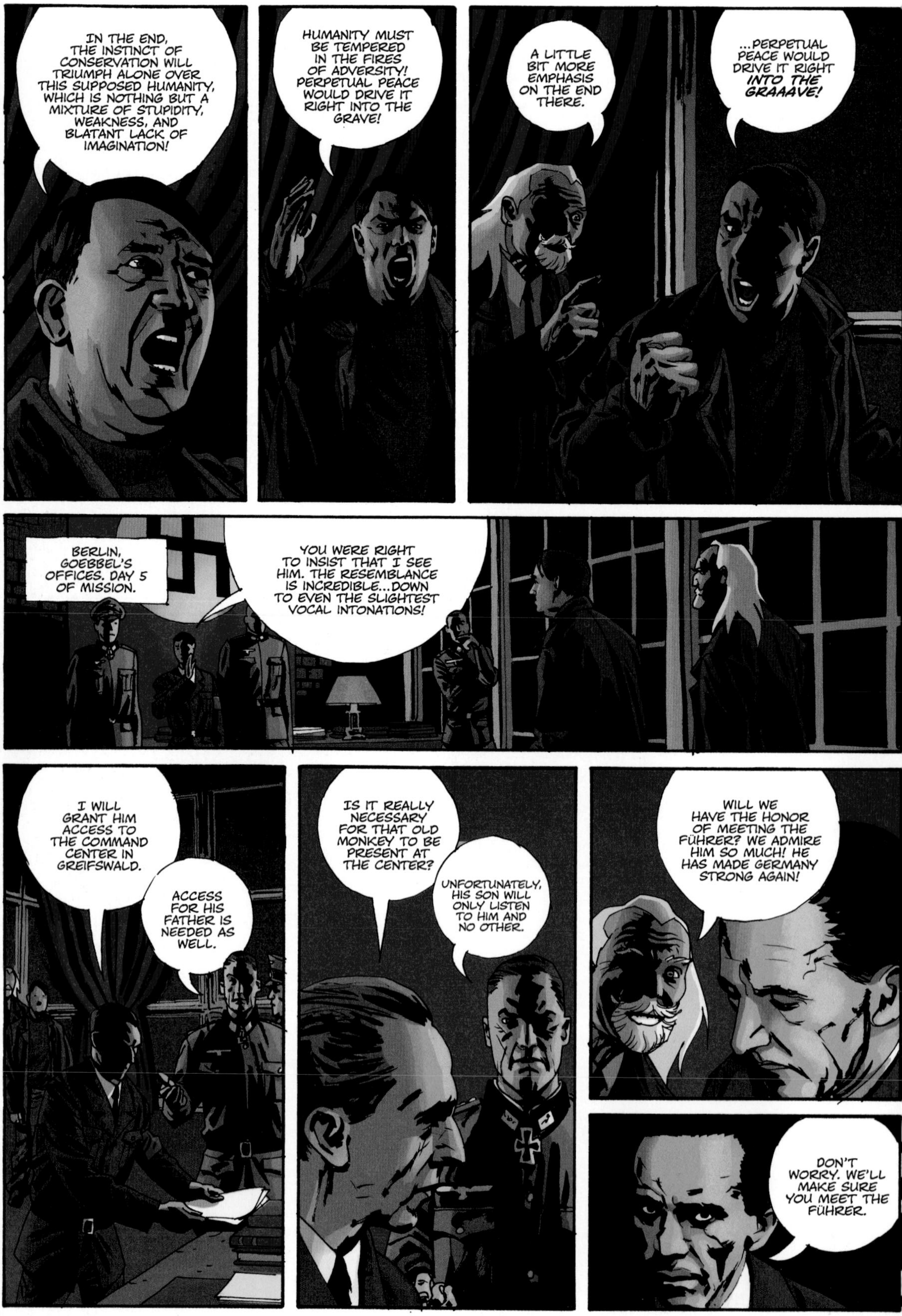
IN THE END, THE INSTINCT OF CONSERVATION WILL TRIUMPH ALONE OVER THIS SUPPOSED HUMANITY, WHICH IS NOTHING BUT A MIXTURE OF STUPIDITY, WEAKNESS, AND BLATANT LACK OF IMAGINATION!
HUMANITY MUST BE TEMPERED IN THE FIRES OF ADVERSITY! PERPETUAL PEACE WOULD DRIVE IT RIGHT INTO THE GRAVE!
A LITTLE BIT MORE EMPHASIS ON THE END THERE.
...PERPETUAL PEACE WOULD DRIVE IT RIGHT *INTO THE GRAAAVE!*
BERLIN, GOEBBEL'S OFFICES. DAY 5 OF MISSION.
YOU WERE RIGHT TO INSIST THAT I SEE HIM. THE RESEMBLANCE IS INCREDIBLE...DOWN TO EVEN THE SLIGHTEST VOCAL INTONATIONS!
I WILL GRANT HIM ACCESS TO THE COMMAND CENTER IN GREIFSWALD.
ACCESS FOR HIS FATHER IS NEEDED AS WELL.
IS IT REALLY NECESSARY FOR THAT OLD MONKEY TO BE PRESENT AT THE CENTER?
UNFORTUNATELY, HIS SON WILL ONLY LISTEN TO HIM AND NO OTHER.
WILL WE HAVE THE HONOR OF MEETING THE FÜHRER? WE ADMIRE HIM SO MUCH! HE HAS MADE GERMANY STRONG AGAIN!
DON'T WORRY. WE'LL MAKE SURE YOU MEET THE FÜHRER.

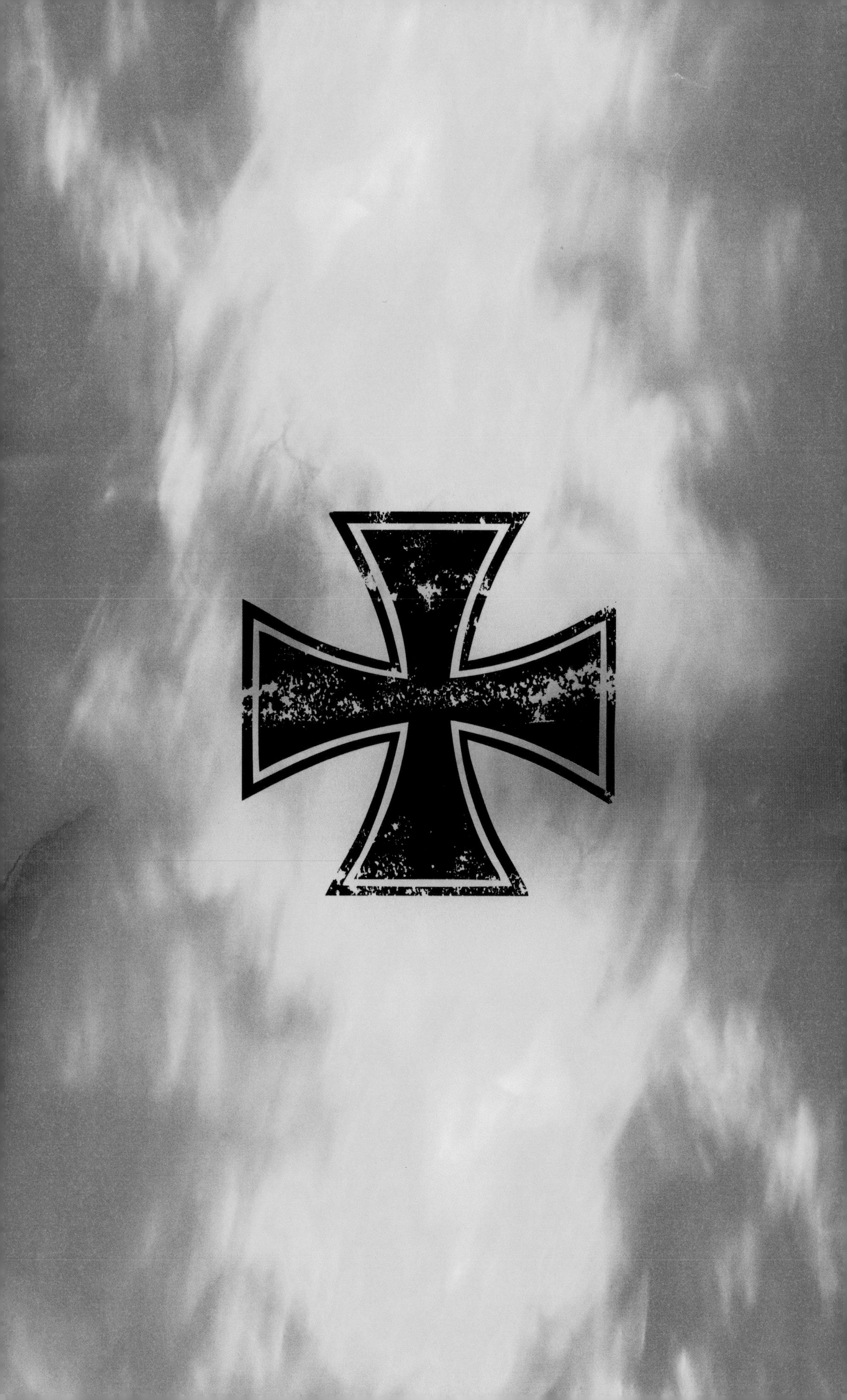

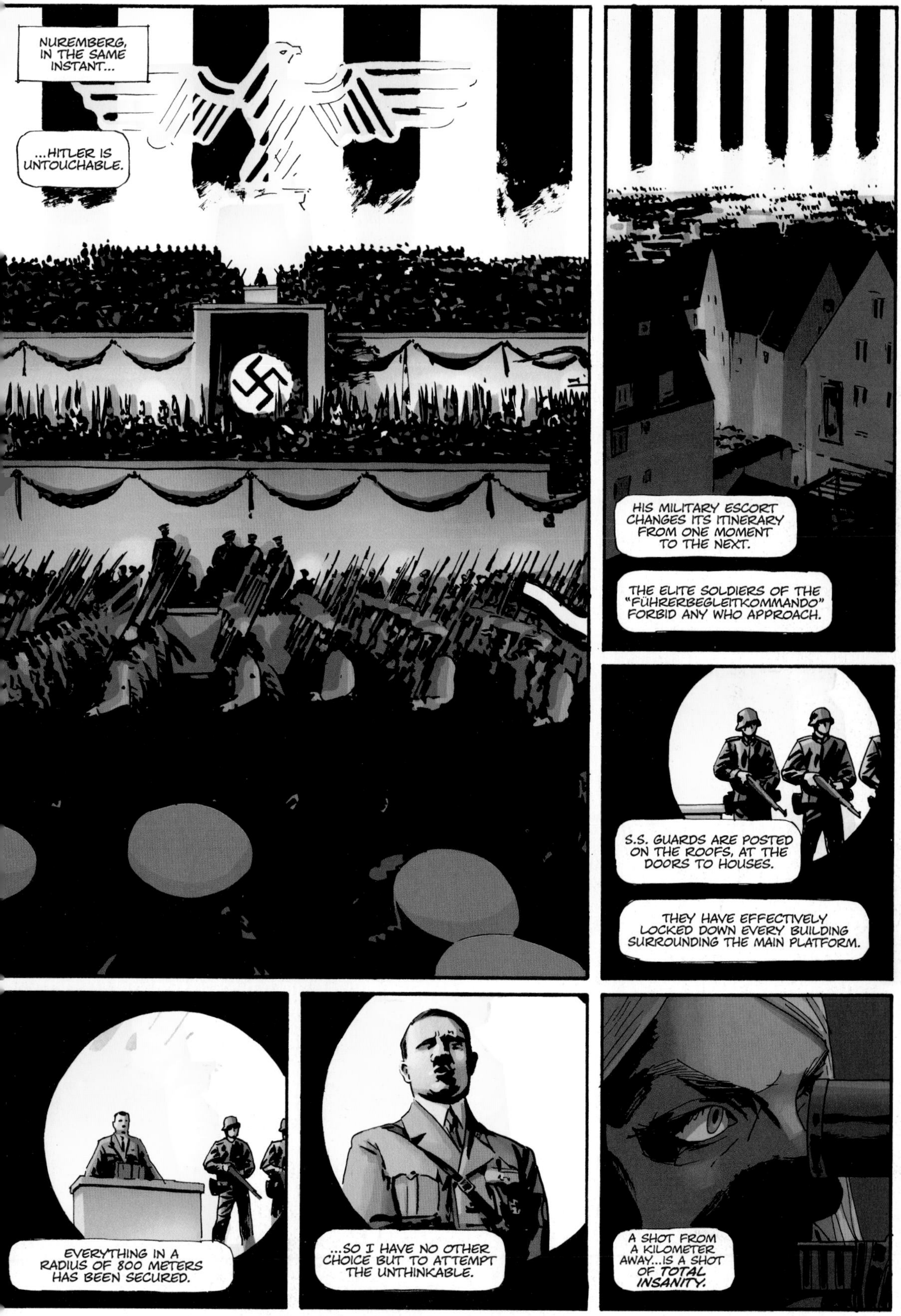
NUREMBERG, IN THE SAME INSTANT...
...HITLER IS UNTOUCHABLE.
HIS MILITARY ESCORT CHANGES ITS ITINERARY FROM ONE MOMENT TO THE NEXT.
THE ELITE SOLDIERS OF THE "FÜHRERBEGLEITKOMMANDO" FORBID ANY WHO APPROACH.
S.S. GUARDS ARE POSTED ON THE ROOFS, AT THE DOORS TO HOUSES.
THEY HAVE EFFECTIVELY LOCKED DOWN EVERY BUILDING SURROUNDING THE MAIN PLATFORM.
EVERYTHING IN A RADIUS OF 800 METERS HAS BEEN SECURED.
...SO I HAVE NO OTHER CHOICE BUT TO ATTEMPT THE UNTHINKABLE.
A SHOT FROM A KILOMETER AWAY...IS A SHOT OF *TOTAL INSANITY.*

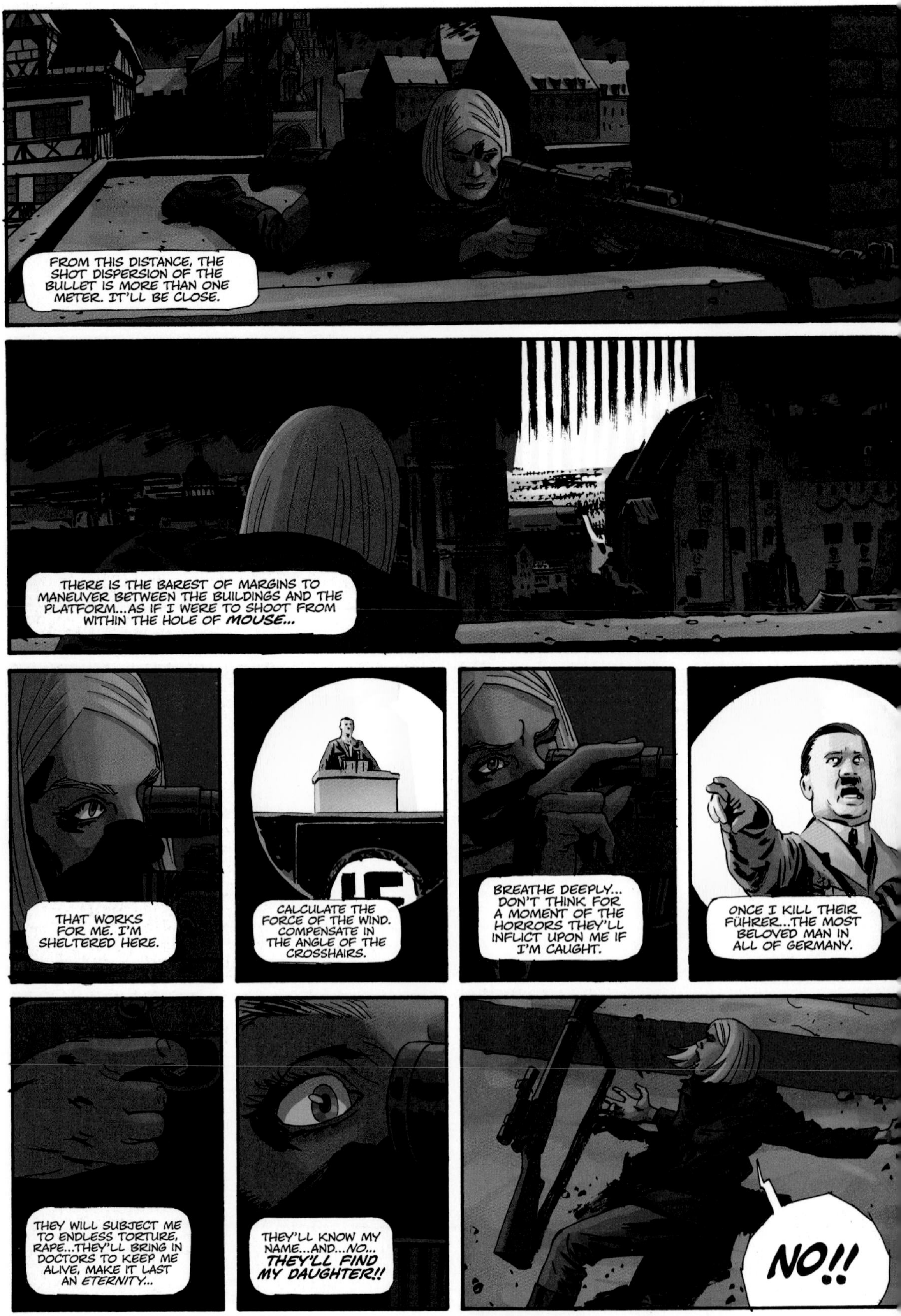
FROM THIS DISTANCE, THE SHOT DISPERSION OF THE BULLET IS MORE THAN ONE METER. IT'LL BE CLOSE.
THERE IS THE BAREST OF MARGINS TO MANEUVER BETWEEN THE BUILDINGS AND THE PLATFORM...AS IF I WERE TO SHOOT FROM WITHIN THE HOLE OF *MOUSE...*
THAT WORKS FOR ME. I'M SHELTERED HERE.
CALCULATE THE FORCE OF THE WIND. COMPENSATE IN THE ANGLE OF THE CROSSHAIRS.
BREATHE DEEPLY... DON'T THINK FOR A MOMENT OF THE HORRORS THEY'LL INFLICT UPON ME IF I'M CAUGHT.
ONCE I KILL THEIR FÜHRER...THE MOST BELOVED MAN IN ALL OF GERMANY.
THEY WILL SUBJECT ME TO ENDLESS TORTURE, RAPE...THEY'LL BRING IN DOCTORS TO KEEP ME ALIVE, MAKE IT LAST AN *ETERNITY...*
THEY'LL KNOW MY NAME...AND...*NO...* ***THEY'LL FIND MY DAUGHTER!!***
NO!!

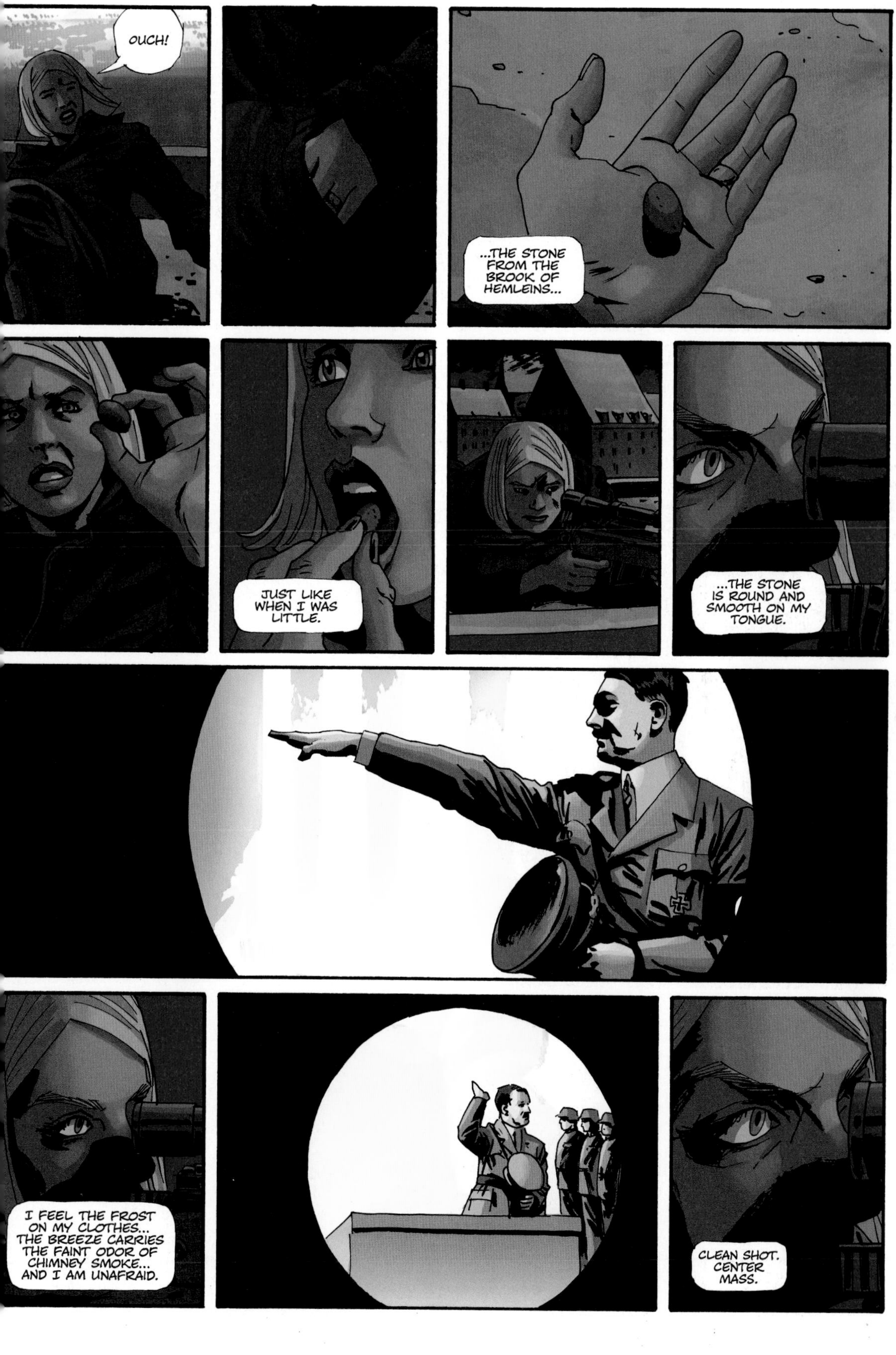
OUCH!
...THE STONE FROM THE BROOK OF HEMLEINS...
JUST LIKE WHEN I WAS LITTLE.
...THE STONE IS ROUND AND SMOOTH ON MY TONGUE.
I FEEL THE FROST ON MY CLOTHES... THE BREEZE CARRIES THE FAINT ODOR OF CHIMNEY SMOKE... AND I AM UNAFRAID.
CLEAN SHOT. CENTER MASS.

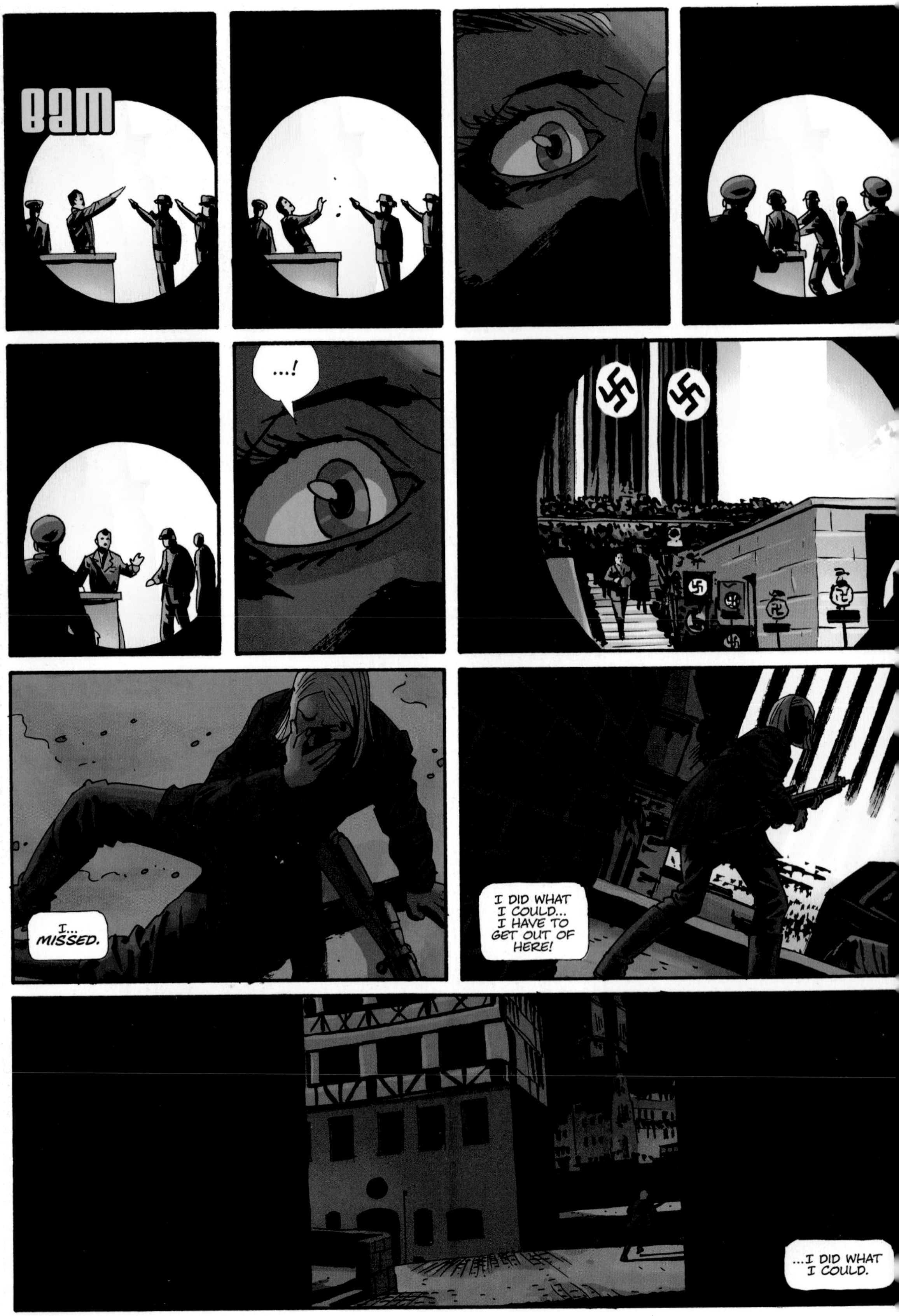
BAM
...!
I... MISSED.
I DID WHAT I COULD... I HAVE TO GET OUT OF HERE!
...I DID WHAT I COULD.

REGION OF GREIFSWALD, DAY 7 OF MISSION.

WHAT'LL WE DO WHEN WE MEET HIM? WE DON'T HAVE ANY WEAPONS!

RELAX, WILLY... MY YEARS OF INTERNMENT HAVE TAUGHT ME MANY THINGS. NOT THE LEAST OF WHICH IS HIDING A KNIFE.

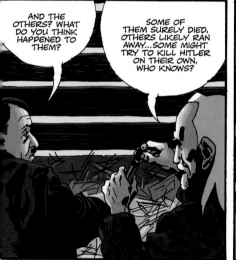

AND THE OTHERS? WHAT DO YOU THINK HAPPENED TO THEM?

SOME OF THEM SURELY DIED, OTHERS LIKELY RAN AWAY...SOME MIGHT TRY TO KILL HITLER ON THEIR OWN, WHO KNOWS?

EXCEPT SMITH...HE'S SURELY FLOATING SOMEWHERE IN THE SKY, TURNING SLOWLY IN THE EVER RISING CURRENTS.

CIRCLING WITH THE ALBATROSS, THE NORDIC GODS, THE DANDELIONS AND ALL THINGS CARRIED BY WIND AND FATE.

EVER CLOSER TO THE BLINDING CLARITY OF THE SUN.

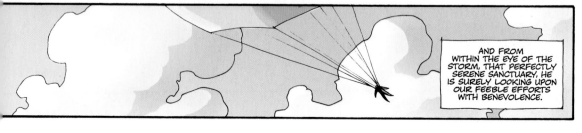

AND FROM WITHIN THE EYE OF THE STORM, THAT PERFECTLY SERENE SANCTUARY, HE IS SURELY LOOKING UPON OUR FEEBLE EFFORTS WITH BENEVOLENCE.

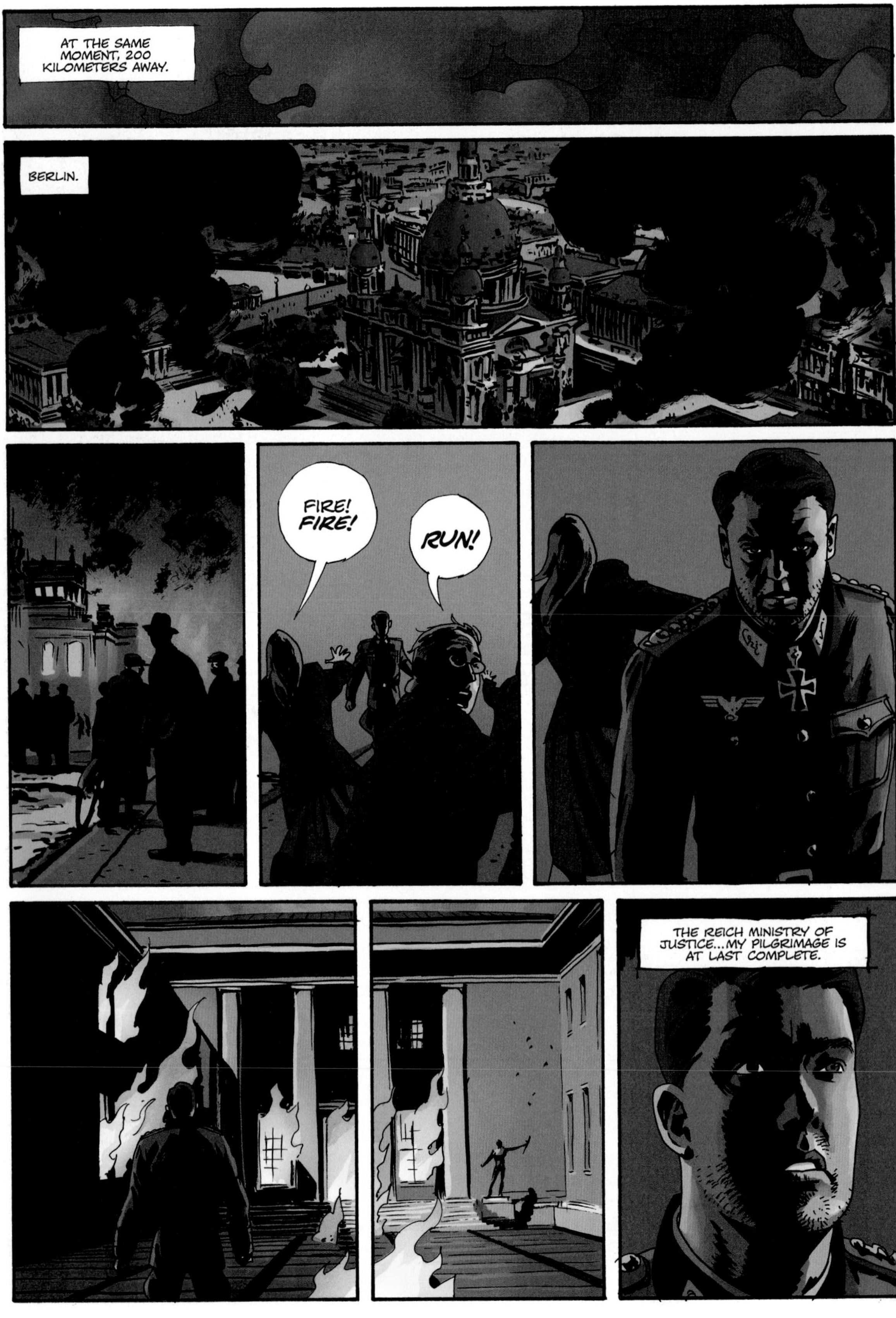
AT THE SAME MOMENT, 200 KILOMETERS AWAY.
BERLIN.
FIRE! FIRE!
RUN!
THE REICH MINISTRY OF JUSTICE...MY PILGRIMAGE IS AT LAST COMPLETE.

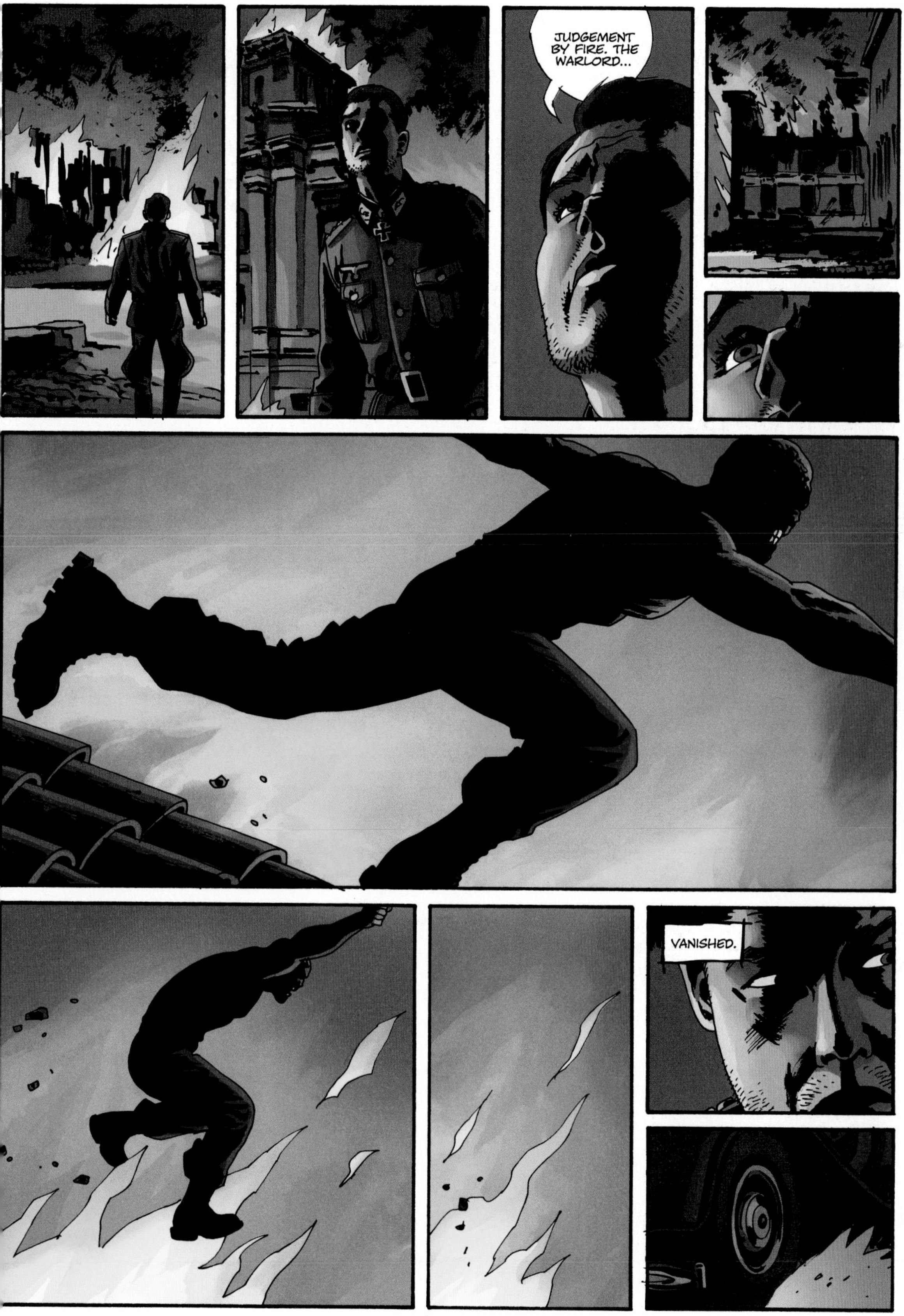
JUDGEMENT BY FIRE. THE WARLORD...
VANISHED.

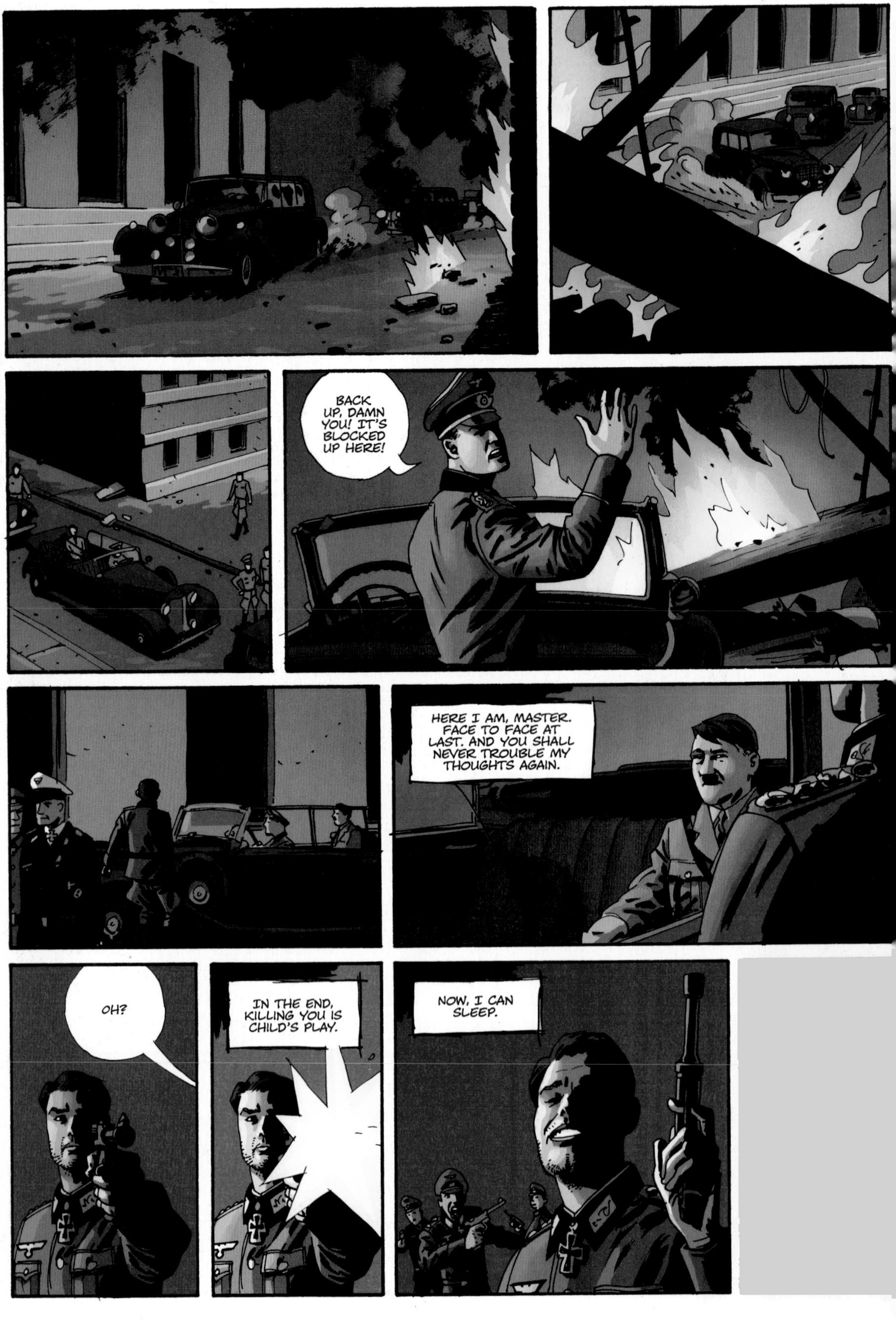
BACK UP, DAMN YOU! IT'S BLOCKED UP HERE!
HERE I AM, MASTER. FACE TO FACE AT LAST. AND YOU SHALL NEVER TROUBLE MY THOUGHTS AGAIN.
OH?
IN THE END, KILLING YOU IS CHILD'S PLAY.
NOW, I CAN SLEEP.

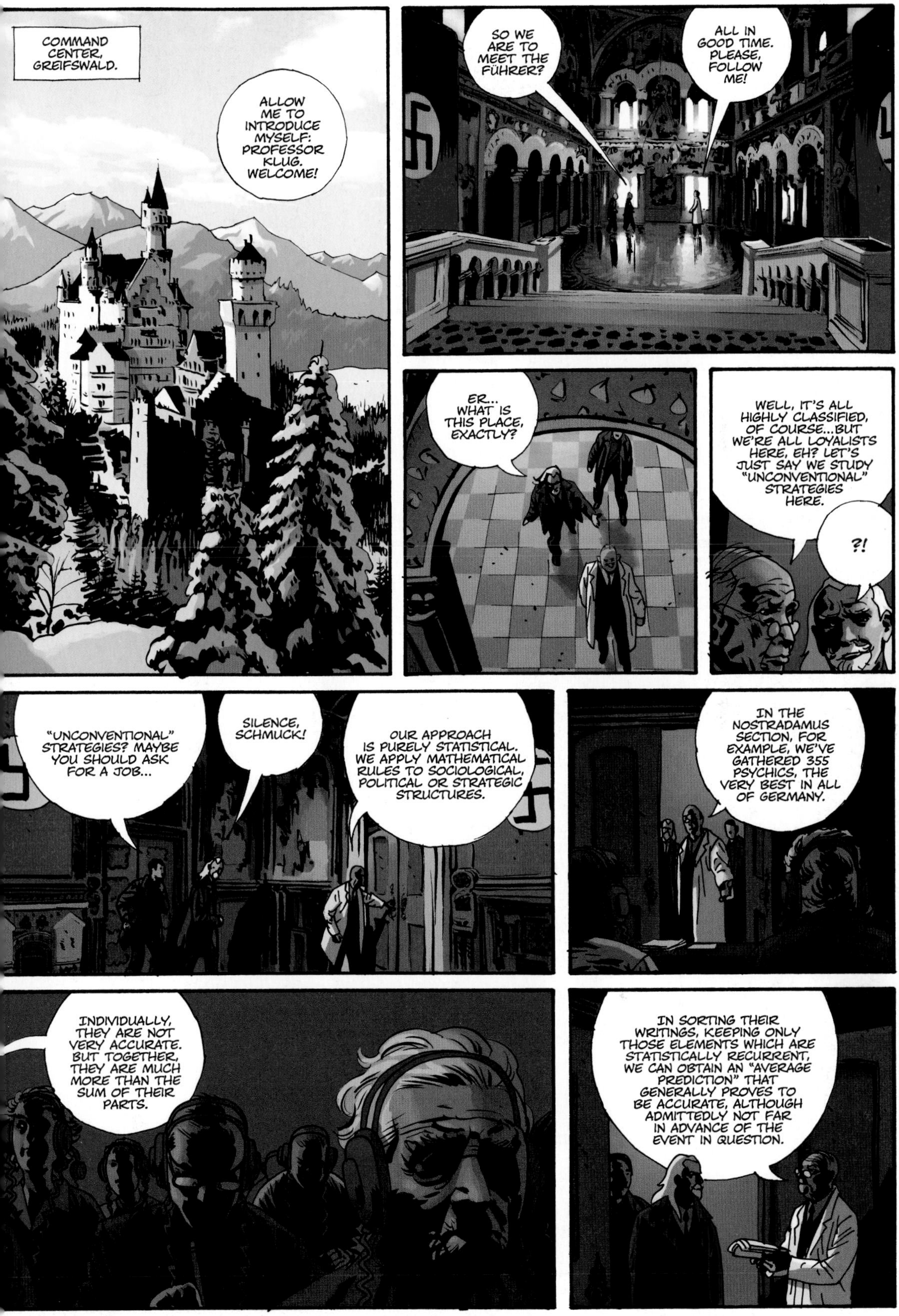
COMMAND CENTER, GREIFSWALD.
ALLOW ME TO INTRODUCE MYSELF: PROFESSOR KLUG. WELCOME!
SO WE ARE TO MEET THE FÜHRER?
ALL IN GOOD TIME. PLEASE, FOLLOW ME!
ER... WHAT IS THIS PLACE, EXACTLY?
WELL, IT'S ALL HIGHLY CLASSIFIED, OF COURSE...BUT WE'RE ALL LOYALISTS HERE, EH? LET'S JUST SAY WE STUDY "UNCONVENTIONAL" STRATEGIES HERE.
?!
"UNCONVENTIONAL" STRATEGIES? MAYBE YOU SHOULD ASK FOR A JOB...
SILENCE, SCHMUCK!
OUR APPROACH IS PURELY STATISTICAL. WE APPLY MATHEMATICAL RULES TO SOCIOLOGICAL, POLITICAL OR STRATEGIC STRUCTURES.
IN THE NOSTRADAMUS SECTION, FOR EXAMPLE, WE'VE GATHERED 355 PSYCHICS, THE VERY BEST IN ALL OF GERMANY.
INDIVIDUALLY, THEY ARE NOT VERY ACCURATE. BUT TOGETHER, THEY ARE MUCH MORE THAN THE SUM OF THEIR PARTS.
IN SORTING THEIR WRITINGS, KEEPING ONLY THOSE ELEMENTS WHICH ARE STATISTICALLY RECURRENT, WE CAN OBTAIN AN "AVERAGE PREDICTION" THAT GENERALLY PROVES TO BE ACCURATE, ALTHOUGH ADMITTEDLY NOT FAR IN ADVANCE OF THE EVENT IN QUESTION.

I'M AFRAID I'M NOT FOLLOWING... WHAT EXACTLY DOES MY **SON** HAVE TO DO WITH THIS?

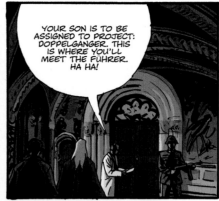

YOUR SON IS TO BE ASSIGNED TO PROJECT: DOPPELGANGER. THIS IS WHERE YOU'LL MEET THE FÜHRER. HA HA!

?!... GENTLEMEN, I'M GOING TO ASK YOU TO WAIT HERE A MOMENT...

I MUST LOOK INTO THIS. IT APPEARS THE PSYCHICS HAVE CALCULATED A 75% CHANCE OF AN IMMINENT INCIDENT...

THE FÜHRER IS THROUGH HERE?

WELL, LET'S NOT MAKE YOUR PSYCHICS INACCURATE, HM?

ARRR!!

SEVEN DAYS INTO OUR MISSION, WE'VE BEEN GIVEN THIS CHANCE. WE WON'T GET ANOTHER.

RHAAA!!!

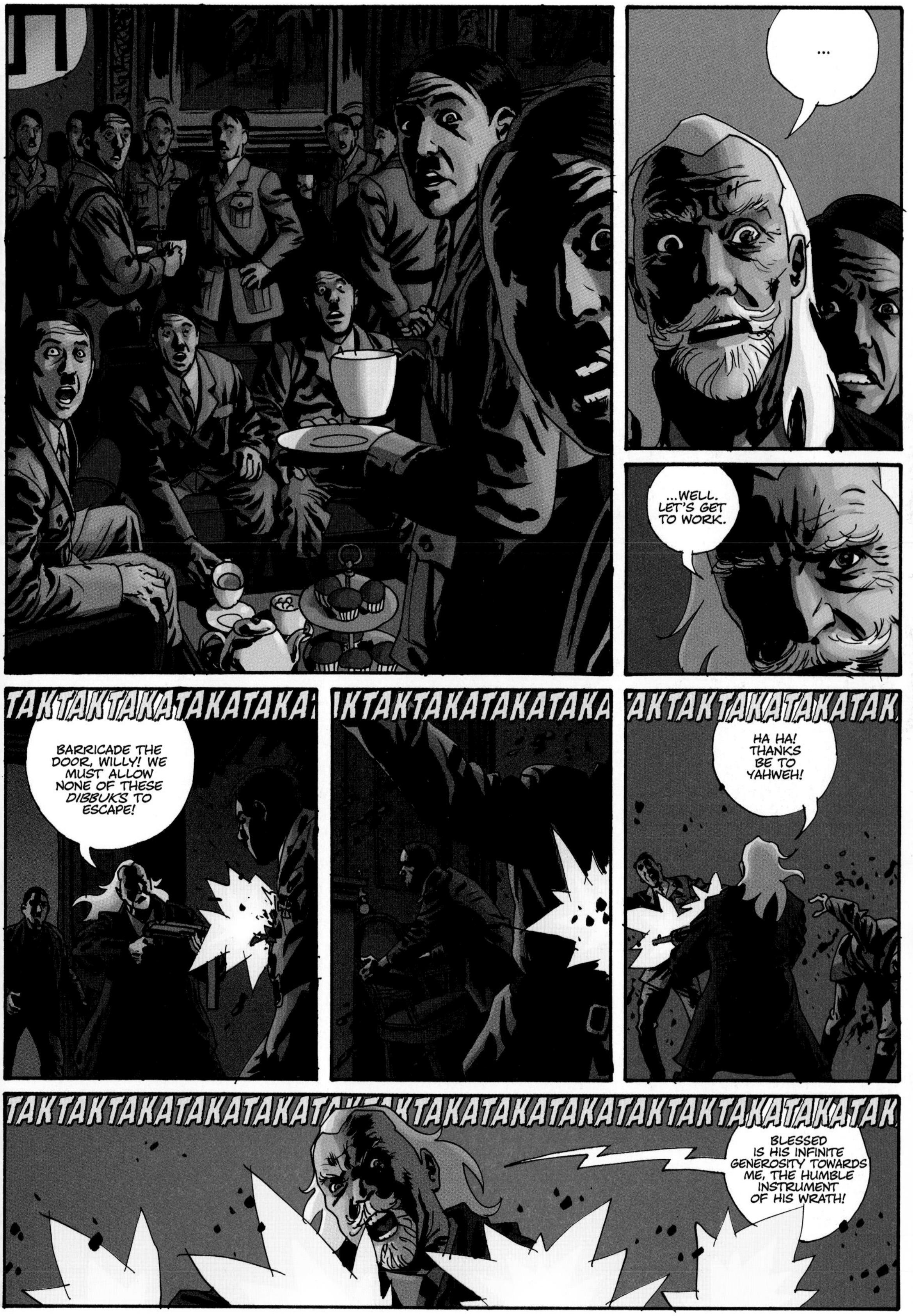
...
...WELL. LET'S GET TO WORK.
TAKTAKTAKATAKATAKA
BARRICADE THE DOOR, WILLY! WE MUST ALLOW NONE OF THESE DIBBUKS TO ESCAPE!
KTAKTAKATAKATAKA
TAKTAKTAKATATAK
HA HA! THANKS BE TO YAHWEH!
TAKTAKTAKATAKATA
TAKATAKATAKTAKTAKATAK
BLESSED IS HIS INFINITE GENEROSITY TOWARDS ME, THE HUMBLE INSTRUMENT OF HIS WRATH!

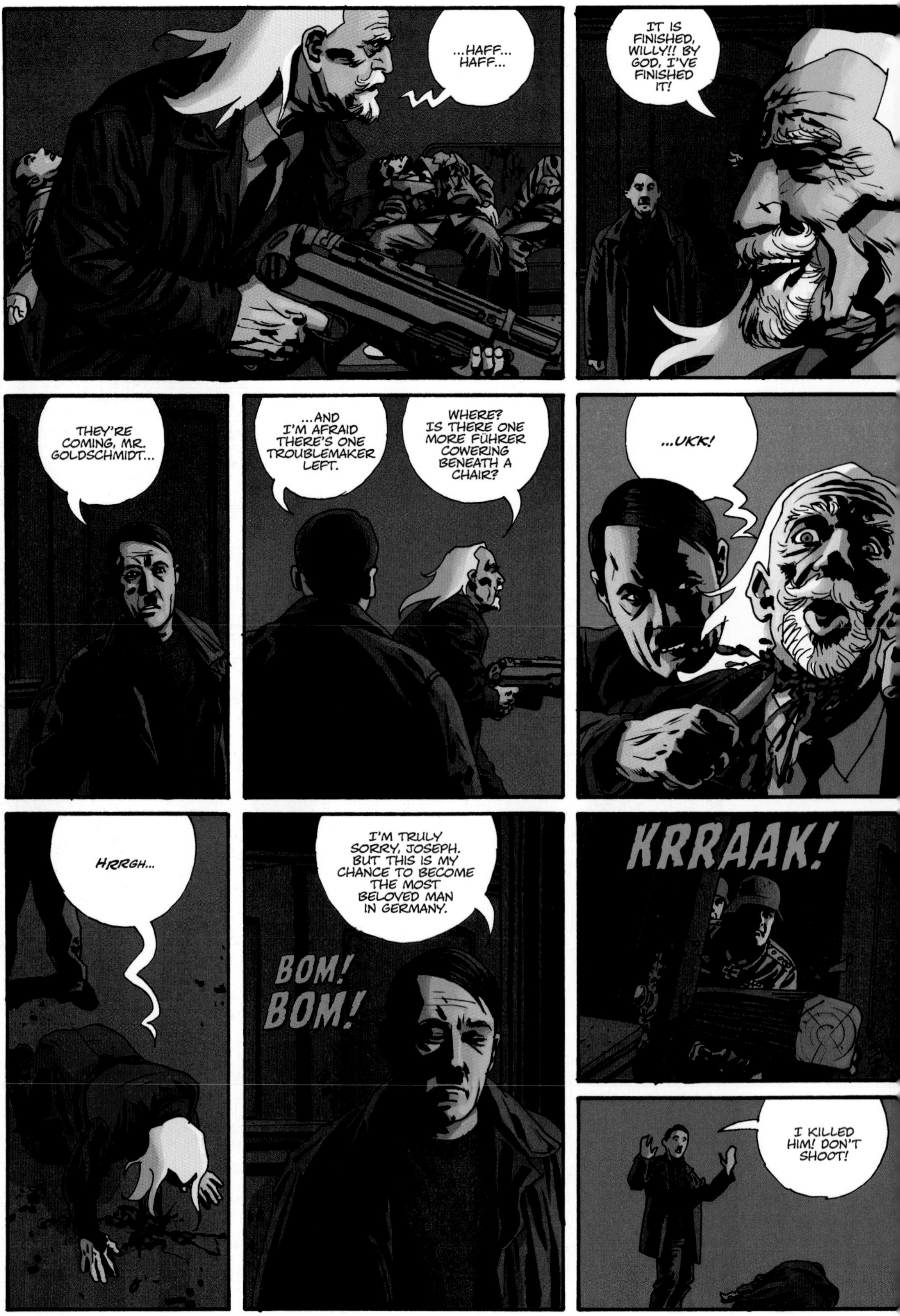
...HAFF... HAFF...
IT IS FINISHED, WILLY!! BY GOD, I'VE FINISHED IT!
THEY'RE COMING, MR. GOLDSCHMIDT...
...AND I'M AFRAID THERE'S ONE TROUBLEMAKER LEFT.
WHERE? IS THERE ONE MORE FÜHRER COWERING BENEATH A CHAIR?
...UKK!
HRRGH...
I'M TRULY SORRY, JOSEPH. BUT THIS IS MY CHANCE TO BECOME THE MOST BELOVED MAN IN GERMANY.
BOM! BOM!
KRRAAK!
I KILLED HIM! DON'T SHOOT!

WE MUST HURRY...YOU ARE THE LAST ONE!

THE LAST ONE? WHAT DO YOU MEAN?!

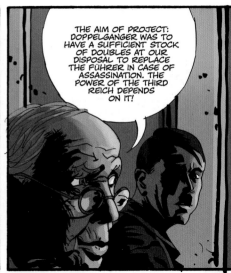

THE AIM OF PROJECT: DOPPELGANGER WAS TO HAVE A SUFFICIENT STOCK OF DOUBLES AT OUR DISPOSAL TO REPLACE THE FÜHRER IN CASE OF ASSASSINATION. THE POWER OF THE THIRD REICH DEPENDS ON IT!

BUT THE S.S. HAS JUST INFORMED ME OF THE MURDER OF DOPPELGANGER #19, AT THE MINISTRY OF JUSTICE!

"DOPPEL-GANGER #19"?!

THE ONE WHO HAD JUST REPLACED #18, WHO WAS KILLED BY A SNIPER DURING A MEETING IN NUREMBERG TWO DAYS AGO...DO YOU UNDERSTAND?

WE HAD DISCHARGED #19 IN BERLIN WHILE WE WERE CHOOSING DOPPELGANGER #20...

NOW BOTH ACTIVE DOUBLES HAVE BEEN ASSASSINATED, AND OUR STOCK HAS BEEN DEPLETED ALL IN THE MATTER OF DAYS! THIS IS--WELL, IT'S STATISTICALLY *IMPOSSIBLE!*

YOU ARE OUR LAST AVAILABLE FÜHRER! WE MUST GET YOU TO SAFETY!

BUT... WHAT ABOUT THE REAL FÜHRER?!

OH, HIM? KILLED BY A BOMB IN MUNICH IN 1939.

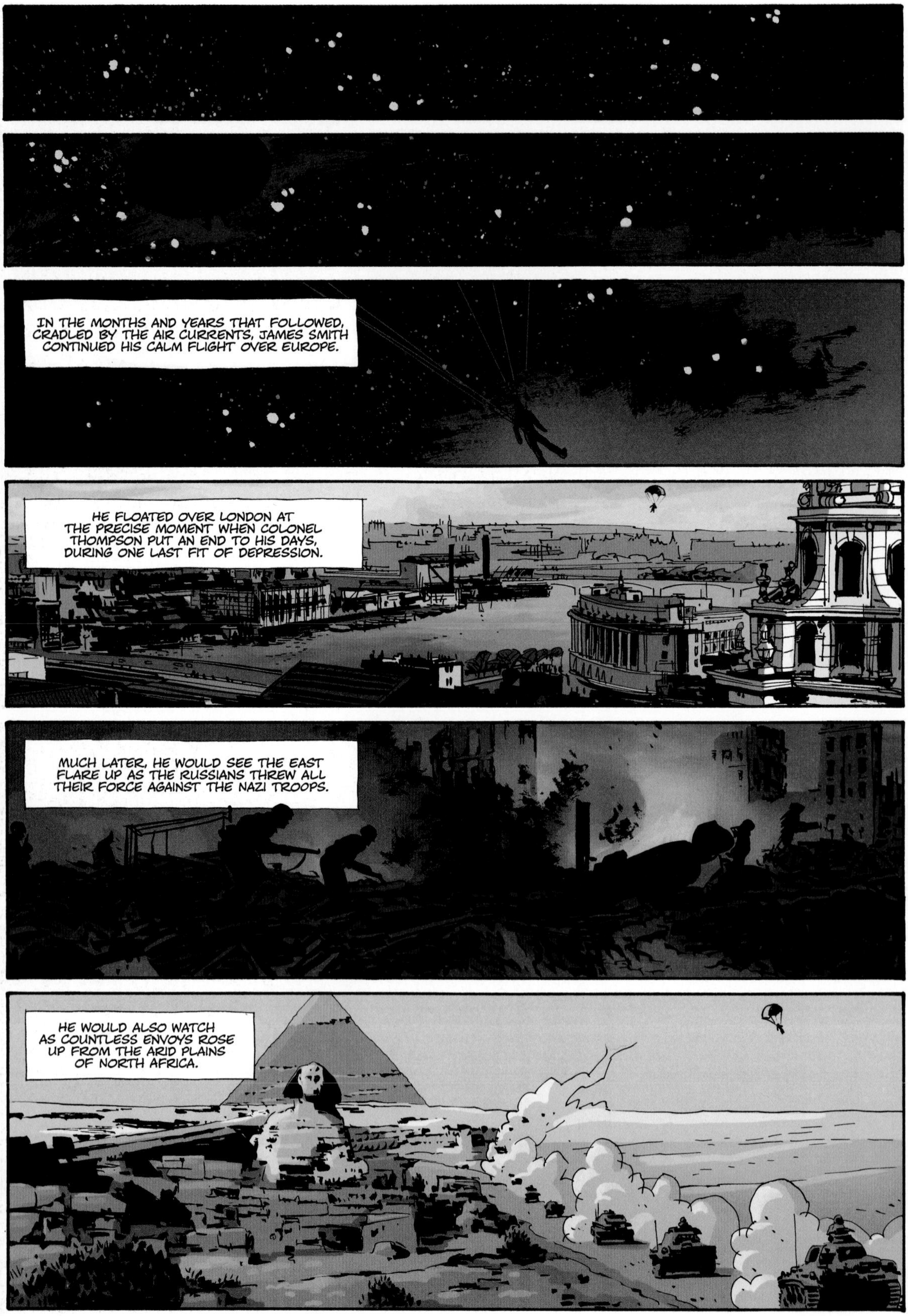
IN THE MONTHS AND YEARS THAT FOLLOWED, CRADLED BY THE AIR CURRENTS, JAMES SMITH CONTINUED HIS CALM FLIGHT OVER EUROPE.
HE FLOATED OVER LONDON AT THE PRECISE MOMENT WHEN COLONEL THOMPSON PUT AN END TO HIS DAYS, DURING ONE LAST FIT OF DEPRESSION.
MUCH LATER, HE WOULD SEE THE EAST FLARE UP AS THE RUSSIANS THREW ALL THEIR FORCE AGAINST THE NAZI TROOPS.
HE WOULD ALSO WATCH AS COUNTLESS ENVOYS ROSE UP FROM THE ARID PLAINS OF NORTH AFRICA.

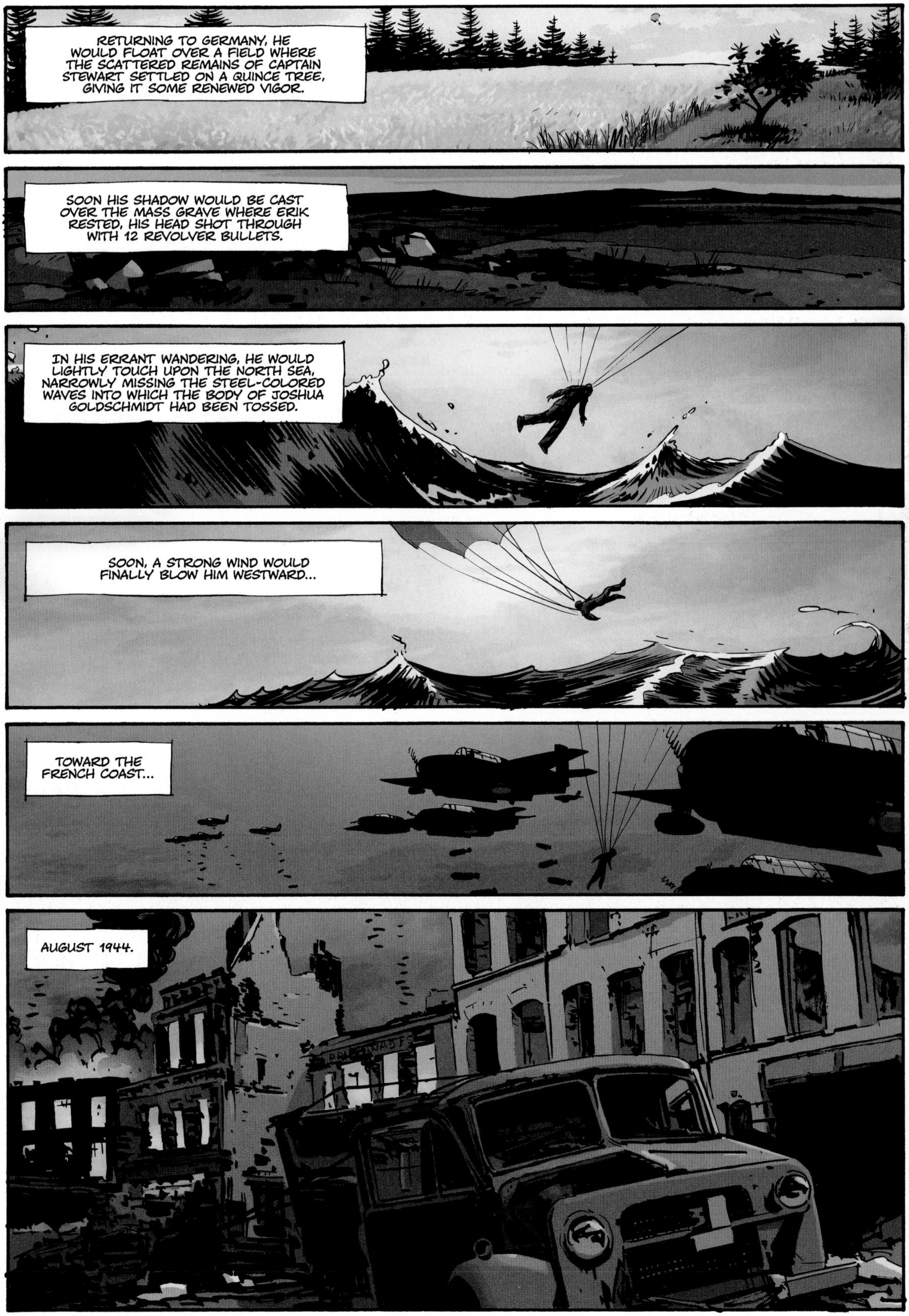
RETURNING TO GERMANY, HE WOULD FLOAT OVER A FIELD WHERE THE SCATTERED REMAINS OF CAPTAIN STEWART SETTLED ON A QUINCE TREE, GIVING IT SOME RENEWED VIGOR.
SOON HIS SHADOW WOULD BE CAST OVER THE MASS GRAVE WHERE ERIK RESTED, HIS HEAD SHOT THROUGH WITH 12 REVOLVER BULLETS.
IN HIS ERRANT WANDERING, HE WOULD LIGHTLY TOUCH UPON THE NORTH SEA, NARROWLY MISSING THE STEEL-COLORED WAVES INTO WHICH THE BODY OF JOSHUA GOLDSCHMIDT HAD BEEN TOSSED.
SOON, A STRONG WIND WOULD FINALLY BLOW HIM WESTWARD...
TOWARD THE FRENCH COAST...
AUGUST 1944.

ENGLAND IS SO CLOSE...I CAN ALMOST FEEL IT!

ALL THESE HORRIBLE MONTHS SPENT HIDING IN CAVES, MOVED ABOUT BY THE GERMAN RESISTANCE. FOREVER HUNTED BY THE S.S. WITH NO WAY TO GET HOME...

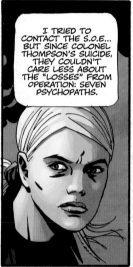

I TRIED TO CONTACT THE S.O.E... BUT SINCE COLONEL THOMPSON'S SUICIDE, THEY COULDN'T CARE LESS ABOUT THE "LOSSES" FROM OPERATION: SEVEN PSYCHOPATHS.

I KNOW I CAN GET TO THE FRONTLINES. I JUST NEED TO FOCUS...PUT MY LUCKY STONE BACK ON MY TONGUE...

WHO'S TAKING CARE OF MY DAUGHTER NOW? I...NO! DON'T THINK OF THAT NOW! KEEP MOVING!

I DON'T KNOW HOW LONG THIS WAR WILL RAGE...I ONLY KNOW I HAVE TO GET HOME TO *HER*...

OH!

AAGH!

?!

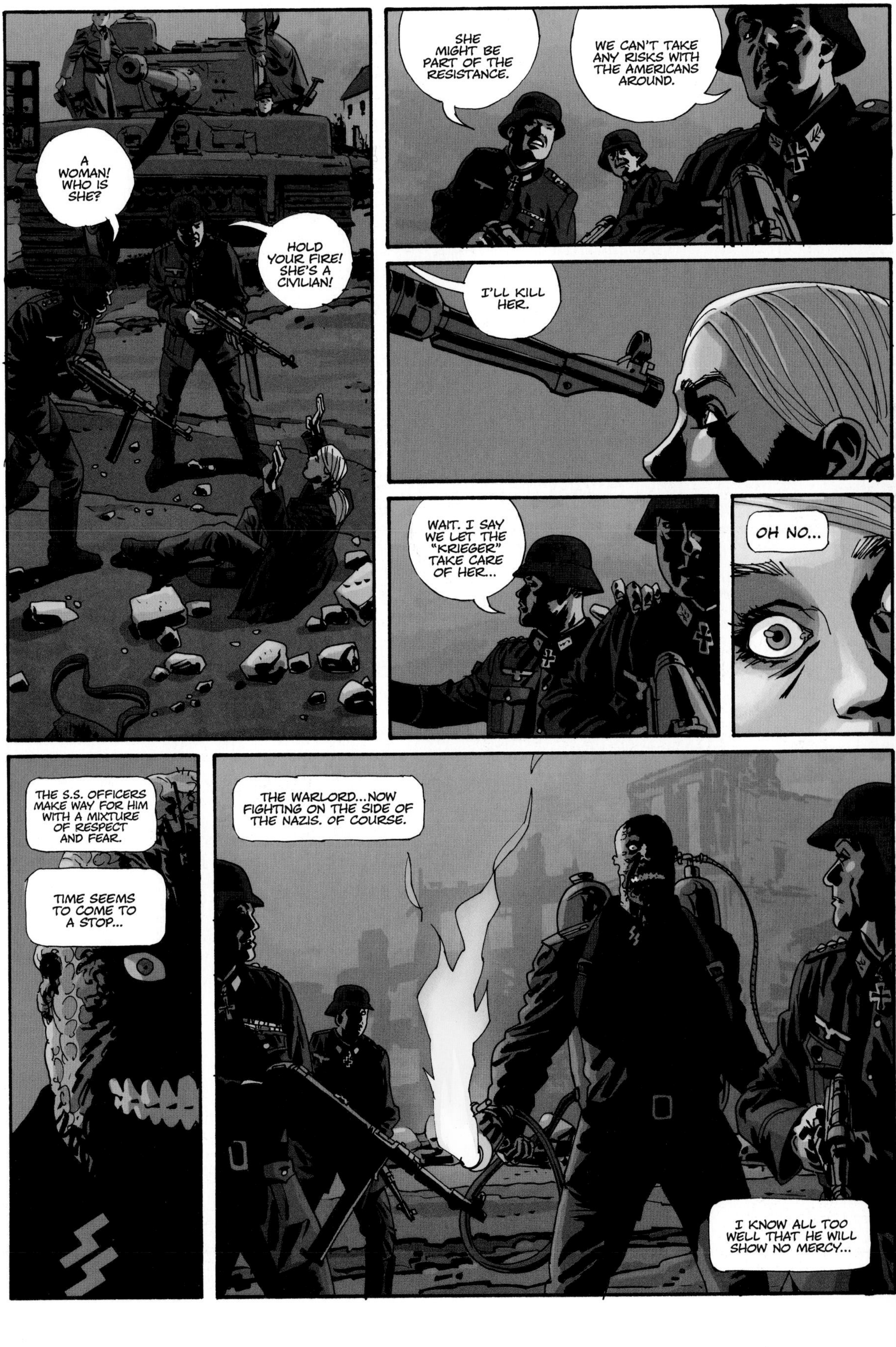
A WOMAN! WHO IS SHE?
HOLD YOUR FIRE! SHE'S A CIVILIAN!
SHE MIGHT BE PART OF THE RESISTANCE.
WE CAN'T TAKE ANY RISKS WITH THE AMERICANS AROUND.
I'LL KILL HER.
WAIT. I SAY WE LET THE "KRIEGER" TAKE CARE OF HER...
OH NO...
THE S.S. OFFICERS MAKE WAY FOR HIM WITH A MIXTURE OF RESPECT AND FEAR.
TIME SEEMS TO COME TO A STOP...
THE WARLORD...NOW FIGHTING ON THE SIDE OF THE NAZIS. OF COURSE.
I KNOW ALL TOO WELL THAT HE WILL SHOW NO MERCY...

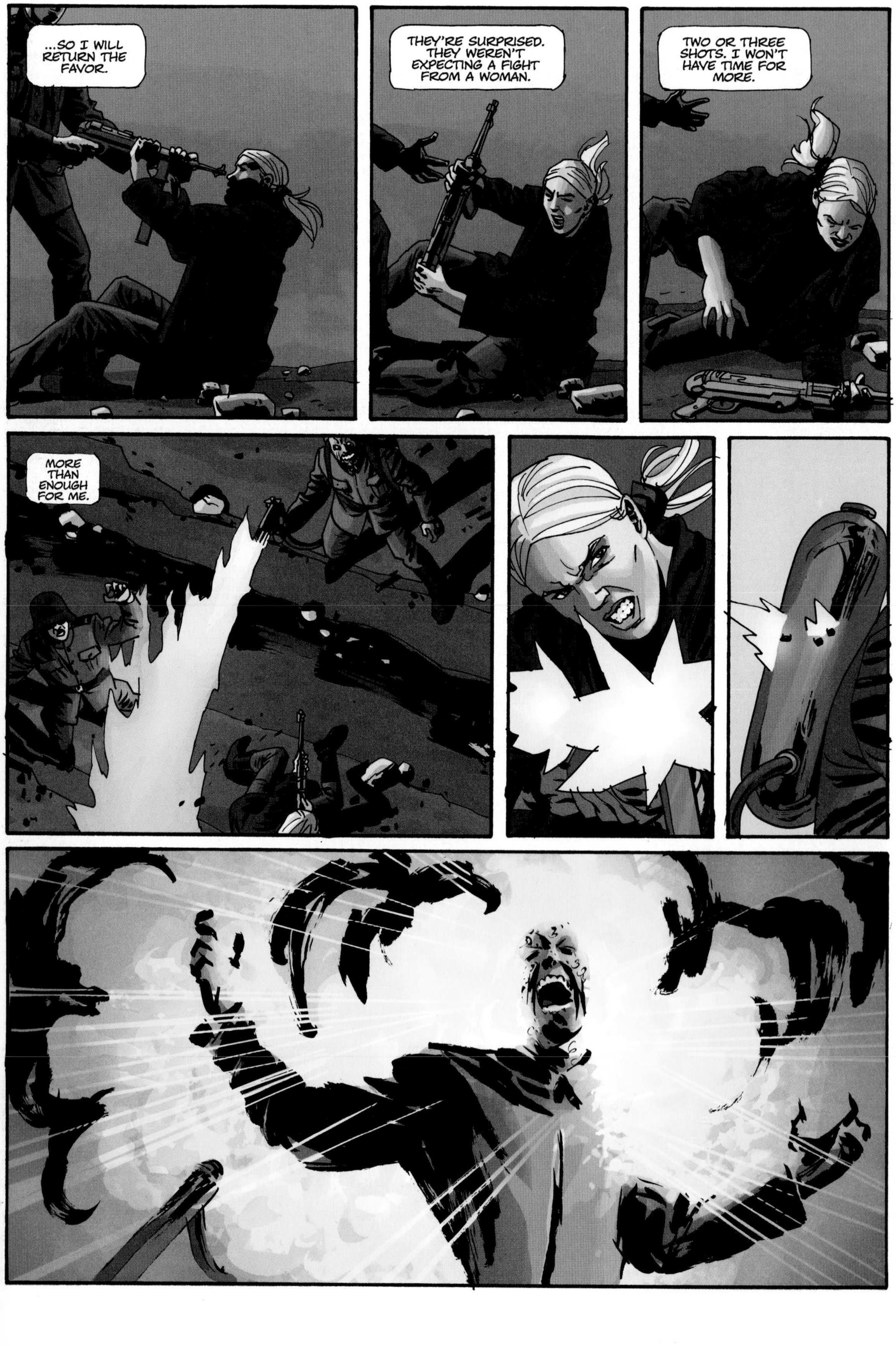
...SO I WILL RETURN THE FAVOR.
THEY'RE SURPRISED. THEY WEREN'T EXPECTING A FIGHT FROM A WOMAN.
TWO OR THREE SHOTS. I WON'T HAVE TIME FOR MORE.
MORE THAN ENOUGH FOR ME.

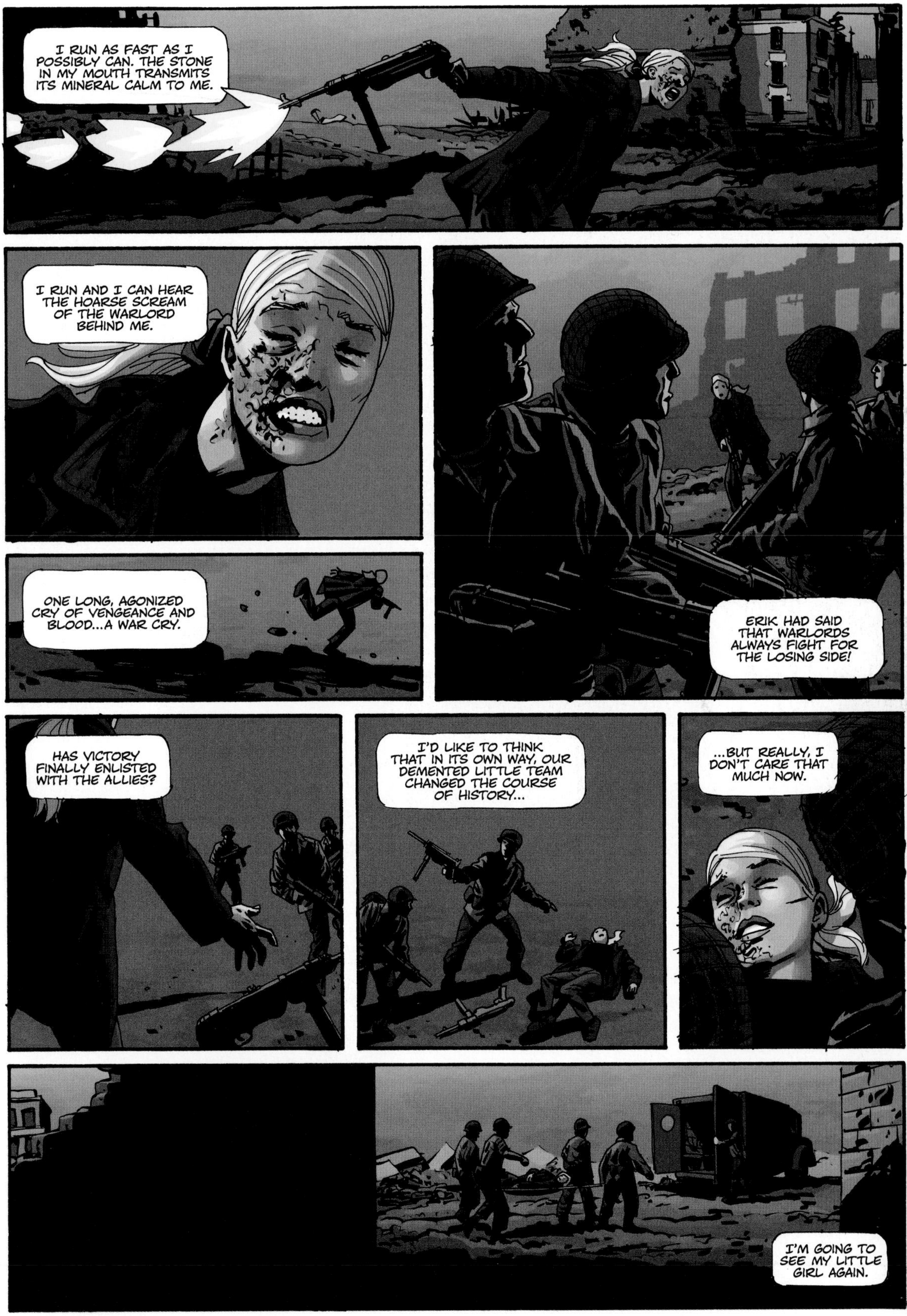
I RUN AS FAST AS I POSSIBLY CAN. THE STONE IN MY MOUTH TRANSMITS ITS MINERAL CALM TO ME.
I RUN AND I CAN HEAR THE HOARSE SCREAM OF THE WARLORD BEHIND ME.
ONE LONG, AGONIZED CRY OF VENGEANCE AND BLOOD...A WAR CRY.
ERIK HAD SAID THAT WARLORDS ALWAYS FIGHT FOR THE LOSING SIDE!
HAS VICTORY FINALLY ENLISTED WITH THE ALLIES?
I'D LIKE TO THINK THAT IN ITS OWN WAY, OUR DEMENTED LITTLE TEAM CHANGED THE COURSE OF HISTORY...
...BUT REALLY, I DON'T CARE THAT MUCH NOW.
I'M GOING TO SEE MY LITTLE GIRL AGAIN.

...THEY'RE ALL GATHERED AT MY SIDE, TO GIVE ME ADVICE OR TO AWAIT MY ORDERS.

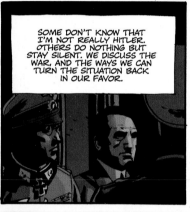

SOME DON'T KNOW THAT I'M NOT REALLY HITLER. OTHERS DO NOTHING BUT STAY SILENT. WE DISCUSS THE WAR, AND THE WAYS WE CAN TURN THE SITUATION BACK IN OUR FAVOR.

AROUND ME SECRET ALLIANCES AND FATAL BETRAYALS ARE STILL BEING ESTABLISHED, AS WELL AS REMORSELESS BROTHERLY STRUGGLES TO SEIZE POWER.

MOST OF THESE INTRIGUES ARE TOTALLY BEYOND ME. I'M HAPPY TO CARRY OUT THIS DECEPTION, TO PLAY THE ROLE EXPECTED OF ME.

....JUST AS WHEN I WAS PLAYING THE PSYCHIC, I LET MYSELF BE OVERTAKEN BY UNKNOWN FORCES, FORCES BEYOND EVERY SINGLE PERSON AT THIS TABLE.

LED AGAINST OUR WILL BY GHOSTS OF THE PAST, WE ARE ALL FORCED INTO A JOYOUS HEADLONG RUSH INTO THE FUTURE...

AS BEFORE, THERE IS NOTHING I CAN DO TO CHANGE THAT. NOTHING.

THE END.

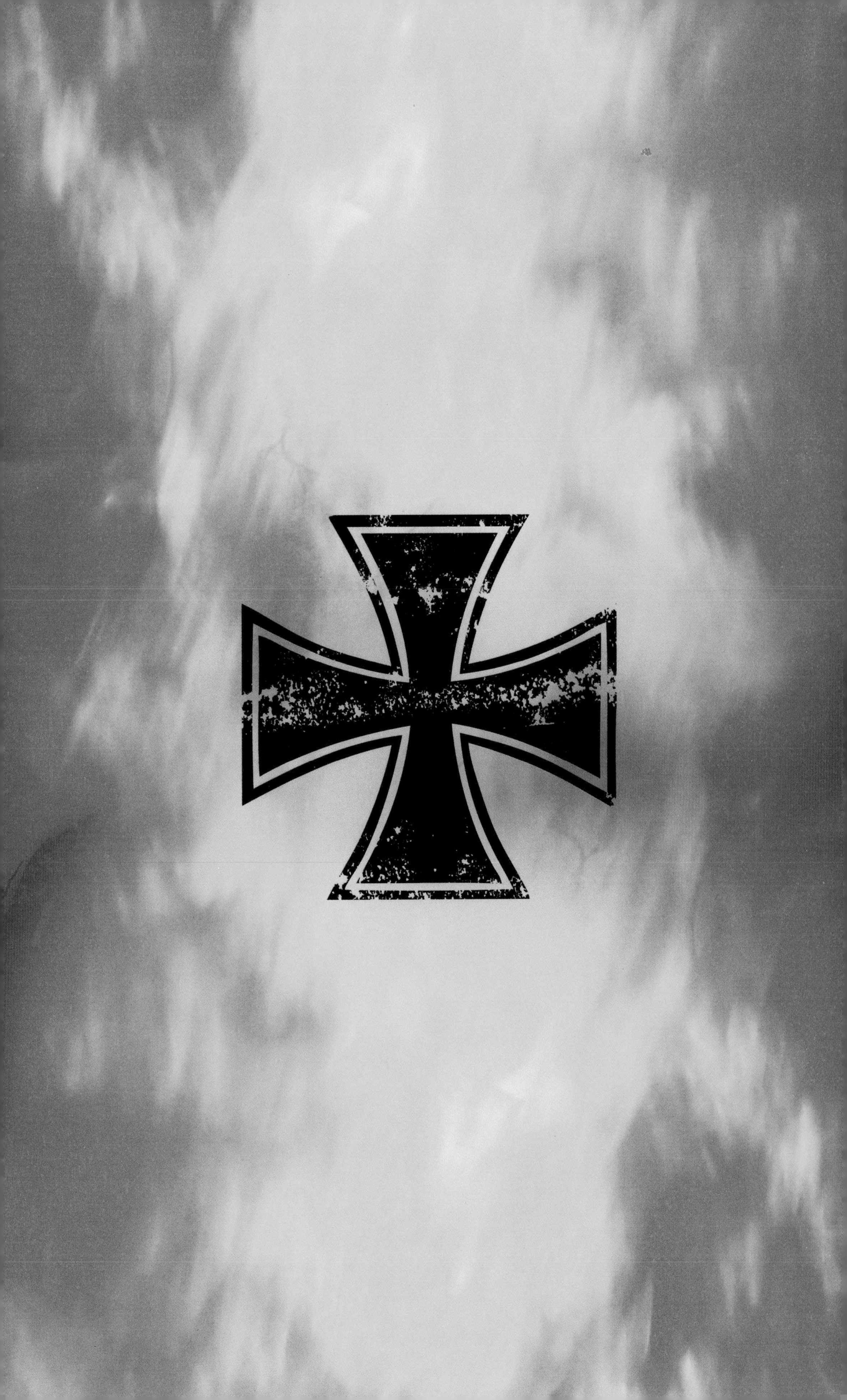

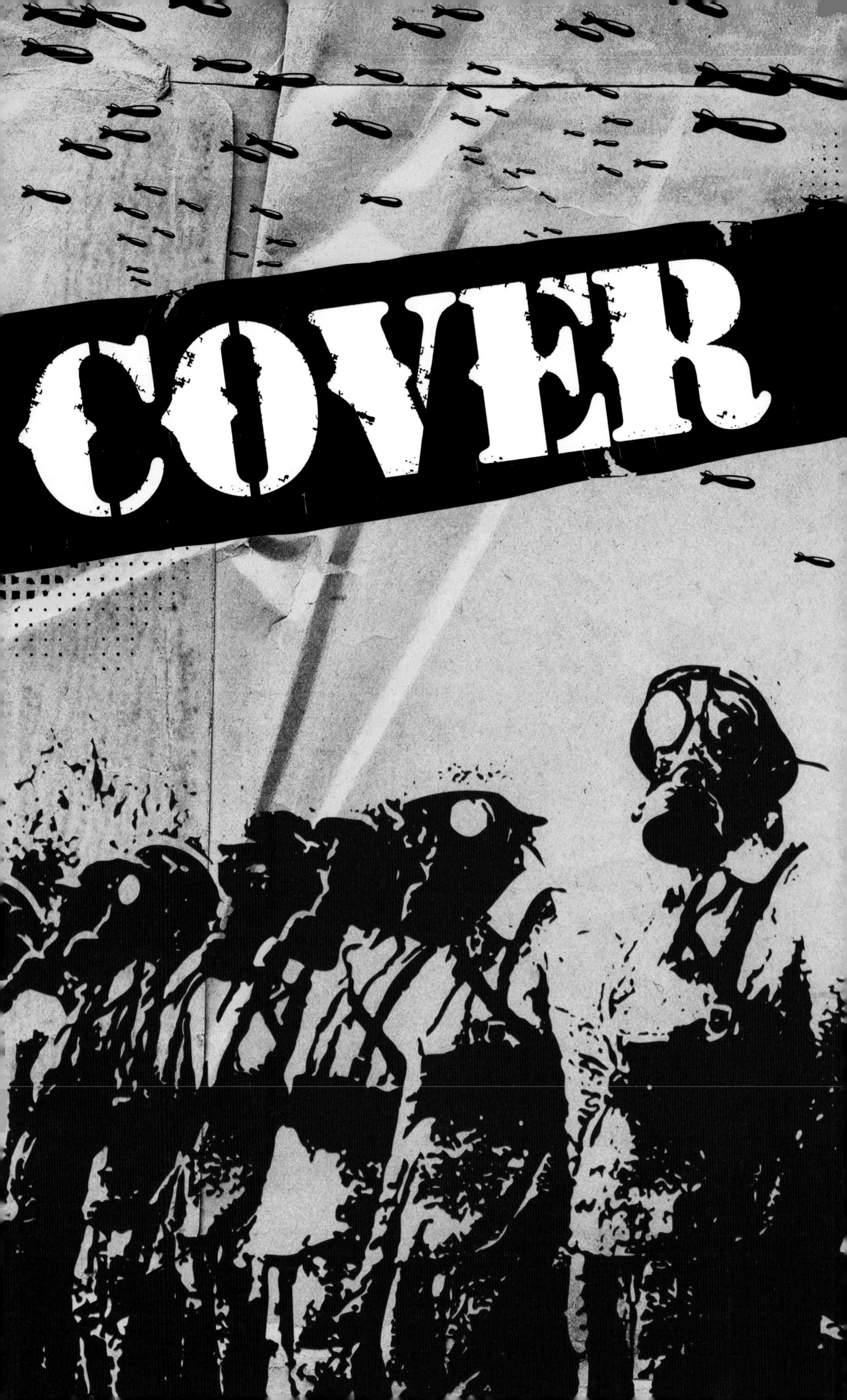
COVER

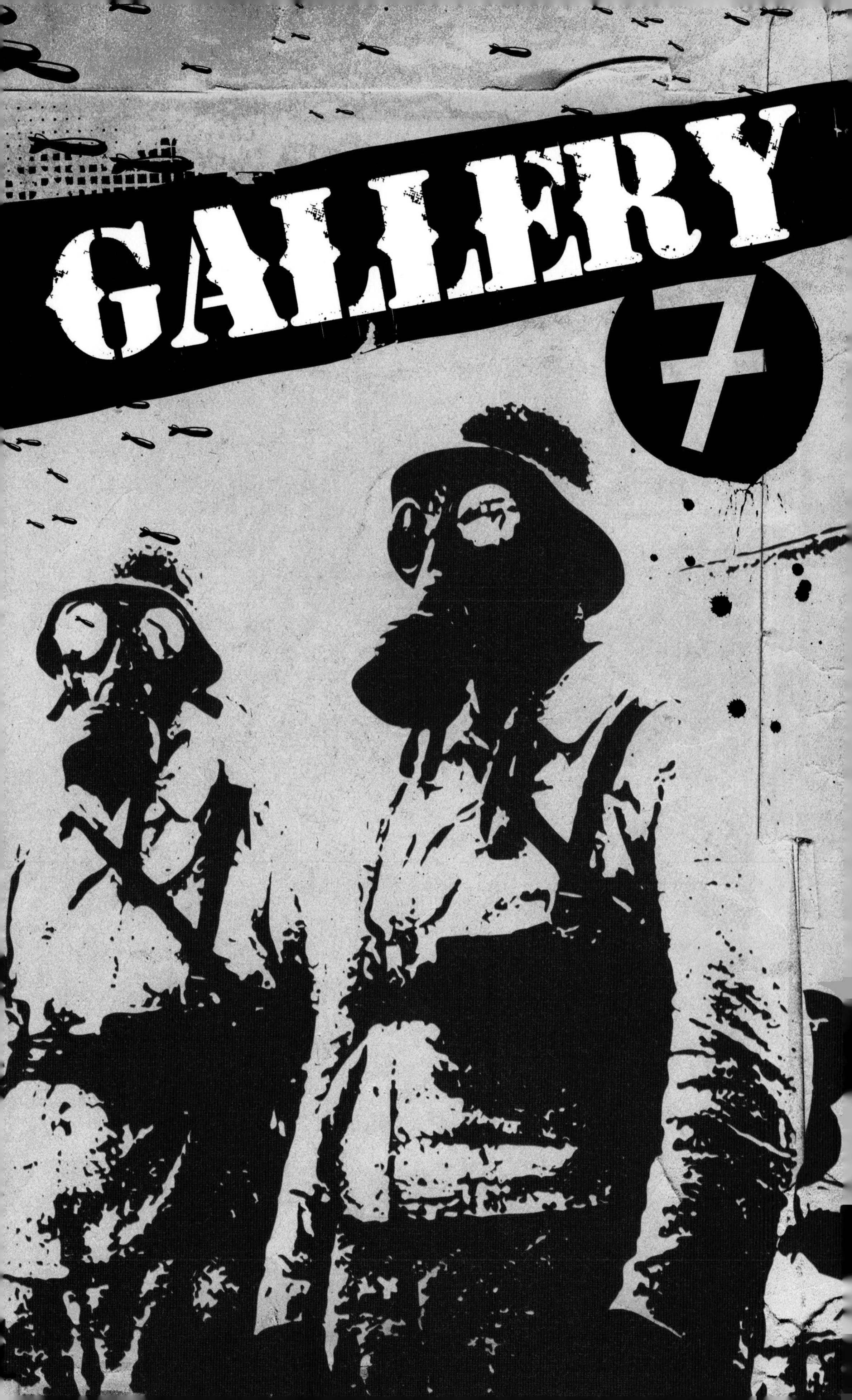
GALLERY
7

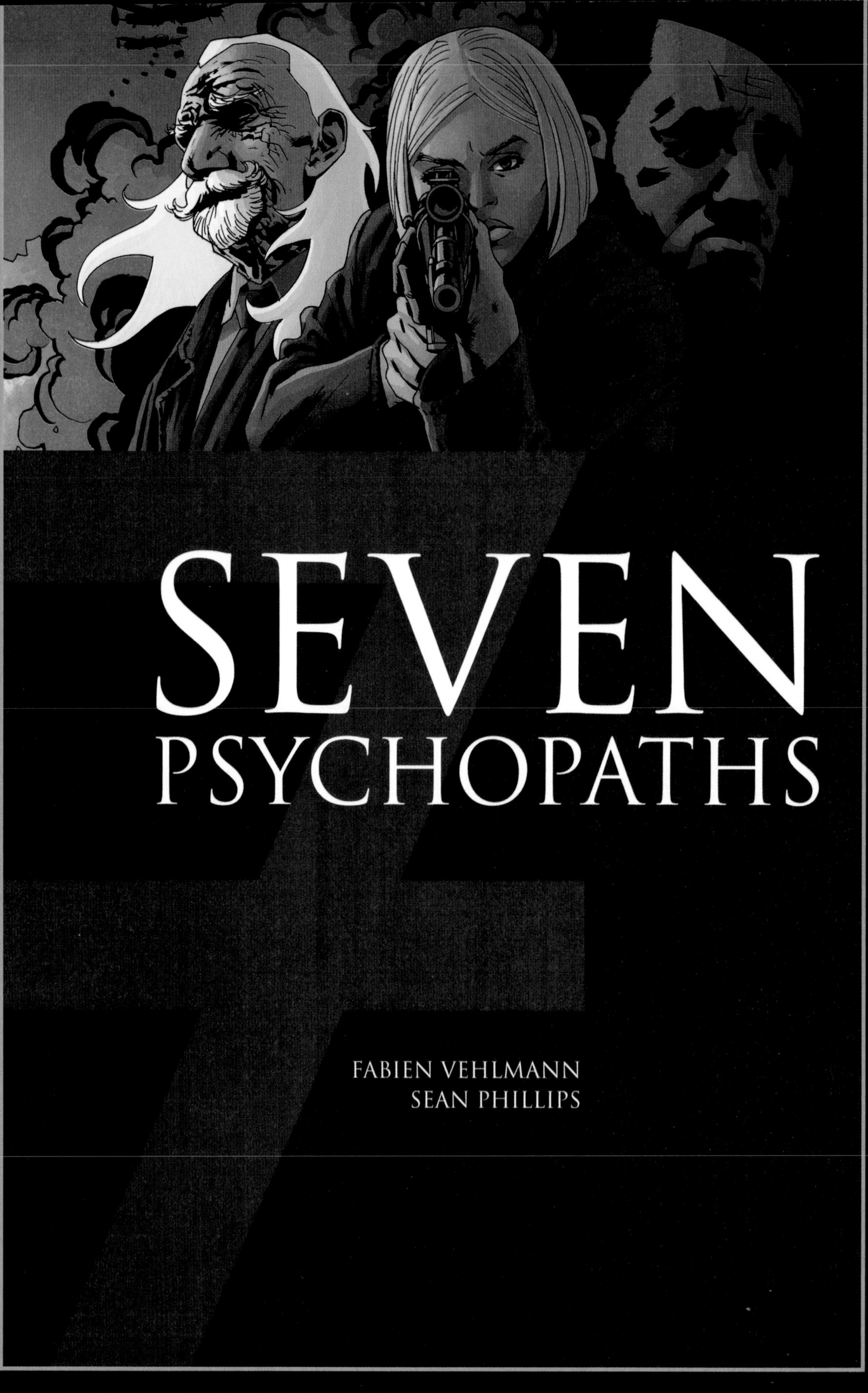
SEVEN
PSYCHOPATHS
FABIEN VEHLMANN
SEAN PHILLIPS

COVER 1: SEAN PHILLIPS

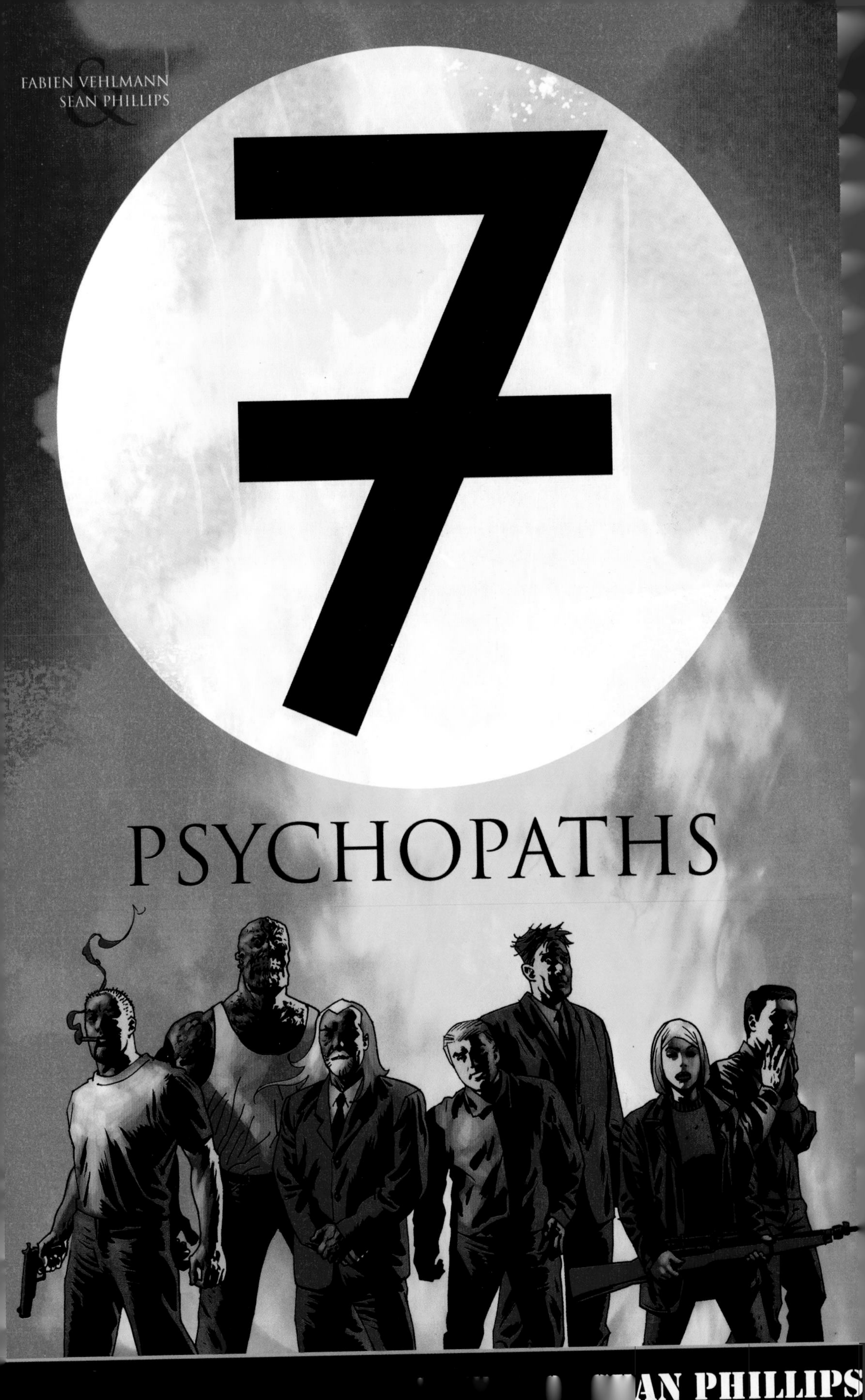
FABIEN VEHLMANN
&
SEAN PHILLIPS
7
PSYCHOPATHS

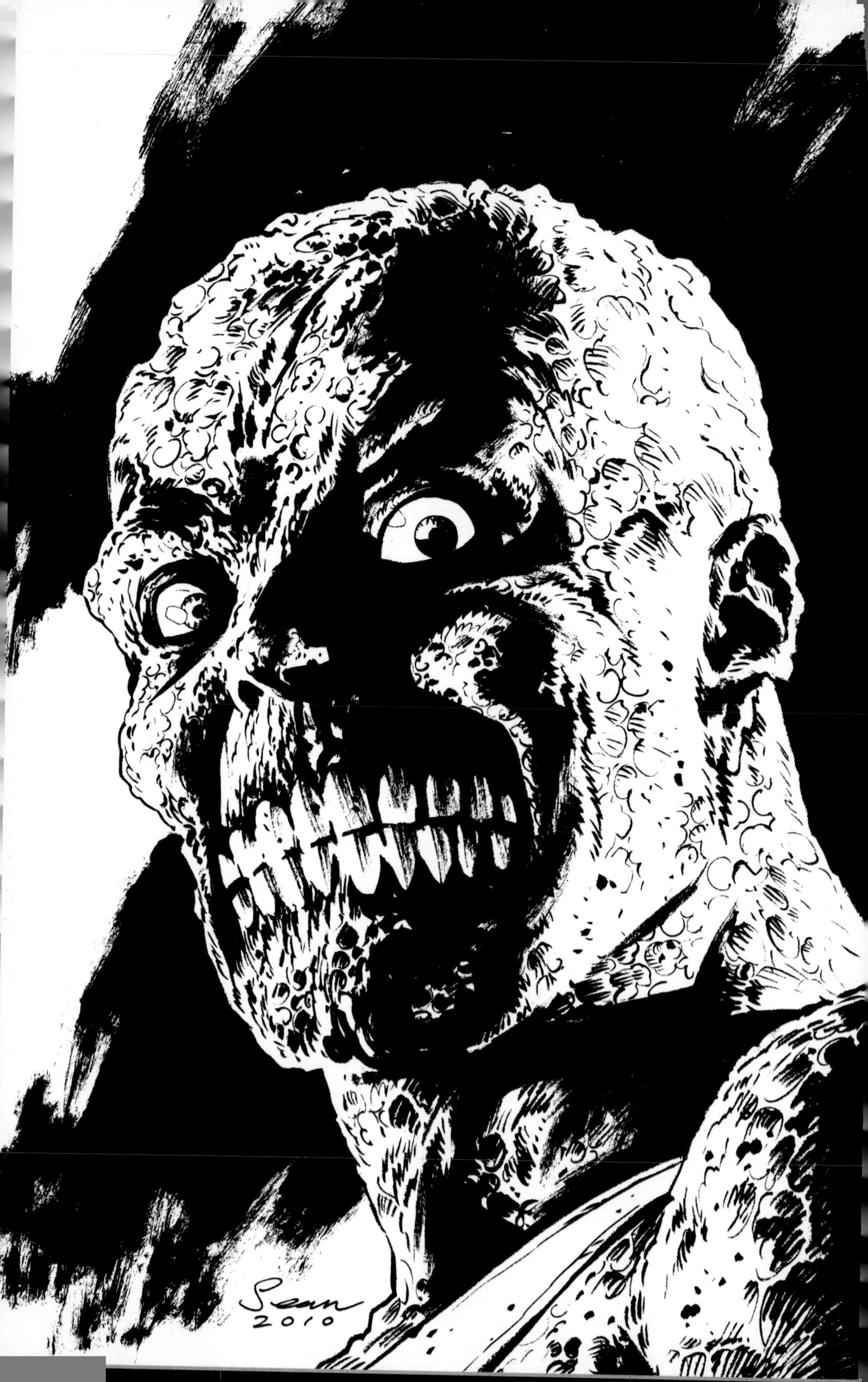
Sean
2010

3 INK

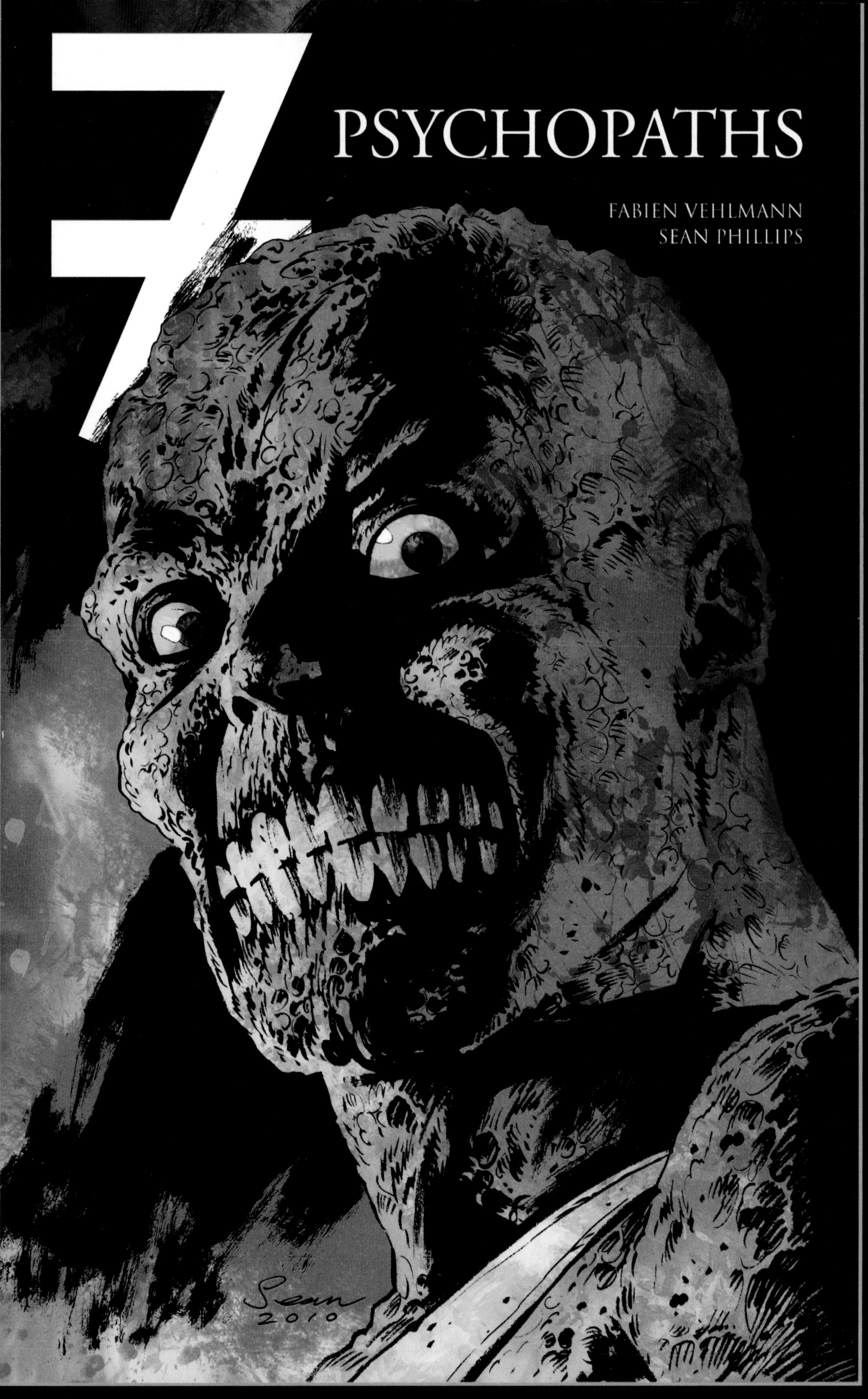
7
PSYCHOPATHS
FABIEN VEHLMANN
SEAN PHILLIPS
Sean 2010

COVER 3: SEAN PHILLIPS

7 SKETCH GALLERY

SEAN PHILLIPS

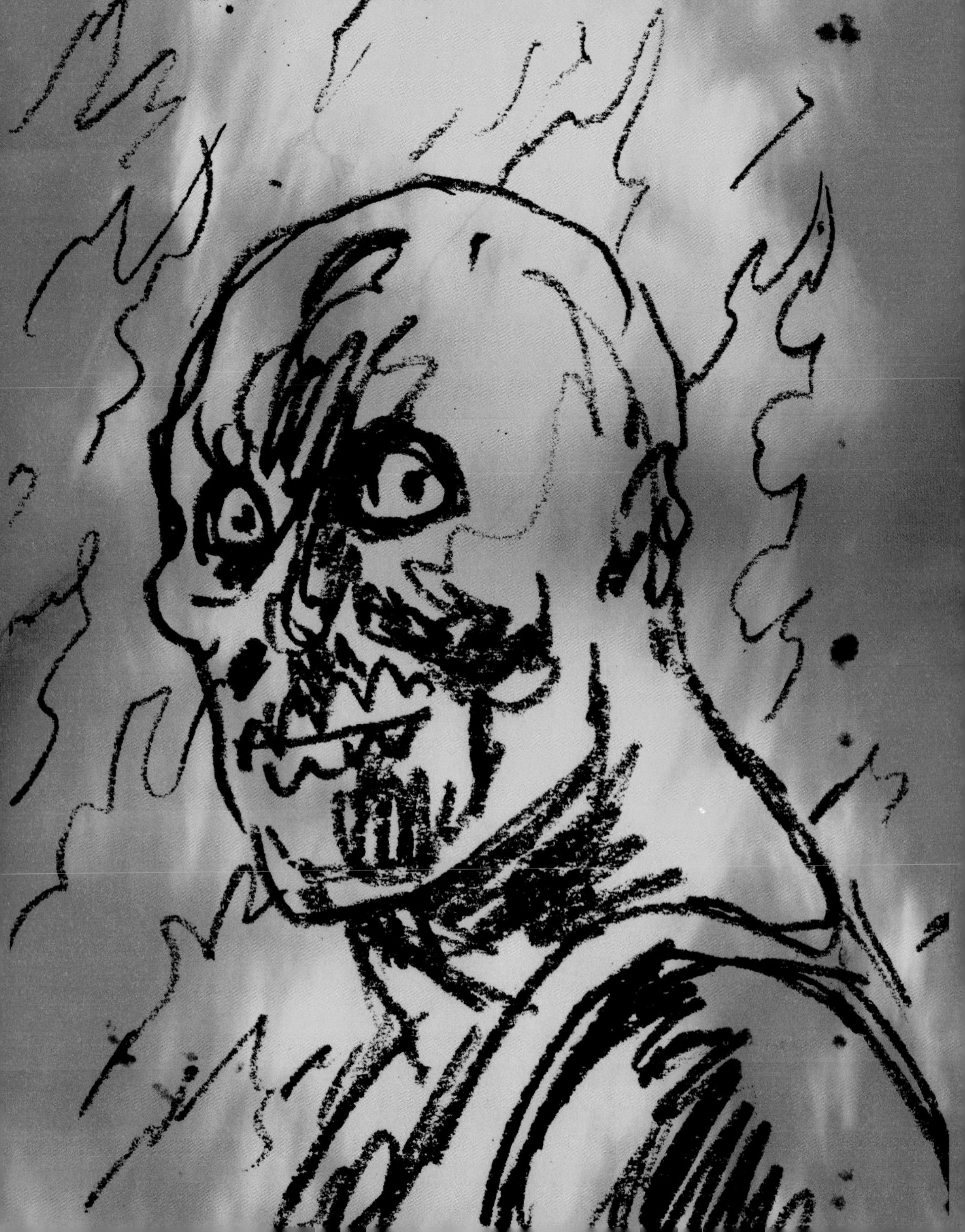

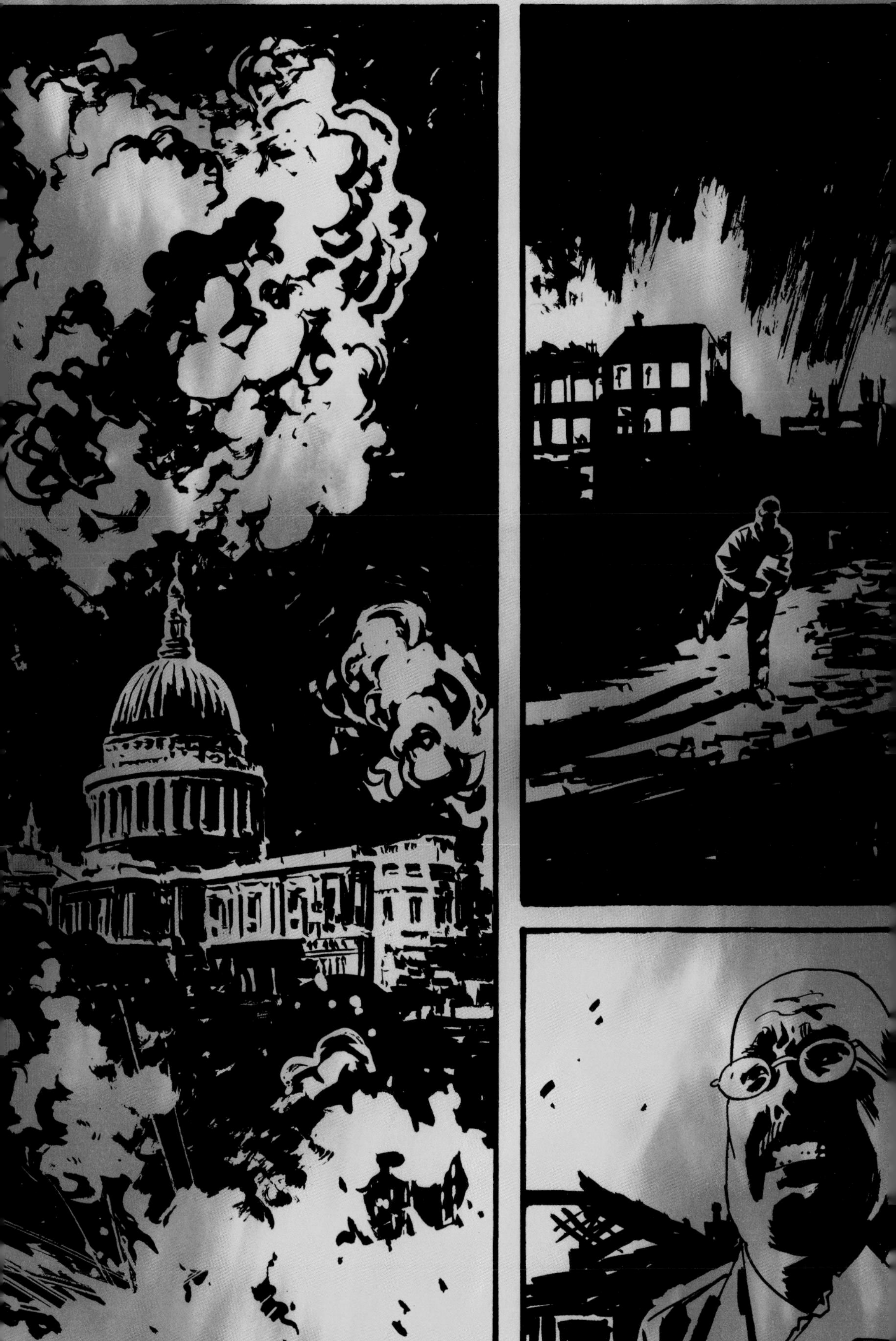

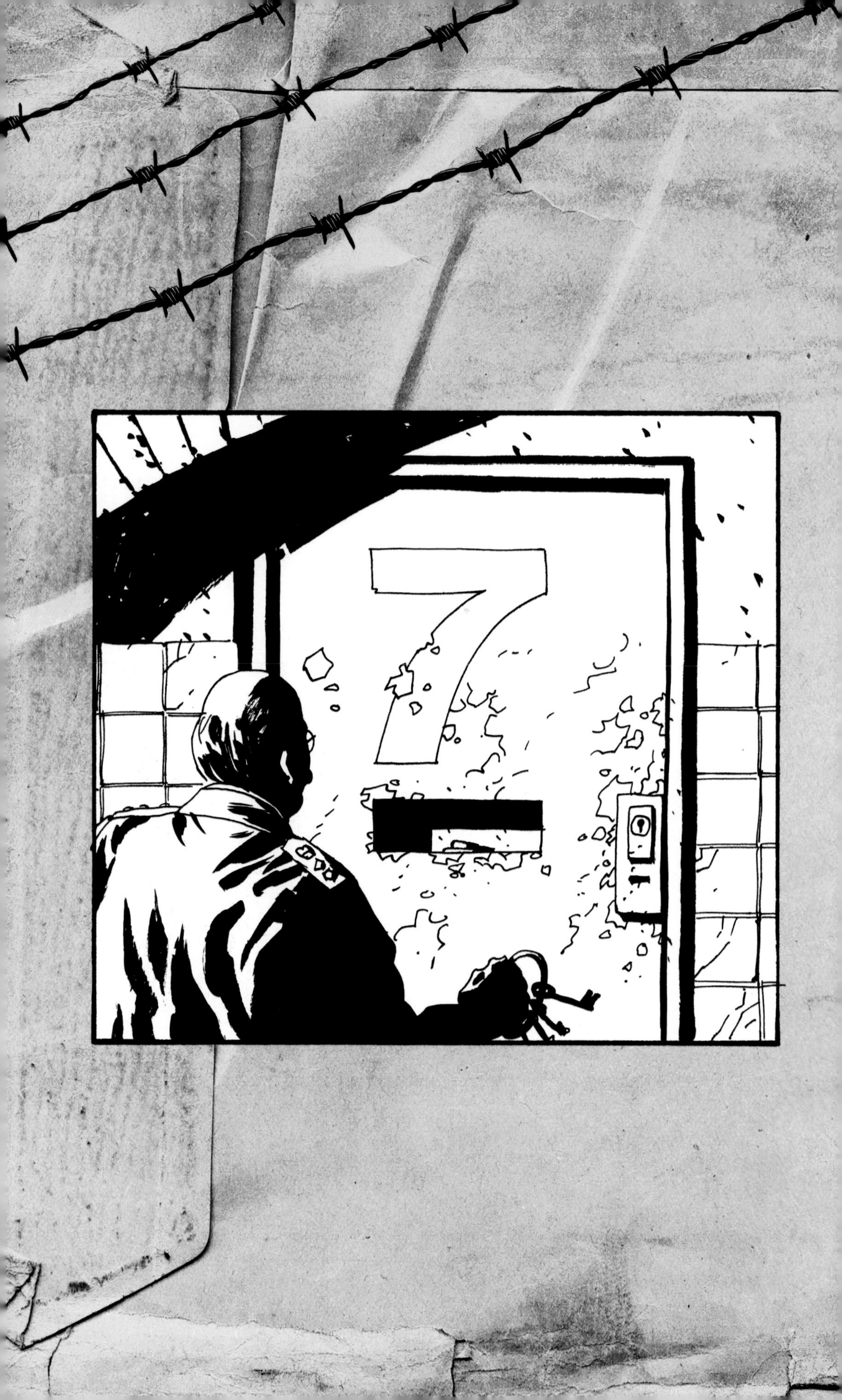
7

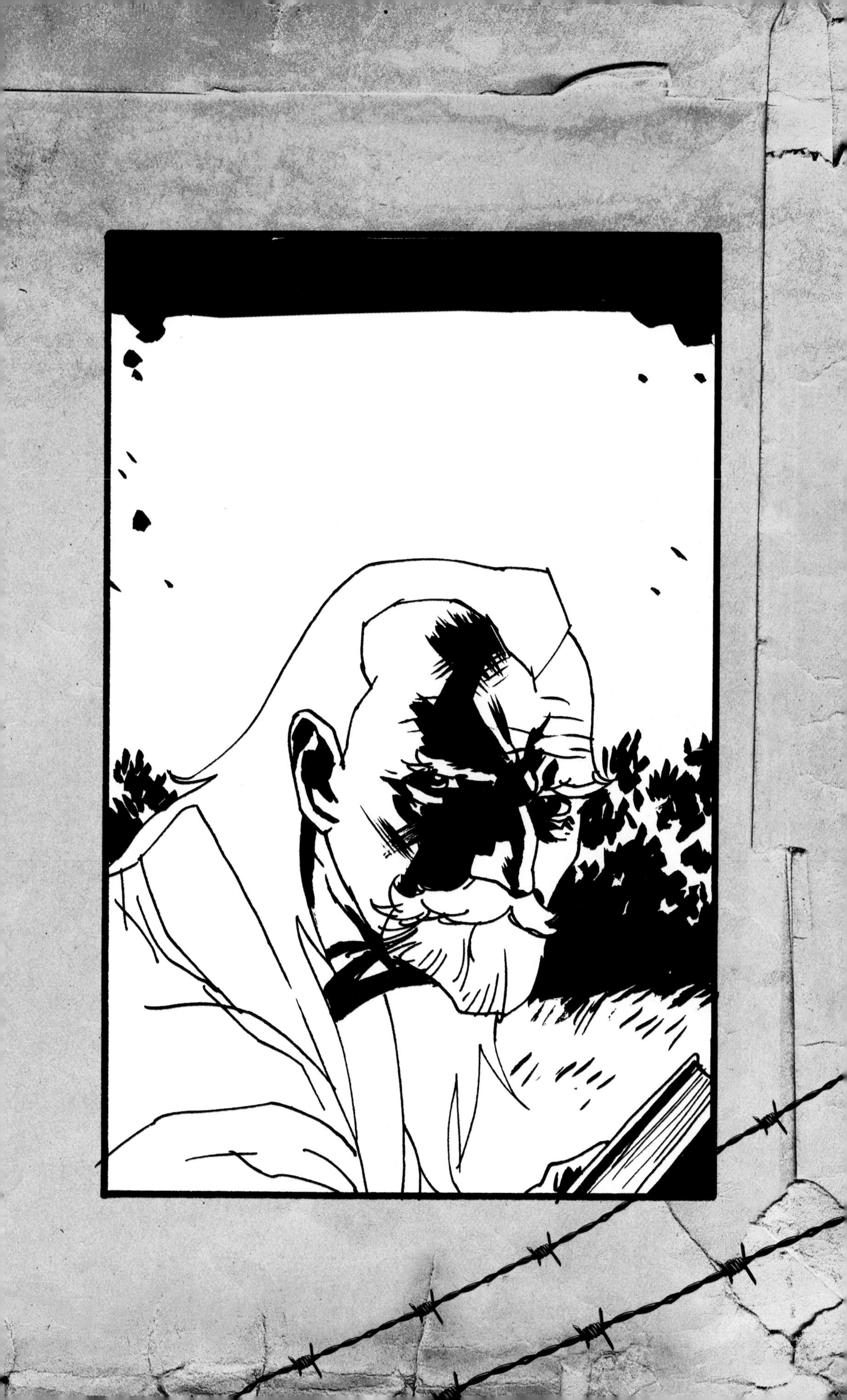

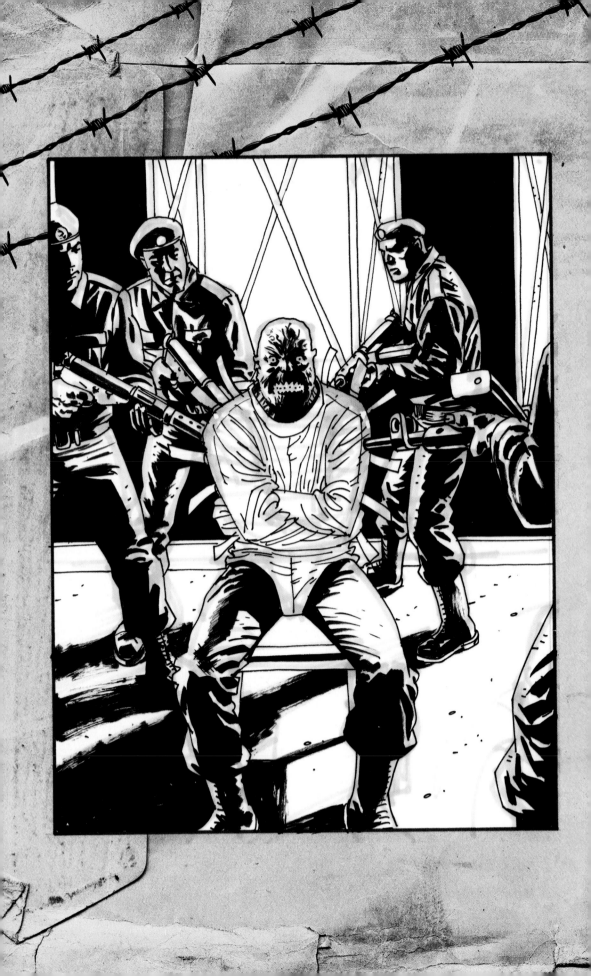

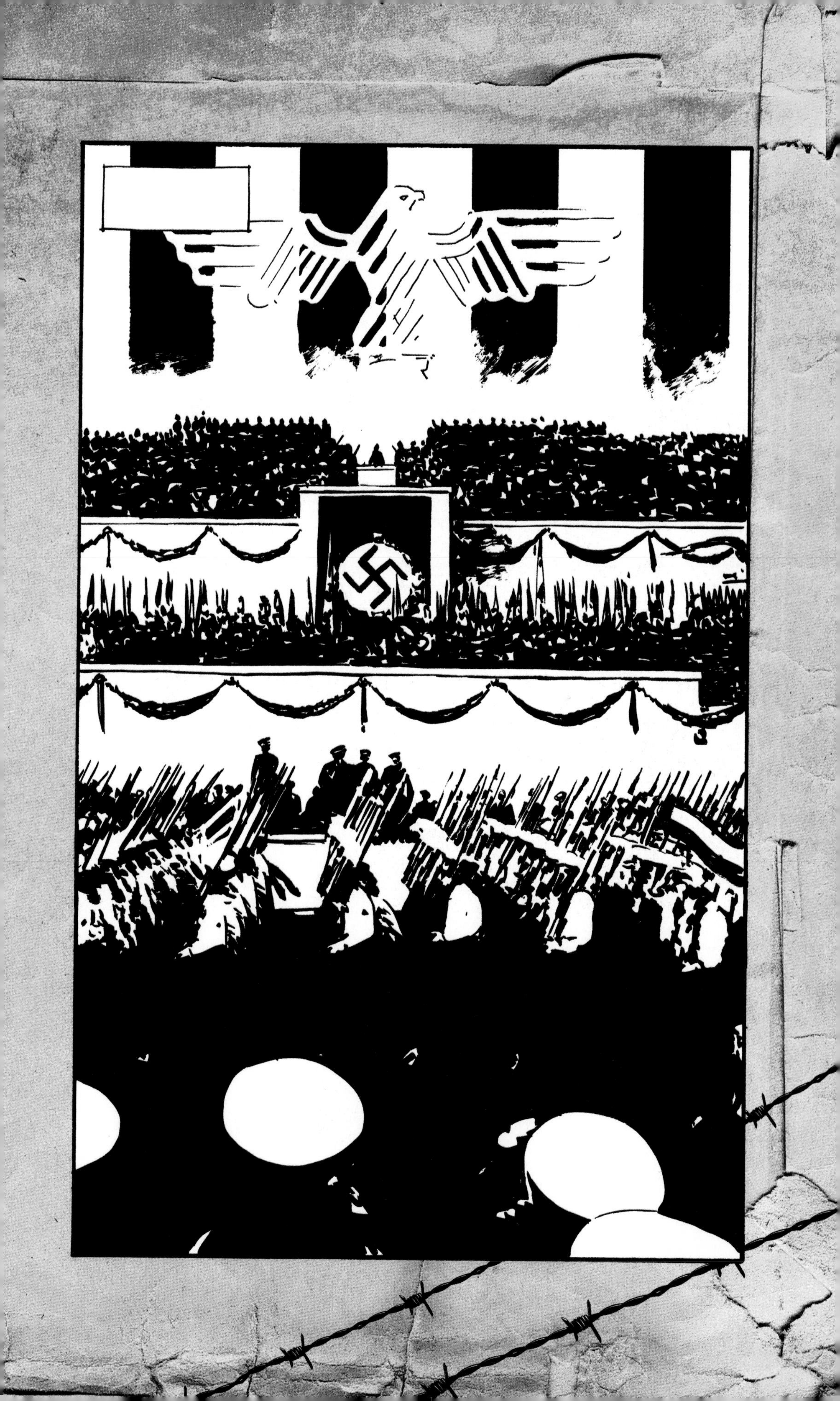

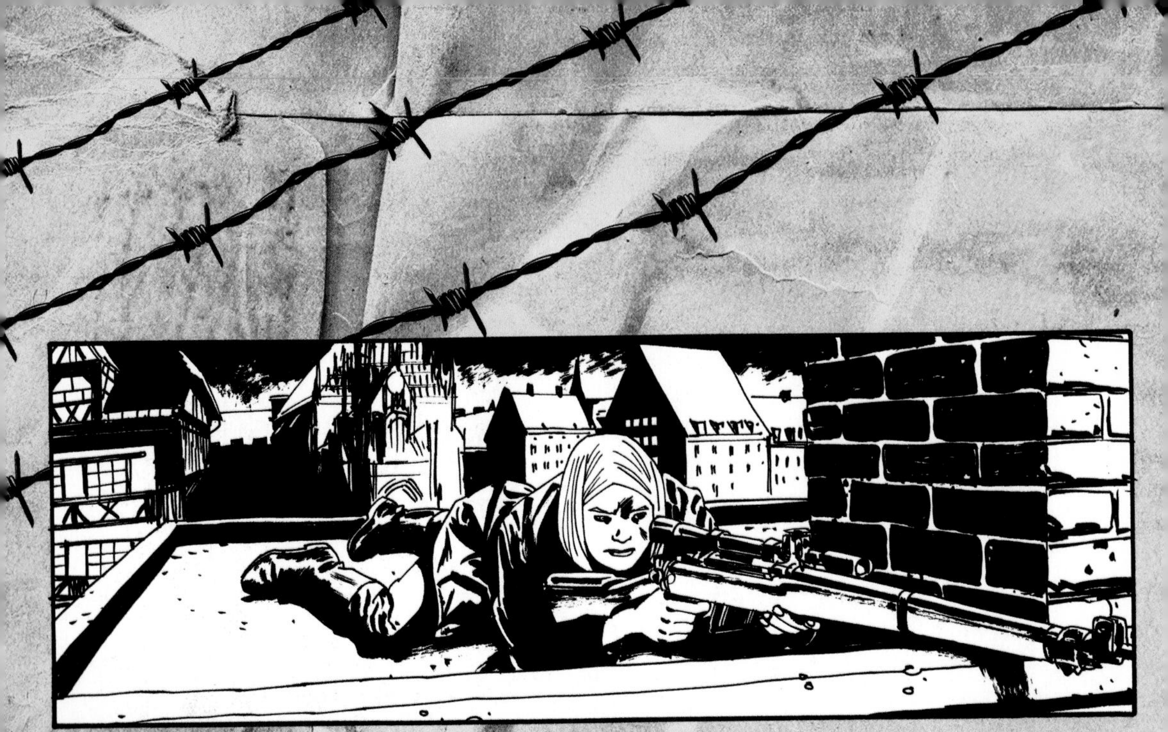

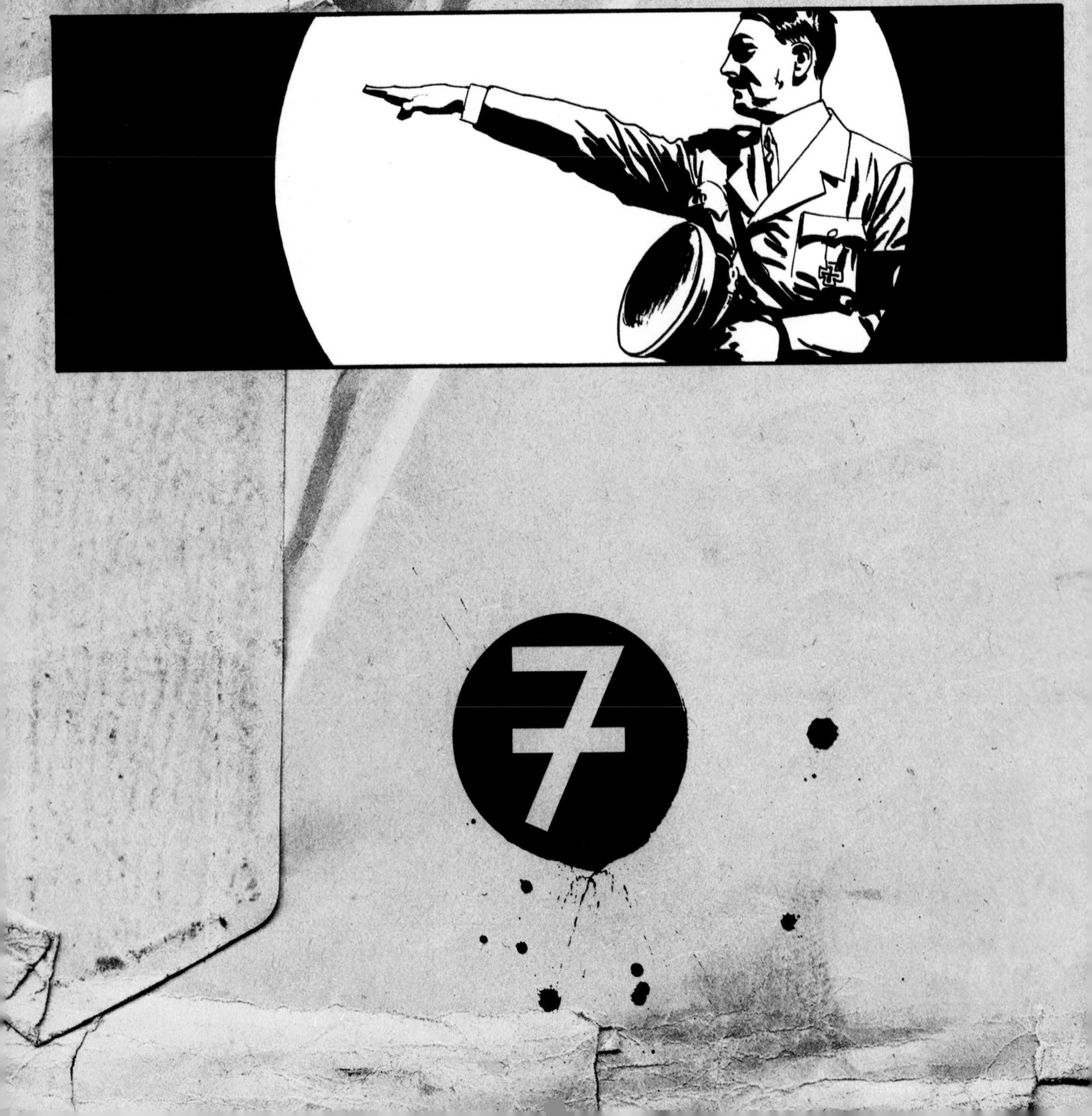

7

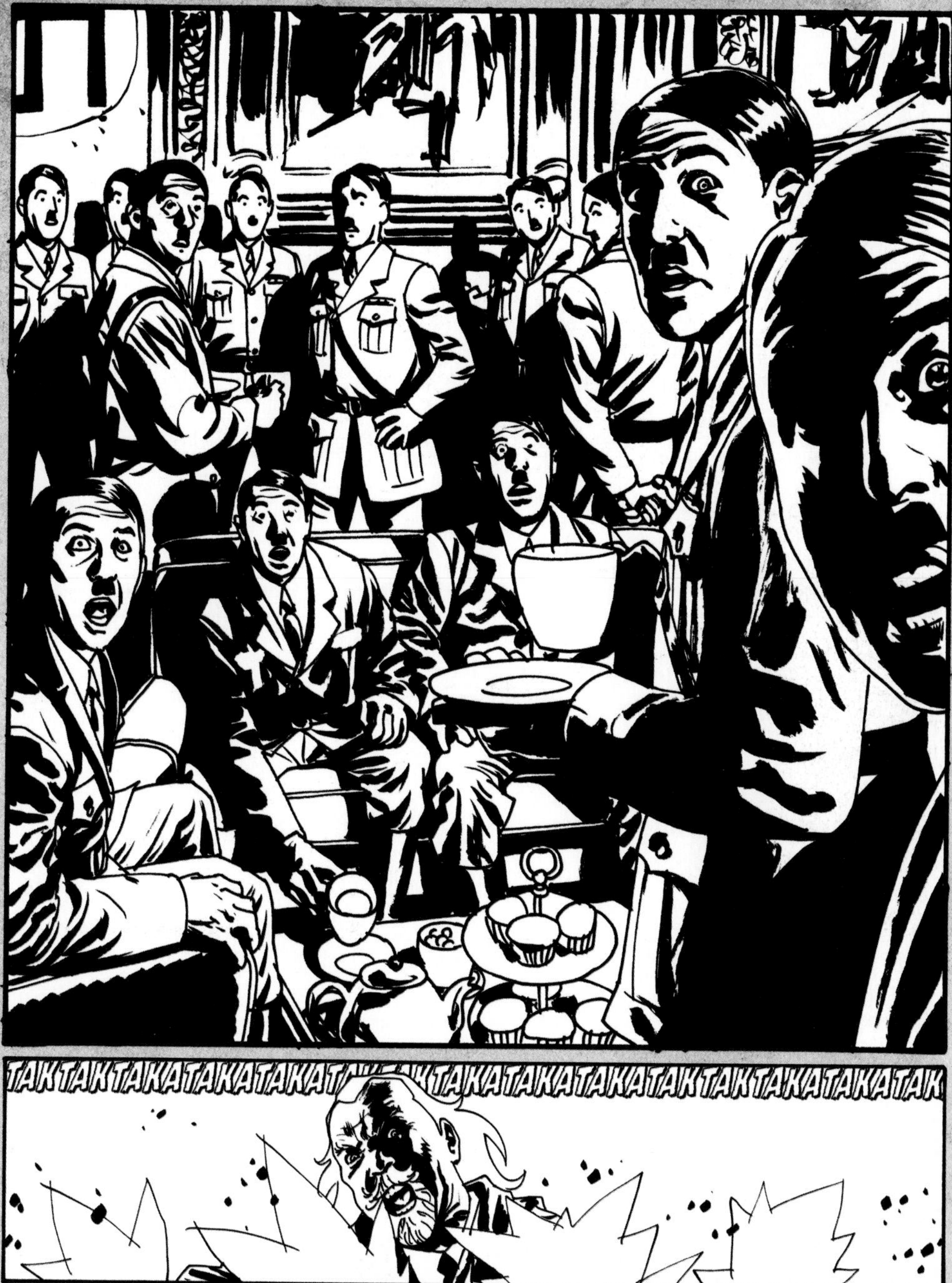
TAKTAKTAKATAKATAKATA
KTAKATAKATAKATAKTAKTAKATAKATAK

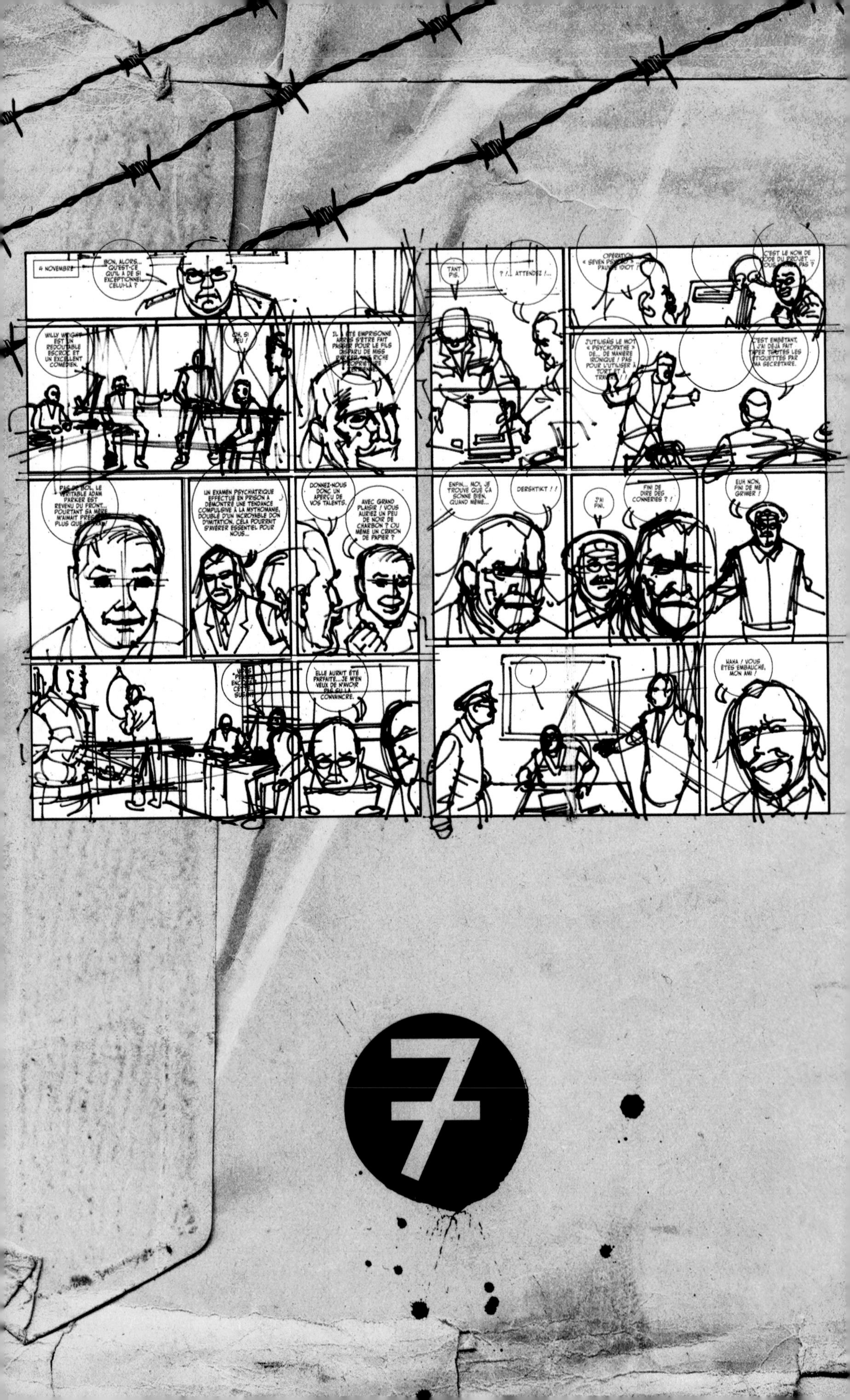
4 NOVEMBRE
BON, ALORS... QU'EST-CE QU'IL A DE SI EXCEPTIONNEL CELUI-LÀ ?
OH, SI PEU !
UN EXAMEN PSYCHIATRIQUE EFFECTUÉ EN PRISON A DÉMONTRÉ UNE TENDANCE COMPULSIVE À LA MYTHOMANIE, DOUBLÉ D'UN INCROYABLE DON D'IMITATION. CELA POURRAIT S'AVÉRER ESSENTIEL POUR NOUS...
DONNEZ-NOUS DONC UN APERÇU DE VOS TALENTS.
AVEC GRAND PLAISIR ! VOUS AURIEZ UN PEU DE NOIR DE CHARBON ? OU MÊME UN CRAYON DE PAPIER ?
ELLE AURAIT ÉTÉ PARFAITE... JE M'EN VEUX DE N'AVOIR PAS SU LA CONVAINCRE.
TANT PIS.
? !... ATTENDEZ !...
C'EST EMBÊTANT, J'AI DÉJÀ FAIT TAPER TOUTES LES ÉTIQUETTES PAR MA SECRÉTAIRE.
ENFIN... MOI, JE TROUVE QUE ÇA SONNE BIEN, QUAND MÊME...
DERSHTIKT ! !
J'AI FINI.
FINI DE DIRE DES CONNERIES ? !
EUH NON, FINI DE ME GRIMER !
!
HAHA ! VOUS ÊTES EMBAUCHÉ, MON AMI !
7

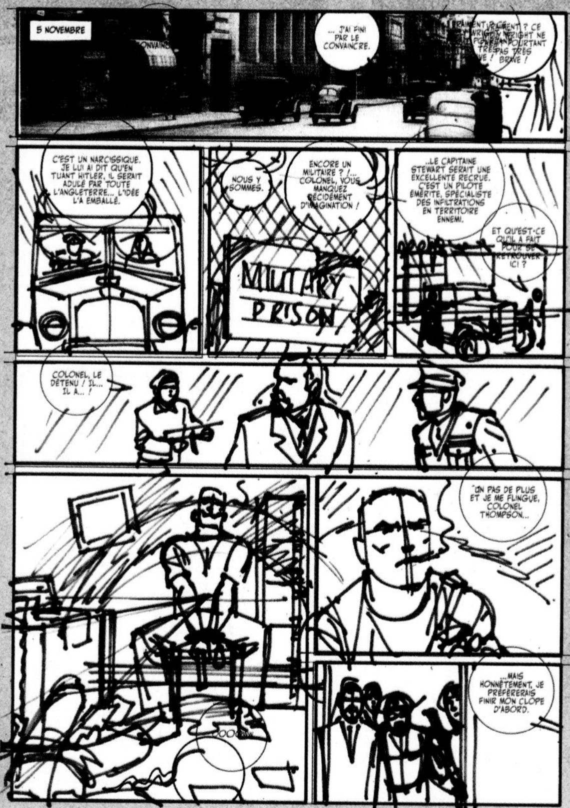
5 NOVEMBRE
... J'AI FINI PAR LE CONVAINCRE.
C'EST UN NARCISSIQUE. JE LUI AI DIT QU'EN TUANT HITLER, IL SERAIT ADULÉ PAR TOUTE L'ANGLETERRE... L'IDÉE L'A EMBALLÉ.
NOUS Y SOMMES.
ENCORE UN MILITAIRE ? /... COLONEL, VOUS MANQUEZ DÉCIDÉMENT D'IMAGINATION !
MILITARY PRISON
..LE CAPITAINE STEWART SERAIT UNE EXCELLENTE RECRUE. C'EST UN PILOTE ÉMÉRITE, SPÉCIALISTE DES INFILTRATIONS EN TERRITOIRE ENNEMI.
ET QU'EST-CE QU'IL A FAIT POUR SE RETROUVER ICI ?
COLONEL, LE DÉTENU ! IL... IL A... !
UN PAS DE PLUS ET JE ME FLINGUE, COLONEL THOMPSON...
...MAIS HONNÊTEMENT, JE PRÉFÉRERAIS FINIR MON CLOPE D'ABORD.

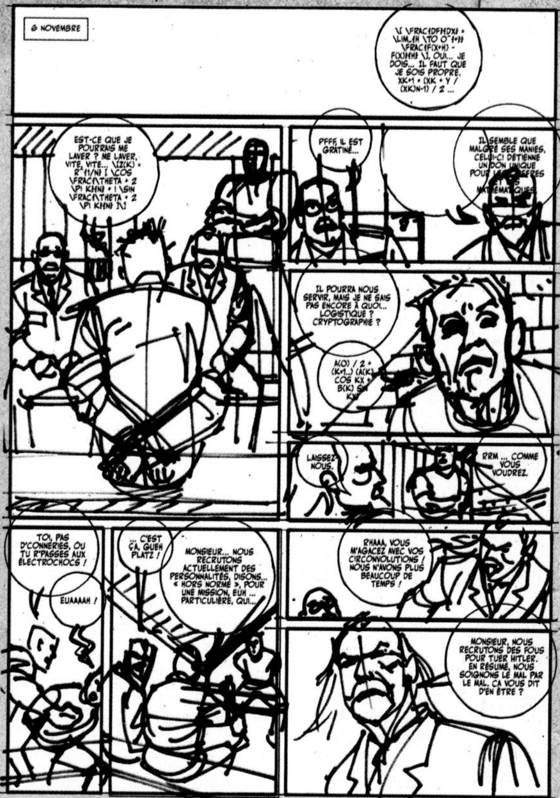
6 NOVEMBRE
OUI... JE DOIS... IL FAUT QUE JE SOIS PROPRE.
EST-CE QUE JE POURRAIS ME LAVER ? ME LAVER, VITE, VITE...
PFFF, IL EST GRATINÉ...
IL POURRA NOUS SERVIR, MAIS JE NE SAIS PAS ENCORE À QUOI.. LOGISTIQUE ? CRYPTOGRAPHIE ?
LAISSEZ-NOUS.
RRM ... COMME VOUS VOUDREZ.
TOI, PAS D'CONNERIES, OU TU R'PASSES AUX ÉLECTROCHOCS !
EUAAAAH !
... C'EST ÇA, GUEH PLATZ !
MONSIEUR... NOUS RECRUTONS ACTUELLEMENT DES PERSONNALITÉS, DISONS... « HORS NORME », POUR UNE MISSION, EUH ... PARTICULIÈRE, QUI...
R'HAAA, VOUS M'AGACEZ AVEC VOS CIRCONVOLUTIONS ! NOUS N'AVONS PLUS BEAUCOUP DE TEMPS !
MONSIEUR, NOUS RECRUTONS DES FOUS POUR TUER HITLER. EN RÉSUMÉ, NOUS SOIGNONS LE MAL PAR LE MAL. ÇA VOUS DIT D'EN ÊTRE ?

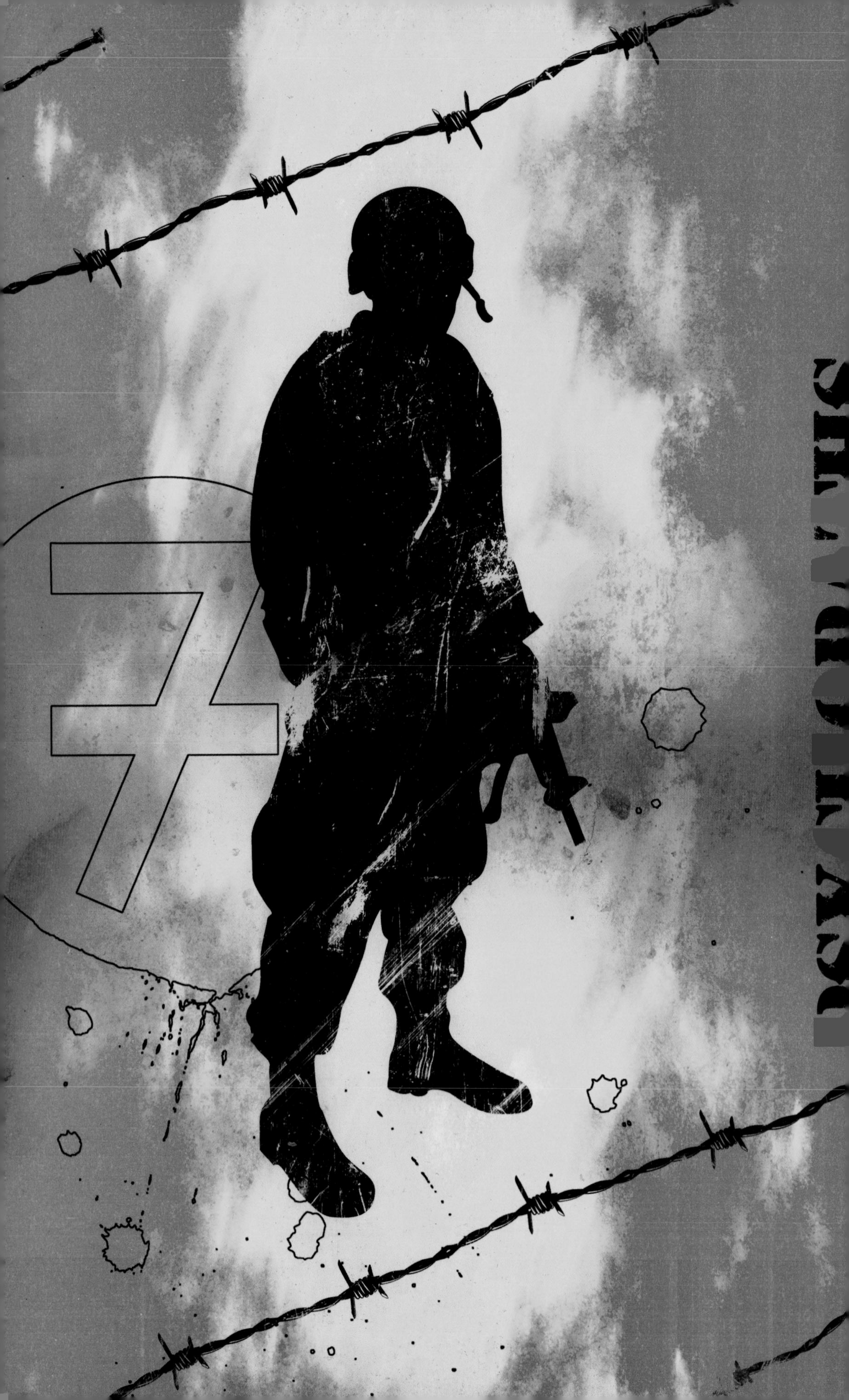